HARCOURT BROWN, Emeritus Professor of French in Brown University, is now living in Parry Sound, Ontario. He has been a member of the History of Science Society since 1934, and is the author of *Scientific Organizations in Seventeenth-Century France* and editor of *Science and the Creative Spirit*.

New scientific theories, methods, and objectives exert subtle and often unnoticed influences on literary creation. The development of the attitudes and aspirations of French scientists between the Renaissance and the Revolution and the impact of these new outlooks on French literature form the theme of this book by an authority in the interdisciplinary treatment of science and literature.

Implicit in the author's exploration is the view that in the development of the scientific revolution there was no overall design, but rather random growth; human beings turn up at various moments, some of them appropriately, some of them not, so that the record is in part a story of successful endeavour, in part a comedy little short of farce. In the historical panorama of this book, four authors, each known for his ironic, even comic, insight into the human condition, are chosen to illustrate the theme. As men of letters, Rabelais and Voltaire exhibit well-defined scientific interests, while Pascal and Maupertuis were drawn from their scientific vocation into the discussion of ideas in literary forms. Consideration of their similarities and differences suggested the title, *Science and the Human Comedy*.

This work is a valuable contribution to our understanding of the historical and cultural conditions accompanying the advancement of science in a critical period, as well as of several ways in which the process was reflected, sometimes directly, more often indirectly, in literature.

HARCOURT BROWN

Science and the Human Comedy

NATURAL PHILOSOPHY
IN FRENCH LITERATURE
FROM RABELAIS TO
MAUPERTUIS

University of Toronto Press

TORONTO AND BUFFALO

© University of Toronto Press 1976
Toronto and Buffalo
Printed in Canada

Library of Congress Cataloging in Publication Data

Brown, Harcourt, 1900-
  Science and the human comedy.
  (University of Toronto romance series; 30
  ISSN 0082-5336)
  Includes index.
  1. French literature—History and criticism.
  2. Literature and science. I. Title.
  PQ142.B7   840'.9'38   74-84353
  ISBN 0-8020-5324-6

A portion of chapter 8 of this volume has been revised from 'From London to Lapland:
Maupertuis, Johann Bernoulli I, and *La Terre applatie*, 1728-1738,' by Harcourt Brown, pub-
lished originally in *Literature and History in the Age of Ideas: Essays Presented to George R.
Havens*, edited by Charles G.S. Williams. Copyright © 1975 by the Ohio State University Press.
All rights reserved.

La poésie, l'histoire et la philosophie ont toutes le même objet, et un très grand objet, l'homme et la nature. La philosophie décrit et dépeint la nature; la poésie la peint et l'embellit; elle peint aussi les hommes ... l'histoire ne peint que l'homme, et le peint tel qu'il est.

(Buffon, *Discours prononcé à l'académie française, le 25 août 1753*)

Contents

Illustrations

Introduction

THIS BOOK is about people, about men who differed in temperament, in style and outlook, and in the manner in which they expressed ideas. They shared a curiosity about the natural world, a concern for new patterns of thought, new methods of exploring the roots of action and change in organisms and matter, and they sought new explanations that might bring order into rapidly accumulating random facts. Linked by the part they played in the effort to understand the natural world, to put constructive ideas into circulation among contemporaries, their work took form in books, expository and theoretic as well as in the form of romance and satire, comedy and verse. The mind and culture of Europe was transformed in the two centuries and more between Francis I and Frederick the Great, and French men of letters and science changed with the times; of those changes these pages will offer no theory, nor even a complete and connected survey. Rather we shall isolate figures of some importance, to emphasize salient variants in the general development.

This is not, then, a history of science nor yet of literature; the narrative has gaps where research does not yield valid links. The chronology is broken, between Rabelais and Pascal, between Pascal and Voltaire. Men and books of note that perhaps belong in these pages are not mentioned, and large branches of science as well as massive areas of literature are left untouched. The generic divisions of literary creation — Pléiade, baroque, classical, rococo, or lyric, theatre, epic, novel, criticism — rubrics which lend their names to divisions in the usual manuals, are of little use in this book, whose purpose lies in an attempt to describe an outlook found with some frequency in France. The scientific vein surfaces in various literary forms at different times through the centuries from the Renaissance to the early years of Louis XVI and beyond.

The austerity of science does not efface the human traits of the scientist any more than the impersonal study of mankind destroys the sensitivity of the novelist or poet. In assuming the external bearing of a profession, the inner man is not fundamentally changed. He is still emotionally responsive to whim or need, as capable of indiscretion and frailty as of penetrating vision into the ways of nature and the events of daily life. The drama of the world of humanity embraces the scientist as much as the man of books, just as truly as it displays the money-lenders, the drapers, the musicians, the pharmacists, and the bankers whose diversity delighted Honoré de Balzac, whose idiosyncrasies he portrayed.

The dozen articles on which the chapters of this book are based were written at intervals over about thirty years, with no intent of assembling them into a book. Some represent responses to immediate situations, a challenge to debate or to rectify a statement of historic fact; an answer to an open question, or perhaps the elaboration of a point of view that somehow had escaped development in the synthesis of history. Still others reflect discoveries chanced upon as an investigation led into libraries not much used in the ordinary course of research. One or two articles used here are reproduced with little revision. In others, statements of fact have been corrected, and opinions and conclusions revised, even to the altering of points of view.

The impulse to pursue the line of investigation these chapters represent was strengthened as I found that the accepted objectives in the teaching of French literature had lost touch with the methods and purposes visible in other historical and critical disciplines, that studies stemming from the philological traditions of the nineteenth century were almost hopelessly closed to the innovations that were fertilizing other fields. The institutionalized vulgate of the subject as understood in the 1920s did not reflect current analysis of French thought, and still less did it bear a useful relationship to the outlook of men and women of the time, or even to the philosophy and science of a country that had made and was still making important contributions to the civilization and technology of Europe. The emphasis on classicism, viewed mainly as a doctrine of restraint and moderation, morally useful perhaps, yet imposing limits to the imagination as well as restrictions on vocabulary and diction, and the correlative view that romanticism was an opposing trend towards unrestrained freedom and self-expression, asked for belief in meaningless categories. Possibly useful as they facilitated memorizing pedagogical formulae, they impeded understanding of the creative processes at work in the periods they attempted to explain.

This failure to relate the phenomena of a great literature to the larger issues of its periods, this lack of a common intellectual vision, demanded study and consideration, and led ultimately to the revision of the foundations on which a teacher's integrity could be based. Tacit assumptions had to be reviewed, and a reconciliation achieved between doctrine and practice in the presentation of the ideas and imaginative literature of France. What was said in class and seminar had to be put in the perspectives of intellectual history gradually becoming clear in other fields of study.

The issue resolved itself into a practical problem, which could be solved by simple means, a return to the texts with a view simply to discovering what they had to say. New insights could be found in the climate of opinion at the time the books in question were composed, a climate often befogged by the consecrated formulae of the usual histories and the repetitious explanations prefacing classic texts. I reopened and reread masterpieces in the fresh light of what I found to be important lines of activity in their time, looking the while for evidence that their authors had been aware of the external world, of the way in which that world was viewed in their own age. In short, I sought the ideas of the seventeenth century in the books of that 'century of genius,' as Whitehead calls it, trying to discover how Corneille and Racine responded to ideas in the air. Perhaps Gassendi and Descartes, with their opposing views of the constitution of matter, meant nothing to Racine; that would be evidence of one sort about the man and his age, but no reflection on atomism or the vortices. Still there was the passage in *Iphigénie* which records the coming of the wind that finally released the ships of the Greeks in the gulf of Aulis:

> Les Dieux font sur l'autel entendre le tonnerre;
> Les vents agitent l'air d'heureux frémissements,
> Et la mer leur répond par ses mugissements;
> La rive au loin gémit, blanchissante d'écume;
> La flamme du bûcher d'elle-même s'allume;
> Le ciel brille d'éclairs, s'entr'ouvre, et parmi nous
> Jette une sainte horreur qui nous rassure tous.

The passing of a windless calm at the rapid approach of a cold front could hardly be better described. Racine conceals the sequence of precisely detailed atmospheric phenomena with his superb classical diction, but the observed facts are there, as clearly recorded as if by a Robert Boyle. The *soldat étonné* of course saw Diana herself descending to accept the incense and the sacrifice, but Racine is too alert to a skeptical audience to put the suggestion in the mind of the subtle Ulysses. He knows the power of the weather in the hands of the tragic poet, and he uses it for its full effect.

For such evidence it was vain to search the usual histories of the literature. In writing the handbooks for a discipline still in the process of defining itself, the professionals of academic criticism exhibited little interest in opening the doors to what might be described as foreign matter, deriving from non-literary experience, which would disrupt the regular narrative sequence of the genres. The time had come to reread the texts without regard for traditional categories, looking at accepted masterpieces as well as at the erratic boulders in the plain, the mavericks in the stable: Fontenelle and his *Entretiens sur la pluralité des mondes*, Voltaire and his *Lettres philosophiques* and *Micromégas*, Molière and *Le Malade imaginaire*. Such works had been accepted for their style or because they were written by men respectable for other writings, not because they were masterpieces in their own right. Representing the oddities of the culture, not the main stream of the literature as the professionals conceived it, such works were exceptional and a little quaint.

In the early years of this century the curricula in departments of literature tended to be static; men and women taught what they had been taught, in much the same way, with little thought of change. Methods and outlook had been only recently defined, on the model of the classic languages, or influenced by the strong philological tendency to find an Indo-European root in every strange word, with no regard for what it meant or how it was used for poetic effect. Those who had been trained in France could not escape the stagnation of the French academic system, with its failure to keep up with the native literature, so that Baudelaire was not admitted to the assigned texts until he had been dead for fifty years. The teacher oscillated in a narrow orbit among half a dozen approved classic plays, a few dozen poems by the Romantics and their school, even including Sully Prudhomme and Félix Arvers, three or four novels by recognized masters of the genre, carefully edited for such passages as could be put *entre toutes les mains*, the least radical parts of Voltaire and Diderot, and a small anthology of the Renaissance poets. Neither Pascal nor Rabelais nor Montaigne was taught in those days; such authors raised too many questions with which the philologically trained professor could not cope. The vicious circle was hard to break.

From this limited range the docile student gained an idea of French literature and thought as something edifying, correct in diction and orthodox in imagination, limited in vocabulary and ideas, conservative in politics and religion. He could be excused for finding it dull if he had not picked up something from the historians, the philosophers, the social scientists, and the students of the arts and music.

A new outlook had to be found, and among many, one of the most promising seemed to be that offered by the history of science and technology, a field in which France and Frenchmen have had enormous influence over the last three centuries. In the 1920s, two or three events coincided to make this direction inevitable. In 1925 Alfred North Whitehead published his *Science and the Modern World*, a book in which most of the interests of modern man could find food for thought; and the History of Science Society was founded, in part to give George Sarton a haven for his work in the new world, but also to respond to the rising interest in the subject shown by a number of scientists, engineers, historians, and philosophers who recognized that the half-century bisected by the year 1900 had seen tremendous changes due to science and technology, and that much could be done to record this progress and preserve its annals and its artifacts. There was also a vitalizing influence in science itself: William Bateson could fill a vast hall with a thousand students to hear a technical lecture on genetics, while Einstein and the word relativity were discussed, with little comprehension, on campus and in some classrooms as well. In Toronto, in particular, the isolation of insulin and the award of a Nobel Prize to Canadians had its effect on the impressionable even if they were not devoted to biochemistry.

Such events were reflected in the creative literature of the time. *Back to Methuselah* was read and talked about, and the two Huxleys, Julian and Aldous, were replacing H.G. Wells, while in French literature Dr Knock was taking readers from that other doctor, Georges Duhamel. Jules Romains' twenty-seven volumes of *Les Hommes de bonne volonté* record much of the excitement and frustration of the period from the perspective of the thirties, with full awareness of the science of the time. Such stirrings in creative literature suggested to the inquiring mind that similar ferments must have been at work in other days, and that perhaps the façade of the classroom and the traditionalist professor must be penetrated to find what was going on when Milton and Molière were young, or when Voltaire and Swift, Pope and Boileau, had to meet the men of the academies of science and render some account of their contact.

Pursuing the subject, one could hardly fail to be impressed by the coincidence that in France the immense development of modern literature and science had begun in the same decades and followed a curiously parallel course. Rabelais' cycle of novels was published from 1532 to 1552, while the work of Vesalius, which stems from the Paris faculty of medicine, where Rabelais' formal medical education began, took form in the years 1538 to 1543. The original work of Ambroise Paré rises by reaction from the humanist medical publications of such men as Guido Guidi, professor in the Collège royal, who edited the chief classical texts of ancient surgery in his fine volume, the *Chirurgia* of 1544, for whose illustrations Primaticcio was briefly diverted from the adornment of Fontainebleau.

It is not necessary to trace in detail the sequence through the four centuries that follow. In common with everyone else, French writers have lived through a scientific revolution and its industrial counterpart, with their philosophic and material implications. To write of the general development of modern literature without taking account of these distinctive features of modern life, without attempting to identify and evaluate the scientific component, positive or negative, in the literary and imaginative thrusts of those centuries, is to falsify history and distort the pattern.

A full account of the scientific aspects of the modern mind is impossible here. Only a few of the more striking and relevant circumstances can be discussed, and briefly. That a historian applies scientific criteria in his analysis of events does not necessarily mean that he accepts an exclusively mechanist explanation or a materialist philosophy; positivist terminology is only one of several available to him. The scientific view seeks integrated and verified observations, leading to a hypothesis that may in turn be replaced by more exact descriptions to be studied with correspondingly exact logic and insight. At any point in the sequence there is room for intuitive perception, for free and imaginative extrapolation from the data. Neither history nor science are haphazard formulations derived from prejudices in real or potential conflict with one orthodoxy or another, nor are they private matters to be understood by intuition and sympathy and learned by rote. Their methods are not the result of prejudice, nor something evanescent and ephemeral, a *mystique*, to use a word once popular.

This scientific method has changed our view of the situation of the earth among other bodies in the universe, has revised our concepts of the place of nations in their mutual relations, and has effectively altered the status of racial and religious groups in the community of men and that of individual men among their like. No person now can write of this planet among the Ptolemaic heavens, as did Rabelais in his *Tiers Livre*, when he imagined man visiting the taverns of the Zodiacal signs. Scientific truth about the universe has had its influence on our sense of possible fact, on our interpretation of fancy and falsehood. In fact, science has given fantasy a new kind of life, freeing the mind from the dogmas of rationality, the necessity of reconciling what is thought anew with traditional teachings. Fantasy has its values still: the poet or the story-teller can remake the universe of Newton or Einstein at will on any pattern or in any mould, subject only to the day when a critic will attack the axioms of his fictitious science. We may reconstruct our frames of reference at any point; but in nationalisms and in religious teachings we know that we call many things true because in the long run we want them so.

Thus the scientific revolution that has accompanied the rise of modern literature has been much more than mere technology, tremendous and irresistible as that influence may have been. The atmosphere has been pervaded by an emphasis on detachment, on being *disponible* in the face of new facts and new urgencies. The finalisms have been taken away, the doors have been opened to an unimaginable diversity of theme and outlook, and the scope of our dreams, and the range of fantasy, have been enriched accordingly. Scientific necessity has not hindered the development of imagination, because the outlook of the scientist cannot abolish poetry or inhibit music. On the contrary, it has offered channels for expression and suggested problems for analysis, and in one sense or another it has been a partner in all the movements which have created new modes of perception and imagery from the Renaissance to the present day.

And so the theme that connects the various chapters of this book is the proposition that science is a wholly human activity, shared in one form or another by almost everyone, involving the intellect and the imagination as well as manual skills and an understanding of the ways in which the external world may be manipulated for human ends. Only too often science has been presented as an obstacle to the spirit, an enemy of the human being, a massive figure allegorically seated on a pedestal of unchanging and unquestioned knowledge, untouched by the passional and emotional needs of man, something to be subordinated to religion, the sentiments, and imagination, or subjected to the articulate claims of theology, aesthetics, ethics, or sheer fantasy. Too often the historian of literature and ideas, even when writing of eighteenth-century France, has found no place in his pages for science as a fundamental and continuing activity. Yet for Voltaire, as for Diderot, Montesquieu, and even Rousseau, and for countless individuals of other generations (not professional men of science, either), the urge to know positively, to question received opinions concerning the external world of mankind and nature on every level, was the most remarkable and fruitful function of the mind. This was the *mouvement philosophique*, and this questioning was what was meant by *philosophie*.

This book is rooted deep in private history. Beyond the fruitful associations of maturity among two or three generations of colleagues lie the origins of literary and scientific interests in a childhood spent among treasured books, where the Bible and Victorian poets were quoted and old novels read, where Galileo and Boyle, Darwin and Dalton were explained. Parental thrust transformed the experience of school into an adventure in which the particular warmth and varied insights of Milton Sorsoleil, H.B. Tapscott, E.A. Hardy, Janie Thomas, and John Jeffries, among others , created a foundation for higher studies. With changing circumstances, horizons widened among men of rarer talents, chief among them George Sidney Brett, philosopher and historian of psychological thought, complemented by Joseph Stanley Will, Herbert Davis, and Barker Fairley, teachers of literature with individual visions. Still later, the counsel of Frederick Barry and the writings of George Sarton contributed a sense of history in science, and Arthur Livingston brought the perspective of Pareto into the discussion of Voltaire. Adding nuances, Louis Cons subtly interpreted François Villon, and Gilbert Chinard discovered intellectual patterns in books of many genres and sometimes inauspicious aspect.

No book assuming the perspective of history can be quite free of the influence of contemporary thought and opinion, and it is natural that the content and focus of these pages should reflect immediate circumstance and the presence of colleagues. The intellectual climate in which these ideas have developed has been provided by several universities, and scholars in various disciplines have contributed to their formulation. Travel and research grants from the American Council of Learned Societies, the American Philosophical Society, and Brown University have made it possible not only to look more particularly at certain problems, but also to seek out relevant books and documents abroad. To this end, I have visited some fifty European libraries, from Belfast and Glasgow to Rome and Copenhagen, including, after the British Museum and the Bibliothèque nationale, such collections as those in the Bodleian, the Arsenal and the Mazarine in Paris, the Laurenziana and the Nazionale in Florence, the Institut et Musée Voltaire in Geneva, the Westdeutsche in Marburg, and the library of the University of Göttingen.

Research in Europe would not have been useful without much preliminary reading in North America. I owe much to libraries at various universities —Toronto, Queen's, Columbia, Rochester, Washington at Saint Louis, and in particular Brown University, where highly favorable circumstances and cooperative librarians, led by Henry Bartlett Van Hoesen and David Jonah, facilitated my research for thirty-five years. On occasion, collections at Harvard and Princeton have been of great value, as have libraries at Yale and McGill. To the staffs of all these and of other institutions, as well as those of New York and Boston public libraries, I am greatly indebted.

One cannot leave this context without recalling that the early stages of research leading to this book and to other publications were in large part oriented by the rich and varied resources of the library and manuscript archives of the Royal Society of London. Access to these indispensable collections was smoothed by the understanding assistance of the genial and talented librarian, Henry Robinson, whose wide acquaintance with the hold- ⁄

ings of the library, as well as with relevant material in London generally, was freely placed at the service of the itinerant scholar. His skilful attention to the needs and desires of the visitor was a matter of daily wonderment and delight.

The perspective of the book, as it emerged at last from the series of disconnected investigations of which these pages are a partial record, was more and more historical. Underlying the separate episodes from three centuries there appeared more and more clearly the continuity of what has been called the scientific revolution – the gradual transformation of the mind of the west by the acceptance of the organizing principles of the exact sciences, in particular mathematics and physics. Discussions with scientists like R. Bruce Lindsay and J. Walter Wilson, the reading of historical studies, of journals like *Isis* and *Annals of Science*, the consideration of various points of view as they were expressed in critical, expository, and imaginative writings, yielded fruit as the parts fell into place, and influences from unexpected quarters became effective. In particular, while it may be doubtful whether Charles Perry Stacey will realize how far his ironic sense of factual evidence has been influential here, it is probable that Roger Hahn will find some reaction to his impressive *Anatomy of a Scientific Institution* in these pages, and possible that Charles Coulston Gillispie will discover a reflection of his incisive thinking as set forth in his *Edge of Objectivity*. Furthermore, two or three of these chapters have been read by a younger scholar whose interests are in anthropology and ethnohistory, with whom I have had many profitable exchanges; her comments on early drafts have been of great benefit.

The books and manuscripts on which this essay is based have, in general, been read and quoted in versions as nearly contemporary with the moment of their composition as could be found. Passages cited have been reproduced with a minimum of alteration of spelling, accents, or punctuation. For certain authors, e.g. Molière or Racine, authentic early texts are not easily found, and such authors have been quoted from accepted modern editions. On the other hand, the writings of Rabelais, Pascal, and much of Voltaire, including the correspondence of the last-named, are available in books, old or new, that permit quotation with good assurance that what the author wrote and intended is at hand.

Much of the content of this book has been revised from articles published in the United States and elsewhere. Permission to use such material has been graciously accorded by the American Association for the Advancement of Science in respect of chapter one, taken from *Scientific Monthly* 83 (1956); by Taylor and Francis of London, England, for chapter two, originally appearing in *Annals of Science* 27 (1971); by Dr Theodore Besterman, Director of the Voltaire Institute, publisher of *Studies on Voltaire and the*

Eighteenth Century, for parts of chapters three and eight (*Studies* 55 [1967] and 24 [1963] respectively); by Professor Philip Wiener, editor of the *Journal of the History of Ideas* for chapter four (JHI 33, 1972); and by the American Academy of Arts and Sciences for the title and content of chapter six. Part of chapter five has been much revised from an article in *Isis,* published by the History of Science Society in 1948, and part of chapter three and most of seven from *Explorations* V and the *University of Toronto Quarterly* 13 (1943) respectively, published by the University of Toronto Press.

The orthography used in this volume does not correspond with the usage of the University of Toronto Press; it represents rather the personal preferences of the author.

A grant from the Humanities Research Council using funds provided by the Canada Council, and similar help from the Publications Fund of the University of Toronto Press, have been of appreciated material aid in the publishing of this book. In a very different mode, the encouragement and patient midwifery of Ron Schoeffel and the ecumenical tolerance of Margaret Parker as she wrestled with an author's orthographic idiosyncrasies have made the last stages of preparation of the typescript a somewhat elongated delight. To them, as to their colleague in the Press, R.I.K. Davidson, I bow with respect and gratitude for their forbearance.

Beyond the invaluable support and interest accorded by numerous colleagues and other associates, named and unnamed, in the course of writing these chapters, more personal obligations must be acknowledged. My immediate family has demonstrated their imaginative confidence in this enterprise by their consistent encouragement of its every stage. Their understanding acceptance of a studious preoccupation with books and documents, which has sometimes been accompanied by neglect of other duties, places this writer deeply in their debt, a debt that can be repaid only in small part by the affectionate dedication of these pages to my wife Dorothy, and to our daughter Jennifer and her family.

Parry Sound
December 1975

SCIENCE AND THE HUMAN COMEDY

CHAPTER ONE

Science and
the artifact

Qu'il est difficile de proposer une chose au jugement d'un autre, sans corrompre son jugement par la manière de la lui proposer! Si on dit: 'Je le trouve beau; je le trouve obscur,' ou autre chose semblable, on entraîne l'imagination à ce jugement, ou on l'irrite au contraire. Il vaut mieux ne rien dire; et alors il juge selon ce qu'il est, c'est à dire selon ce qu'il est alors, et selon ce que les autres circonstances dont on n'est pas auteur y auront mis. Mais au moins on n'y aura rien mis; si ce n'est que ce silence n'y fasse aussi son effet, selon le tour et l'interprétation qu'il sera en humeur de lui donner, ou selon qu'il le conjecturera des mouvements et air du visage ou du ton de voix, selon qu'il sera physionomiste: tant il est difficile de ne point démonter un jugement de son assiette naturelle, ou plutôt, tant il en a peu de ferme et stable![1]

IN THE LAST few years of his life, Blaise Pascal turned from experimental physics and mathematics to active support of the Jansenist teachings accepted by his family and friends, many of whom were associated with the Bernardine convent of Port-Royal. The shift from objective exposition of fact and theory to persuasive eloquence in the discussion of moral issues and the interpretation of Christian doctrine necessitated a change in style and manner quite as much as in content, and the transformation of many of the qualities of his

---

1 Blaise Pascal, *Pensées*, Zacharie Tourneur and Didier Anzieu eds., Bibliothèque de Cluny (Paris, A. Colin 1960) 2: 92, no 587. Here and elsewhere in this book, the *pensées* are referred to by their numbers in this edition; based on the manuscripts and including variants, these volumes permit the reconstruction of the process by which Pascal's fragments were composed.

scientific writing. Impersonality and economy of statement had to be sacrificed if assent to his new message was to be won. Numerous fragments in his manuscripts illustrate his problems, while others discuss questions of style and the means by which effective belief could be created. Of these, one of the most notable is the paragraph quoted above; into it, as into many similar passages, one can read a scientist's embarrassment as he turns from the criteria of experimental truth and logical argument to his new role as apologist.

These lines reflect much that he had learned in various groups he had known, in the scientific and philosophic milieu of the cell of the Minorite Marin Mersenne, and, in contrast, in the social literary assemblies in the house of the Duchesse d'Aiguillon, niece of the Cardinal de Richelieu. In these circles, Pascal had become accustomed to the impersonal standards of mathematical exposition as well as to the allusive speech of men and women gathered in a salon, where meanings are caught in a word half heard, a sentence half completed. From such circles the physicist had discovered the importance of gesture and facial expression, of tone of voice, timing, and silence. He had become sensitive to the impact of personality on the communication of ideas, on the speaker himself as on those who listened. Language was capable of as many interpretations as there were hearers; modified by tonal quality, by movement of eyebrow or hand, words conveyed values sometimes remote from their precise semantic content. In order to speak and write so that these nuances should contribute to communication, Pascal found he had much to learn; the fragments of his manuscripts devoted to eloquence, as much as those which developed his view of man's place in the universe, suggest that the shift in direction had produced much tension in him.

On the threshold of what was to be his last great effort, uncertainties are apparent in the state of his papers, in their endless revisions, erasures, and restatements. Pascal was clearly uncomfortable in the presence of a new variable, the reader to be persuaded, whose emotional state had to be reckoned with, who had to be reached by means other than pure logic on the basis of impersonal experiment. He was finding that historical fact, moral perceptions, and religious truths were not as easily discovered as the qualities and quantities of the natural world. His dilemma over the question of style and language offers an opportunity and a model for the exploration of a boundary still unmarked, still open to troublesome debate whenever scientists and humanists meet to define purposes and reach towards a new synthesis.

Broadly, one may say that, while the sciences are concerned with knowledge of the natural world, with the formulation of laws that explain the development and behavior of natural objects, the humanistic disciplines study objects produced by human ingenuity and skill, discovering and evaluating artifacts, from the crude arrowhead of earliest man or the song and story of primitive tribes to the complicated and meaningful product of evolved civilizations. On certain levels – for instance those characterized by projectile points, scraping tools, and communal middens – the scholar must be content to reconstruct the culture, typing the artifact and the artisan in comprehensive classes, Acheulian, Algonkian, Folsom, and so forth. There is joy when a touch of individuality in carving, or in modeling clay, or in a daub of paint reveals an original craftsman, allowing the archaeologist to go beyond the class or type, to sense the presence of an artist under the mass of statistics and the rubbish left behind by tribe or band. So far, the work has been close kin to science, the establishment of regularities in something resembling the natural world of higher primates, the great apes. Now the archaeologist becomes a humanist, finding a mind, a will to add to the mass of classified data. Ends and values, the marks of the rocky irreducible individual, demand new categories in the filing cabinet of science. Something has been reached which cannot be further subdivided, which in the long run cannot be completely described in the usual terms.

In other words, the problems faced by students of the humanities are rarely susceptible of resolution by strictly scientific means. Books may, of course, be thought of as physical objects, their bindings, paper, printer's ink, type and ornaments, studied for their material appearance, analyzed chemically, or examined by reconstruction of the mechanics of production. The scholar who neglects the results of skilled analysis of such material features does so at his peril. Certain celebrated forgeries of English poetry attributed to the artifices of Thomas J. Wise should warn him of the risks run by those who neglect the science and insight of the expert bibliographer.[2]

On the other hand, the scholar who hopes to establish the date and textual value of a document by the exclusive use of such methods would be making a mistake. Accurate dating of books, pamphlets, or broadsides often defies scientific analysis. Paper made of rags, and kept away from light and air, is durable. Type fonts and ornaments were used for many years after they were first cast from metal or cut from wood. Furthermore, the arts and taste of printer and binder change so slowly that ten years is a minimum and a quarter or even half a century a much safer margin to allow when dated testimony is lacking. When one adds to the factor of slow change in the printer's craft the

2 The forgeries associated with the name of Thomas J. Wise have been discussed by J. Carter and G. Pollard in *An Enquiry into the Nature of Certain Nineteenth-Century Pamphlets* (London and New York 1934) and by W. Partington, *Thomas J. Wise in the Original Cloth* (London 1946).

marked lag found in the techniques and equipment of the small provincial shop as compared with enterprises of larger cities, the scholar finds that priorities cannot be set up on circumstantial evidence alone. He needs a credible witness with an acceptable date rather than the clues that chemistry or the techniques of printing and binding may afford. Positive scientific attacks on these problems yield approximations only, less valid than an honest and undeceived written word.

For example, among innumerable undated plays of the Golden Age in Spain, careful analysis of content, even carried on by an amateur, has shown itself successful where the scientific methods of competent scholars had produced only fairly satisfactory probabilities. Skilfully devised techniques of the palaeographer and bibliographer had been used on the documents, printed and manuscript; vocabulary and content, style, versification, and structure had all been analyzed with assiduous care, so that an acceptable chronology had been achieved. Yet there remained a lingering doubt that the results really permitted the recognition of a sequence on which the historian could base a definitive account of the theatre of the period or a biography of the author. There was always a chance that development had not followed the curve of the statistics, that the poet had used verse forms at random, or that he had archaized in language from time to time. Finally certainty was reached from evidence within the texts themselves. A reader not in academic circles, the novelist Thornton Wilder, succeeded in establishing a convincing chronology by using recognizable features of acting companies, the presence in successive plays of a pair of growing children, and the career of a tame and senescent lion.[3] On such intrinsic evidence the humanist scholar rests his case. A coherent record in the texts or the testimony of an honest witness obviates the necessity of non-literary impersonal approximations.

There are other, sometimes less valid, reasons why a humanist scholar disregards, or at least underestimates, the efficacy of scientific methods. Statistics have been used in the study of literary language; the worth of such researches depends on the discrimination used in sorting the raw material, and the recognition of the limited purposes for which the results may be used. It is interesting to discover the native content of the vocabulary of *Paradise Lost*, or to count the archaisms in a Romantic poet or novelist, and it may be useful to establish a rough chronology of the features – syntax, idioms, and spelling – of a group of texts whose origins are in doubt. Such information may be relevant to the understanding of a period of literature, offering more

3 Thornton Wilder, 'Lope, Pinedo, some child-actors and a lion,' *Romance Philology* 7 (1953-4): 19

knowledge of persons and cultures, and perhaps reinforcing intuitional perceptions, and contributing to critical analysis and the synthesis which is the goal of scholarly work. Yet in spite of all this, arithmetic and the computer are not enough; the scholar is happier when the scientific linguist leaves the language of poetry alone and devotes his efforts to pidgin English and Minoan B. Discovery of what an author meant is one thing, the statistics of the raw material of speech are something else. A critical account of poetry or drama must allow for the context of artistic pattern, with ear and eye alert for intentional effects, such as the use of popular speech or the illustration of character by the use of *précieux* diction. It need hardly be pointed out that the academic critic who disapproves of the refined solecisms of the *femmes savantes* and the flowery diction of Tartuffe is as far off target as the statistician who uses a raw analysis of the language of the collected works to give us an insight into the personal standards of Molière.

Thus the humanist begins with the careful and imaginative reading of the book, the study of the painting, the hearing of the music, the progressive discovery of the meaning of the total work through perceptive analysis of parts and their function in the whole. His goal is a creative synthesis, a painstaking endeavor to recapture the full purpose of the artist. Whether the subject of study be literature, music, painting, or another art, the effort is to find and participate in the point of view from which the creator worked; to define his purpose and to establish the degree to which purposes may have been mingled. In short, the critic seeks the postulates from which the artifact began, the criteria used in the artist's choice of alternatives, the methods by which he proceeded, the end for which the whole was made. The interest is in the *why*; the scientific *how* is relevant, but no humanist can exorcise the teleological *why* for very long.

It is apparent, therefore, that in humanistic study classification and distribution into genera and species may be achieved only on a high level of abstraction, really at the cost of mutilation, even destruction, of the evidence. Furthermore, while the most complete history of one of the arts may remain as a conscious objective of some humanists as a terminal point of all their studies, it will never replace close contact with the artifacts themselves. The aspects of the arts in which independent historical sequences may be established are innumerable, not to be reduced to a single series, nor even to a manageable cluster of series. Although a new book on an artist or style may complement its predecessors, it will only rarely supersede them, becoming with them part of the total historical sequence. Sooner or later, we go back to earlier interpretations, for understanding as well as for forgotten facts. Audubon can still tell us something about birds, if not as a scientist, at least as a painter. His relation to his subject-matter is kin to that of the scholar and critic in the face of the works of art he studies.

In an early discussion of scientific method, a fragment of a preface to a proposed treatise on vacuum, Pascal pointed out that there are two broad areas of inquiry, that in which truth derives from the authority of documents, and that in which understanding is gained by observation of the external world. If we add to written documents the data obtained from critical examination of artifacts – interpreting this term as broadly as possible – we may continue to accept this rough division, and define the humanist scholar as one who discovers and discusses objects produced by human ingenuity and skill. 'Authority' must now be taken to refer to any statement made by a human being in any of the arts. A statement or a group of data of this nature cannot be made into something else without falsification; what the scholar works with is given to him in its physical substance, in its context, as well as in its form and pattern. Through study of these elements he proceeds to an ever-deepening understanding, a continually enlarging view of the intent of the creative artist. In turn, the product of his thought becomes an artifact for study. Its value lies in the degree to which he can persuade his colleagues, present and future, of the quality of his insight. It is obvious that the writings of scientists are artifacts also, and an appropriate object for humanistic criticism.

But in the scholar's work as a whole there is little resemblance to the procedures of science. The humanist may claim that he, too, is engaged on an endless quest, the rolling back of a constantly expanding frontier, even though the centre of his interest and the boundaries of his survey are both subjective. The fruit of the critic's study, as he examines the works of Michelangelo, Beethoven, Montaigne, Cézanne, or Jean-Jacques Rousseau, is limited only by his inventive capacity. Whether such work has been studied before or not is of no consequence to him, for there can be no prospect of finality in the commentary and evaluation of a great work, no end to the research in progress on its author. Pascal held that the authority of books could be described as limited, in contrast with the infinite complexity of nature, but neither he nor anyone else in his age could foresee the magnitude of our expanding libraries and imagine the problems a librarian faces as he tries to discover which books he may justifiably discard. It is not merely the result of the expansion of areas of articulate human interest; a major difficulty lies in the innumerable vistas opened by a single simple statement, a poem, a miniature, or an ancient brooch, when subjected to the comments of half a dozen moderately sophisticated scholars who look at the object, its historical and cultural context, its technical quality and its aesthetic merit, its precedents and its reverberations.

If it is difficult to define the intuitive comprehension by which a humanist scholar grasps the significance he finds in the subject of his study, one may still attempt to examine the outlook of a scientist as he describes the principles by which he works. From many possible definitions, two may be selected; quite distinct in their purpose and application, each expresses what one scientist thought best characterized an essential feature of his method. Writing in *Scientific Monthly*, M.J. Walker asserts that understanding takes place when a particular phenomenon may be regarded as illustrating a more general law.[4] He cites, for instance, Newton's theory of gravitation, which permitted physicists to 'understand' Kepler's model of the solar system. It is unlikely that any scientist would concede that a humanist scholar understands anything in his special field in quite the manner described; in five decades of literary study, the present writer has not met the kind of relationship between law and experience of which Walker speaks. Many 'laws' or general statements have been suggested, but they operate better in classrooms than in the world where the arts, including literature, are created.

Another formulation comes from a conversation with a physicist for whom 'understanding' occurs when he can take an idea into his laboratory and do something with it, when the idea suggests an operation, an experiment which he can create and which will lead him to a result previously unknown, permitting a deeper penetration of the structure of the natural world. Once more, experience of literary studies is inadequate; one may operate on a poem, experiment with it, write it out like prose, transfer it to another medium, and one finds that the original poem is still there, luminous and indestructible, held together by verbal tensions that will not yield. One has learned something about that poem, but one would hesitate to say that one had found much from which to deduce the nature of other poems, even by the same author.[5] Ideas about poetry may be brought home and applied, but their value lies in their creation of differences, the addition of distinctiveness and individuality to what is known, rather than in regularities and resemblances.

In short, it is difficult to accept the distinction which has been attributed to Turgot, the eighteenth-century statesman and economist, that 'the sciences are immense, as nature is; the arts, which are only relationships with our-

4 *Scientific Monthly* 81 (October 1955): 55

5 Even after hearing Debussy's *Prélude à l'après-midi d'un faune* and witnessing the danced interpretation of poem and music, one returns to Mallarmé's *Églogue* with a sense that nothing has been explained. The final words, 'je vais voir l'ombre que tu devins,' remain as mysterious as ever.

RONDEAV.

A foy, c'eſt fait de moy, car Iſabeau
M'a conjuré de luy faire vn Rondeau,
Cela me met en vne peine extréme.
Quoy treize vers, huict en eau, cinq en eme,
Ie luy ferois auſſi-toſt vn batteau!

En voila cinq pourtant en vn monceau.
Faiſons en huict, en inuoquant Brodeau,
Et puis mettons, par quelque ſtratageme,
        Ma foy c'eſt fait.

Si ie pouuois encor de mon cerueau
Tirer cinq vers, l'ouurage ſeroit beau;
Mais cependant, ie ſuis dedans l'onziéme,
Et ſi ie croy que ie fais le douziéme;
En voila treize ajuſtez au niueau.
        Ma foy, c'eſt fait.

FIGURE I This rondeau by Vincent Voiture succeeds only in reducing *ad absurdum*
the seventeenth-century cult of *la difficulté vaincue*. Facility in overcoming difficult
formal problems was sometimes regarded as the mark of a true poet. From an early
edition of the *Œuvres* of Voiture (Paris 1650)

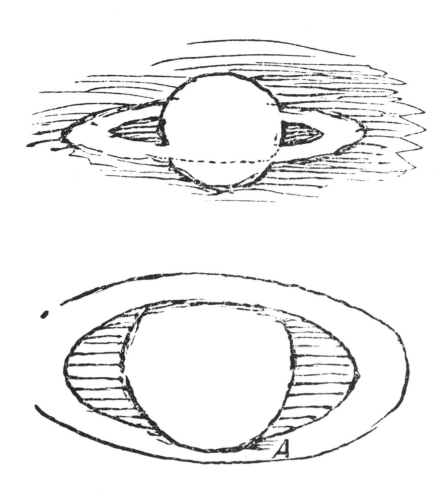

FIGURE 2 In contrast with technical invention of verbal trivia is the first drawing of the planet Saturn with its now well-known ring, as seen by Christiaan Huygens about 1656. This is derived from his original sketch, reproduced in the *Œuvres complètes*, volume 15 (photo University of Toronto Science and Medicine Library).

selves, are limited, as we are.' There seems to be no reason to regard the diversities possible in the arts as less baffling or less important than those found in the sciences. Both are mental constructs, with different purposes, principles, and products, and it is no reflection on either to suggest that they are incommensurable.

If a scientist is justified in doubting whether a humanist can be said to understand anything in the way a scientist does, what may we say the humanist is trying to achieve? The savant who divided all intellectual activity into two great branches, theoretical physics and collecting postage stamps, was not a philatelist. The humanist seeks accurate and progressively more complete description, but with only a minor interest in classification, for terms like classical, romantic, symbolist, and surrealist convey very little insight into the poem or play to which they are applied. Aesthetic evaluations are spontaneous and intuitive, susceptible only in the vaguest and most general way to rules. The rationalist Voltaire found that the only bad genre was the *genre ennuyeus*. In the twenty-second chapter of *Candide*, the hero meets an advocate of the most reasonable of styles, the learned scribbler who can recite the pattern of the perfect play, but whose tragedy can never hold the stage because it is so dull. The *je ne sais quoi*, the unknown quality which no classical, nor, for that matter, any other, critic could successfully define, is the indispensable component, the ultimate necessity in every work of art. With it, any irregularity is finally condoned; without it, no perfection of order, no elaboration of ornament can mask the weight of essential dullness.

The goal of the student of the humanities is therefore not the discovery of laws of art in general, nor the elaboration of formulae by which the material elements of a culture may be neatly relegated to oblivion while a textbook or a history takes the place of contact with originals. The physicist does not have to know the creative books and monographs by which the fabric of his science has been created; time and his predecessors have selected the crucial experiments, rewritten the formulae, rephrased the laws, and the supply house can offer him by return post the materials for a rerun of the tests. The blood, sweat, and tears of the great discoverers may be forgotten, but Swift and Voltaire, Raphael and Donatello, cannot be learned from a history book. Only hours spent in assiduous study of the original, in imaginative reconstruction of the particular experience the work embodies, can convey the meaning or meanings of *Gulliver* or *Candide* or 'The School of Athens.' The history or the textbook is a short cut, an abstraction in which one searches in vain for the experience of the flesh and nerves of the creative spirits whose achievements it reports. A guide to the subject may be memorized, but a compendium of information offers no basis on which a new art or a new literature may be founded. In its own way, history may be a creative activity too: Xenophon, Thucydides, Caesar, Commines, Gibbon, Voltaire, and Toynbee produce works of art whose study may be required as a humanistic pursuit; but here, once more, the considerations set forth above apply.

Reduced to objective scholarship, then, the humanist sees himself as a conservative, concerned with the preservation and comprehension of the past, the advocate of the understanding of other cultures remote in time and space, of other forms of human expression. He tends to see science as a major agent of social change, 'its silent appropriation of this dominant function,' as Lord Balfour writes, 'the most vital of the revolutions which have marked the development of modern civilization.' Whether this is a fair description of science or not, it is a conception that bulks large in the minds of many students and teachers of the humanities. They see in science the chief enemy of the traditional cultures, the more dangerous because of its very intentness on progress in techniques and immediate results, without regard to longer trends, or to the ultimate purposes in the culture and civilization as a whole. The ecologist Paul Sears may write that it is not the destiny of science to ease man's labors or prolong his life, or to serve the ends of power, 'but to enable man to walk upright, without fear, in a world which he at last will understand, and which is his home,' but there lingers a doubt whether all the engineers and technologists understand this fully, and a fear lest there be some misunderstanding about our home, which may become uninhabitable if the applications of science advance faster than, and unaccompanied by, understanding of man himself.

The difficulty lies, of course, in the tendency of modern scientific man, not necessarily the scientist, to forget what our world is like without him and his works, his highways and airports, his electronic media, and his efficient machinery of destruction. Many of the liveliest sciences of today are remote from human perceptions of measurement, of cause and effect. The range between erg and dyne, angstrom unit and meson, on one hand, and parsec and megaton on the other, is vastly greater than a Pascal could visualize three short centuries ago, and yet it is in this range of magnitudes that exact measurements are possible today. But plants and animals are within the frame of reference of everybody, and the weather, sickness and death, the comforts and conveniences of the common life, retain the element of hazard, and demand human, even humane, qualities of everyone. Science works on this level too, with its averages and extrapolations, but within the actuarial framework there is enough uncertainty about individual destiny to allow mankind to prefer the intuition of the artist, the tragic sense of a Racine, the cosmic vision of a Milton, the depth and diversity of a Dante, which no science, exact or social or humanistic, can explain away.

All this, of course, is not intended to deny that we are all in one academic boat and breathe a common atmosphere, more or less polluted. The influence of science on the scholarly study of the humanities has been considerable, and much of it has been good. While a scientific vogue in the 1880s led French theorists to discover deterministic elements in the development of the novel, the theatre, and even lyric poetry, a keener sense of what was scientifically possible soon brought about the discard of such analogies and a return to more accurate description of what had actually happened. Awareness of scientific standards of truth has developed the sense of fact, enlarged the capacity to criticize theory and hypothesis, and let much of the wind and water out of our work. It seems safe to say that the change in outlook among literary humanists, and perhaps among historians of art, aesthetics, and religion as well, over the last two centuries, is quite as marked and follows many of the same lines as those found among social scientists and general historians. The modern scholar seeks to avoid predicating occult powers and mysterious faculties; he strives, since the issue of plain and unornamented expression was raised about 1660 in France by Pascal and in England by Thomas Sprat, for a clear and direct manner in discussion of critical fact, so that his methods and results may be demonstrated convincingly to his colleagues.

Other results of the methods and objectives of science have not been quite so beneficial. There has been a trend, perhaps inevitable, towards seeking quick results by a high degree of specialization, not only within the various phenomena of a single culture or the narrow limits of a single method of analysis, but even in the broader fields of comparative literature. Still claiming to be humanists, scholars have become adepts in the trivial, confining their attention to the details of scientific bibliography, to the sociology of a brief period of a national literature, to a 'new criticism' narrowly applied, neglecting the general principle that a true picture of phenomena can only be established if the background is broad and the perspective accurate. Much of this has been undertaken, of course, in the belief that it is useful to seek positive results in a small field, applying familiar criteria to a few creations, in preference to placing those works of artistry in a rich historical and cultural perspective.

This narrowing of outlook is due partly to the increasing complexity of our culture, and partly to timidity in the face of general ideas that are not sheer platitude. It is easier to make up one's mind about Pascal's style than about his religious views or his value as a guide to human circumstance. Likewise, since we are speaking of educational issues, one cannot expect a teacher concerned with linguistic fact or biographic detail, readily absorbed and remembered, to have much time for the identification and discussion of intellectual themes, the tensions between religion and science, body and soul, ethics and the passions, in the authors he explicates. Yet there is no doubt that these issues of meaning, these questions of ends, are much closer to the heart of artist and author. There is a long path from the details of grammar and prosody, sources and influences, to the full understanding of what an author means. Unfortunately, the path is not always followed very far.

And so we return to the vigorous formula of Hippolyte Taine, 'Rien n'existe que par l'individu; c'est l'individu lui-même qu'il faut connaître.' Believing this, we turn away when Taine neglects this outlook in the adopted science of his theory of *race, milieu et moment*, which blights the introduction to his *History of English Literature*, telling us that vice and virtue are products, to be discussed like vitriol and sugar. Unreserved acceptance of this view denies the need for discrimination of ends and purposes, for diversity of methods, for a sense of personality. Taine's own writings cannot be reduced to a single standardized formula; he has a strong individual insight into the books he reads, the poets, novelists, dramatists, and critics he discusses. Neglecting his science of history, the rigorous analysis of abstractions that turn men into statistics, we can delight in his intuitive, spontaneous response to the art and literature of the world.

What has happened to Taine illustrates at least one of the attitudes of modern scholars towards the development of science in recent times. The formulae that propose an analysis of an author, reducing the data by such categories as race, milieu, and momentum, are neglected as science and taken as historical events, as so much raw material for study. They become products of their own coordinates, to be filed away among much other bric-à-brac of nineteenth-century positivism – interesting examples, valuable as we recreate the historic flow. Taine's science becomes, like other sciences, a subject for research, a special and unique activity, product of a personality rather than of biological and environmental factors. Like other events in the history of science, it has certain unique qualities; it is capable of being understood and evaluated in many different ways and terms, from different points of view. The humanist may try to see a scientific event as the scientist sees it, or he may legitimately see it in relation to any one of a number of parallel activities, from which it may derive, to which it may contribute, or towards which it may be antipathetic and harmful. He may, at some peril to the integrity and cogency of his main interests, neglect the contribution that a knowledge of the historical development of science may make to his special study, but this peril is no greater and no less than would be a neglect of the knowledge of the history of theology, politics, or morals. It is even possible that the humanist component is the most necessary ingredient of studies in the history of science.

The situation in which the humanist scholar found himself just a few years ago is well illustrated by the final pages of a book by A.R. Hall, *The Scientific Revolution, 1500-1800*.[6] The general themes of the book were clear; he could state with the optimism of the 1950s that in comparison with modern science, 'capitalism, the nation-state, art and literature, Christianity and democracy, seem regional idiosyncrasies, whose past is full of vicissitudes and whose future is full of dark uncertainty,' adding that modern science sprang from a society which lasted some four hundred years, now in dissolution, which it seemed likely to survive. Appropriately, it is the historical question that puzzles Hall. Science emerged from this intermediate stage, he writes, 'and it is this emergence that we do not adequately comprehend.' Two final pages develop the questions he finds he must ask; to a humanist they appear very familiar indeed, exact parallels of those he has been asking and partly answering these many years.

These questions concern the human factor, the element of uncertainty that is inevitable as soon as the unpredictable individual appears on the scene. Why do men commit themselves to one kind of proposition about nature rather than to another? Why is one type of statement more plausible than another? Why talk of corpuscles rather than of spirits, without factual evidence for either? Why all the talk about the vacuum? Thought was modified in ways that cannot be ascribed to the results of observation and experiment; historical comprehension demands psychological and philosophical insight, and a command of historical facts which is not now available, 'for,' he adds, 'the operation, the incidence, and the impact of the creative intellect are almost unknown.' Finally, Hall remarks that 'we cannot write the full history of science save by reflecting the operations of original thought, which we do not understand; and ... we cannot exclude from science, which is rational, the influence of factors which are irrational.'

It is hard to summarize the principal elements of the study of the humanities. It seems to be essential to expect that there will be a recognizable presence of an individual human being in every investigation. This expectation must, of course, be modified by ironic perception of the limits, not only of human capacities, but also of the subject matter – and all these limits are in themselves relative. The scholar knows his vision will be partial, though he will strive with Pascal to see his subject from as many angles as possible, still recognizing that he may be wrong, even in an area in which he is presumed competent. Thus he will conclude with a surmise, whose accuracy will demand the study of the human being at the heart of any creation in science and the arts; and he must recognize that the unity of knowledge, if it is to

6 (London, New York, Toronto, Longmans, Green 1954) pp. 364-7

explain phenomena usefully, depends on finding unity in man himself rather than on discovering it in the external world.

Somebody (my notes do not say who) has written that James Thurber's *Let Your Mind Alone* is 'about seven times as educational as anything James Harvey Robinson ever wrote, because Thurber has digested his culture; it has turned into Mr. T.'

It may be suggested that the best literature, and perhaps the best scholarship, is that in which science and the other components have been completely absorbed, have 'turned into Mr. T.' In other words, they have penetrated the whole structure, contributing their proper share of understanding and perceptiveness, a sense of relevance to the general range of organized experience. Science, among other things, appears thus in the best of Voltaire's tales, in *Zadig* and in *Micromégas*; less obviously in *Candide*. It is present in Flaubert's *Un Cœur simple,* as in *Madame Bovary,* and in a modern novel like *La Peste* by Albert Camus, as well as in Pascal's *Pensées*. The digestive process is not always complete; in much science fiction it is not uniformly successful. Much literature and art, and many humanists, reject science in any form, or leave it in a state resembling its original condition, an undigested lump, an uncomfortable burden to the sense and to the spirit.

Neither scientist nor humanist scholar should be surprised, therefore, if there is an inevitable lag between the arrival of a new science, a new theory, or even a new view of the universe, and its general and fruitful acceptance by the literate public. A similarly comprehensible delay occurs before a new outlook among artists and scholars is understood by scientists. One can sympathize with the impatience of those who expect immediate synthesis of the two outlooks, but it may be suggested that we are all better off for the presence around us of great diversities of outlook, methods of argument, and investigation, as well as of objectives. Science and humanistic endeavor differ profoundly in many ways, and will remain different as long as man's nature retains its protean capacity. For Balzac, mankind in his time presented a human comedy, in which men and women played many different roles; he was wise in his day, and his vision permits another perspective, historical in its main dimension, scientific in its theme and personalities.

This chapter is revised from a contribution to a symposium of the American Association for the Advancement of Science, Atlanta 1955, published in *Scientific Monthly* 83 (October 1956): 169-75. A byproduct of the work of the Committee on the Humanistic Aspects of Science, set up in 1950 by the American Council of Learned Societies, it is a footnote to Harcourt Brown, ed., *Science and the Creative Spirit,* published for the council by the University of Toronto Press in 1958, reissued in the Scholarly Reprint Series, 1971.

CHAPTER TWO

Pantagruel
and health

RABELAIS has always interested doctors; many have written about him, and professional sympathy and clinical insight have contributed much to the interpretation of his books. Innumerable articles and monographs discuss his knowledge of anatomy, his comments on pregnancy and childbirth, the wounds inflicted in the encounters vividly described in the first two novels of his cycle, and the treatments by which his personages achieve their cures, some of them too marvelous for belief. Occasionally claims are made for him as a surgeon and practitioner which sober reading of the documents will not support – assertions which irritate rather than enlighten, creating skepticism in a reader not predisposed to concede omniscience and omnipotence to the entire medical profession.

Of course doctors know that truth is visible from no one angle, that a professional outlook does not encompass the whole of life, and that a multiplicity of points of view promotes insight. Likewise, the emphasis which critics commonly place on Rabelais as man of letters, as story-teller, or as comic author, their tendency to focus on one or other of a dozen disciplines or modes of thought, on music, on folklore, on the tradition of Erasmus, or the teachings of evangelical preachers, may easily preclude consideration of other aspects of the man and distort essential facts. In the complex case of Rabelais, whose work bears traces of many pervasive influences, the particular problem is that of achieving balance and consistent clarity. In the present context, we ask what training and practice in the medical arts may do to a novelist, what may be the effect of the disciplines of a medical faculty of the Renaissance on the outlook or motives of a man who creates human beings in the pages of romance?

The general question cannot be answered *a priori*. It is more helpful to take a specific case – a writer such as François Rabelais, who studied medicine in his maturity in Paris between 1527 and 1529, before transferring to Montpellier, where he earned degrees in 1531 and 1537. The writing of his fiction coincides with his medical career: *Pantagruel* appeared in 1532, and the puzzling fourth book antedated by about a year his disappearance from public life and presumed death in April of 1553. As personal physician to Cardinal Jean du Bellay he went to Italy in 1534, an episode which gave new directions to his career, in personal relations as well as in intellectual orientation. Viewed in his lifetime as a doctor rather than as an author, Rabelais has become a major figure in the literature of the world, creator of the giant heroes Gargantua and Pantagruel and of the fantastic milieu in which they live, as well as of the lesser characters whose names have come to represent types: the rogue Panurge, the unforgettable Frère Jean, Picrochole drunk with a dictator's power, Judge Bridois with his wise senility, the mad Sibyl of Panzoust, and many others. Characterized by Voltaire as 'our giggling rural vicar,'[1] Rabelais ranks with François Villon, Montaigne, Molière, Honoré de Balzac, and Victor Hugo in the handful of names France has added to the essential library of the world. He may not be the most accessible of authors to a modern reader, but his roots are deep in humanity and his words have left their mark on the language of today. Taste has changed since Madame de Rambouillet brought Italian standards to a Gascon court in Paris, imposing the artful delicacy of a woman's manners on writers and critics, and through them on publishers, booksellers, and the wide reading public.

We may look at once at the difficulties the reading of Rabelais imposes on us. His language is his own private brew, in part remnant of older French, in part dialect or patois (even jargon), in part invented for his own artistic purposes, sometimes from Greek roots when available French words did not lie at hand. Derived from the speech of his day in its rhythms and syntax, it is often obscure, for he was no theorist and had no dreams of establishing norms for posterity. He took no pains to develop commonplaces into the Renaissance equivalents of Horace's brass and oak. He writes for himself and his private public, which he creates as we read. We are expected to join him in his

1 *Letters concerning the English Nation by Mr de Voltaire* (London 1733) p. 215. This phrase, which has no equivalent in the French text of the *Lettres philosophiques*, appears in one of the fourteen letters (the twenty-second) which the present writer regards as having been composed by Voltaire in the English language. See my article, 'The Composition of the *Letters concerning the English Nation*' in W.H. Barber et al., eds., *The Age of the Enlightenment: Studies Presented to Theodore Besterman* (Edinburgh and London, Oliver and Boyd 1967) pp. 15-34.

fun and his commentary on mankind, to recognize and enter his world, which we find includes our own, and to become at last each a private Pantagruel, with 'une certain gayeté d'esprit, conficte en mespris des choses fortuites.' If there is an air of inscrutable mystery about it all, it arises, according to the most Rabelaisian of scholars, Gilbert Chinard, himself a man of Rabelais' *pays de vache*, from the rural trait of deliberate concealment of the truth from outsiders; the answer to a question may be known, but it will not be quickly revealed. In the course of conversation Chinard added that this trait, common in Poitou, was the despair of the German army in 1942 and 1943. The invaders had a limited knowledge of Rabelais.

Not every reader has seen the need of making this cautious effort towards intuitive comprehension. More than most authors, Rabelais develops the speculative vein in his commentators, and as a result innumerable indefensible conclusions have been drawn in the interpretation of his book. There are literally shelves of volumes on him as Rosicrucian, occultist, freemason, and initiate into the arcane, beclouding the issue of his meaning with the dense fog of the private perspectives of well-intentioned souls whose idiosyncrasies have taken over their common sense. The presence in his own age of emblematists, whose influence may be seen in the work of Albrecht Dürer and Hieronymus Bosch, of chemists like Theophrastus Bombastus von Hohenheim (better known as Paracelsus), subtle humanists like Erasmus, erudite men like Guillaume Budé and Jacques Lefèvre d'Étaples, as well as more dynamic figures ranging from Cornelius Agrippa through Jean Calvin, Martin Luther, and Ignatius Loyola to Henry VIII, Francis I, and Charles V, has suggested that Rabelais' big and undisciplined book must include everything and everybody of his time, and that it may be interpreted in terms equally comprehensive and equally undisciplined.

And so there have been books of every kind on Rabelais. The legendary figure is not completely lost from view; the less scholarly encyclopedias still cling to the colorful and improbable tales that early accumulated around the few solid facts in his biography. From the documents research has produced a more plausible Rabelais, but the evidence does not quell the impression that there must have been unique and remarkable personal qualities to put the traditional figure afloat in the history of his era. Whatever may be the proportion of legend, there is no doubt of the genial nature of the man, of his power as a story-teller, of his way with patients. One senses an urbanity, a wit, a keen intelligence, and an alert understanding of the varieties of human nature, qualities that made him the doctor that he was and contributed to the largeness of his vision. This genial accessibility has contributed to his fame; Rabelais has been 'appreciated' uncritically on many convivial occasions, sometimes with useful results when an imaginative and philosophic doctor has penetrated beyond the surface to see his colleague as he thinks about health and disease of body and mind. It would be ungrateful to depreciate the import of such postprandial lucubrations in offering a word of cautious warning.

A few established facts allow us to put François Rabelais in the context of his age. He was born about 1490 in or near Chinon, into a family that was bourgeois and legal, close to the land and local feudal customs. As a boy he was destined for the church, which suggests that his family saw no good way of setting him up in life in any other calling. From the Franciscans he went in his maturity to the Benedictines, where he began Greek and Latin studies with more freedom from monastic restraints, developing at the same time some association with humanists. His legal background was useful in understanding human and social relationships. A new peace of mind came to him as the world of learning opened through the reading of ancient historians, notably Herodotus, modern physicians such as Giovanni Manardo, and, most important, the leaders of humanist thought, Erasmus and Guillaume Budé.

All this made the little world of Poitou seem limited, and Paris beckoned. He went there in 1527, and soon entered the famous medical school, where Günther von Andernach was teaching, and where the patron and protector of scholars suspected of a tincture of Lutheranism was Cardinal Jean du Bellay, Bishop of Paris. Rabelais was no longer an adolescent, and was free from the restricted life of the colleges. One is not surprised to find that there is a record of a widow in Paris seeking legitimization of two children, whose father is said to be one Franciscus Rabelaesus.

In any case, he now left Paris, where there were rising constraints on thought and activity, and in 1530 went to Montpellier, notable for its autonomous faculty of medicine, where students chose their sponsors and teachers, determined and collected fees, and paid the salaries of professors. Freedom of thought prevailed, and students from Germany, the Netherlands, Italy, England, and Spain, as well as from many parts of France, contributed to a cosmopolitan atmosphere that effectively shut out the dogmatic intolerance that was to hamper the growth of the University of Paris for so many years. The linguistic diversity of the student population as well as the concentration on clinical medicine and the consequent emphasis on the patient and his idiosyncrasies had lasting effects on Rabelais and on his books. At Montpellier he gained power as a teacher and found new directions in his writing: for Epiphany 1531 he wrote and produced the student farce which centuries later Anatole France developed into *The Man who Married a Dumb Wife*. Later in the year he was teaching medicine from Greek texts in Ionic characters, as he says, from his own manuscript of Galen.

At Montpellier he became acquainted with the biologist Guillaume Rondelet, author of a treatise on fishes, and Antoine Saporta, later to be chancellor of the university. Thus at forty or thereabouts, Rabelais was bachelor and licentiate in medicine, examining candidates, permitted to exercise his art beyond the immediate environs of Montpellier. He could now accept appointment as surgeon at the general hospital of Lyon, the Grand Hôtel-Dieu du Pont-de-Rhône, sometimes referred to as the Nosocomion, and enter on active practice. He seems to have remained well within traditional limits, a man of the transition between the middle ages and the flowering of modern scientific medicine in the years after Vesalius' *Fabrica* of 1543. The focus of the profession was not yet on experimental techniques and the advancement of the art; there seemed to be no need of penetrating further into the mysteries of anatomy and function than was allowed by means available to Hippocrates and Galen. Although magnifying glasses were used to assist aging eyes, little use was made of them for the study of delicate structure and minute bodies. Invention in the technical arts was confined mainly to the mechanical trades, the arts of war, and engineering. Doctors, concerned with the unchanging processes of health and disease, birth and death, were not inclined to believe that knowledge could be usefully augmented by new devices.

Thus there were as yet few who saw that the combined efforts of a generation of men in possession of a new point of view and the new tools that would derive from it could probe deeply into the human body and its functions. The ancient texts were still the preferred object of study; they could be checked against observation, but with limited means of obtaining clear vision of fine detail, it was thought more probable that the modern observer was in error than the classic text. The habit of argumentation and debate was strong; the truth of an old text was not questioned, and the medical world was not ready to revise procedures on a basis which could not be argued in syllogisms. A young doctor could not readily attack Galen for his errors in observation; what counted was internal consistency in argument, and this had been transferred by tradition and habit into the very foundation of the medical art. Two generations of original genius would be needed to turn the philological humanist into the scientific physiologist of the century of William Harvey.

And so, in spite of the strong clinical interests of the school of Montpellier, it could not be expected that a Rabelais, child and student of the law, should turn quickly to empirical methods and become an apostle of the new sciences and medical reform. He brought to his work an analytical mind, an interest in the traditional problems of the doctor, and a skill in dissection that was praised by his contemporaries. He recognized that health of body was related to health of soul, and that mental attitude was of extreme importance in therapy. He was aware of the impact of social crises on public health, that the conjunction of Mars and Venus led to syphilis and other ills. Good food in moderation was essential; his satire on gormandizers has often been misunderstood. In short, intellectual activities depended on natural good health maintained by moderation in food and drink, in exercise and repose. As Rabelais' Doctor Rondibilis declares, at the end of his counsel to Panurge, 'Mettons-nous neutre en médicine et moyen en philosophie, par participation de l'une et l'autre extrémité et par compartiment du temps, maintenant en l'une, maintenant en l'autre extrémité.'

Just as Rabelais could draw no useful line between the functions of body and soul, so he made no clear distinction between the fine and useful arts. For him language was a tool and a delight, and his power of expression so colors his communication of ideas and opinions with hilarious farce and exuberant poetry that the reader finds he must penetrate beyond the imagery and the vigorous verbs to discover the serious and hidden message of the book. We have been warned in the *Gargantua* prologue that, as philosophic dogs chew marrow bones to extract their hidden treasure, so must we gnaw his text in repeated readings to find 'bien aultre goust ... et doctrine plus absconce, laquelle ... révélera de très haultz sacremens et mystères horrificques, tant en ce que concerne nostre religion que aussi l'estat politicq et vie œconomicque.' This awareness of an ability to express a wealth of meaning in obscure, often fantastic, language, in the firm belief that the intelligent reader will finally understand him in spite of his curious idiom, sets Rabelais apart from other authors more conscious of the reactions of a conservative public. He wrote for a leisurely age; he expected the reader to read his book as he would Herodotus or Plutarch or Lucian, or perhaps Erasmus or *Utopia*, in repeated sessions of vigorous wrestling with the sense. The results for the cooperative student would be twofold: critical delight in the sheer virtuosity of the writing in all its fun and humor, and an understanding of the subtleties which enhance the direct and powerful message perceptible through the ironies of the interplay of deeply etched characters. If the message is obscure today, it is because we have strayed far from the simple evangelical teaching which lies near the heart of every major episode of the book. Learned men have neglected the meaning of Rabelais' work because they are no longer, or never have been, touched by the gospel of Christ, the *philosophia Christi*, which Erasmus, chief of the moderates, expounded with such ironic power in the *Praise of Folly*, and which underlies the *Utopia* of Thomas More.

Thus language was art and tool for Rabelais. It could communicate fact and intellectual method, or it could express details of personality and the finer points of sensation and intuitive experience. Each purpose admitted style and individual differences, the peculiar contribution of the personality of the writer, apart altogether from content and logical arrangement. Like any other art, it could be fine or useful, and was more often both. Man was served in either case, and the rules that governed the arts depended on an inner vision quite as much as on the limitations of sense and nervous endurance and the constraints of a flesh too weak, too easily fatigued.

The view that man is a unity in body and mind runs through all of Rabelais' work, medical as well as fictional, and perhaps indicates the place he should occupy in an account of medical thought and writing in the Renaissance. His first publication, an edition of the *Epistolae medicinales* of Giovanni Manardo, was typical of his interests. Manardo was a doctor of Ferrara, a humanist who, in this work, combined the field study of plants with a discussion of parallel descriptions in Dioscorides — natural history and textual study in one book. In the same year, 1532, Rabelais brought out an edition of the *Aphorisms* of Hippocrates along with three other Hippocratic texts and Galen's little tract *On Medical Art*, in a small volume with annotations on the language. Each duodecimo was prefaced with a dedication in which Rabelais gave some account of his purposes and philosophy, consistent with ideas that recur in his later writings and infuse his work as a whole. This kind of editing was a means of understanding the traditional arts; it taught the reader the vocabulary of the ancient doctors, thus establishing a medium for teaching and discussion on an international scale and discouraging the tendency to use terms of strictly local usage. The Latin used for the notes and dedicatory epistles was refined by Ciceronian criteria, and the newly developed means of circulation in several foreign markets subjected the standards of the editors and printers to criticism from many medical schools. Historians of science now recognize the indispensable nature of the work of the humanists who put ancient texts like these into general circulation in inexpensive pocket formats.

Perspective can be gained by comparing the career of Rabelais with that of Andreas Vesalius. Rabelais had come to medicine late in life, through reading rather than by early vocation. Before he went to Montpellier he had had little or no technical or clinical training; in contrast, Vesalius was studying in Paris under Günther and Sylvius in 1534, at barely twenty. His *Tabulae*, which Singer and Rabin have edited under the title *Prelude to Modern Science*, were printed before he was twenty-four, the *Fabrica humani corporis* at twenty-nine, and his last work, the *China-root Epistle*, in 1546, when he was younger than Rabelais had been on entering the medical faculty at Paris as a student. Vesalius' work was over before he reached the age at which Rabelais began practice. Although Rabelais was aware of a ferment in contemporary thought – his letters of dedication to André Tiraqueau and Geoffroy d'Estissac both speak of it in general terms – yet he could not entirely escape the legalistic conservatism of his family, and he came no nearer to what is today accepted as science than the outlook of an intelligent observer. A brief excursion into productive scholarship as a medical humanist left a mark on him even though he did not return to the editing of Greek texts and Latin translations with marginal commentaries.

His novels are the basis of his fame, and it is from them that one learns to know the man. Published at intervals between 1532 and 1552, the four authentic books are diversified in style, in subject matter, and in artistic purpose. They are inconsistent as narrative; characters appear and disappear, returning in new forms with new traits. The simple plot is largely forgotten in the last two books, and is not much more than a bare skeleton on which the author hangs his enormous commentary on human affairs. The book has a tone of its own, a personal outlook on life, modified as the author ages and gains wisdom as well as mastery of his art. Ranging from outrageous farce to serious comedy, the successive episodes present the nature of mankind in two aspects, body and soul, cooperating or at cross-purposes, a theme that keeps the reader's interest high. Where the doctor sees disease of mind or body, unhealth, the Christian moralist – one remembers that Rabelais was both – sees defect of soul. The two points of view are present, as the obscenely comic ruffian Panurge in *Pantagruel* (1532) develops into the indecisive rogue of the third book (1546) and then into the coward and buffoon of the fourth (1552). In contrast is Pantagruel himself; in 1532 not very sharply drawn, with crude inconsistencies, he reappears in 1546 as a giant model of physical and moral health, giving the tone of the latter part of the whole cycle.

But it is the presence of the anatomy and physiology of man, more carefully and thoroughly portrayed than was usual in his time, that gives a special flavor to Rabelais' novel, and particular resonance to the adjective rabelaisian. Infirmities and health, natural functions, and the brutal unnaturalities of combat are all frankly described in terms whose precision betrays the professional hand, while the burlesque note reveals the *carabin*, the medical student of Paris and Montpellier, more evident in *Pantagruel* than elsewhere, but recurring briefly in the *Tiers Livre*, when Epistemon recalls the Patelinian comedy of the Epiphany of 1531. Parody and farce yield to a more sober note, a sense of hygiene, in *Gargantua* (1534) when the education of the hero is described in detail and at length as the final chapters portray an idealized vision of the life of Renaissance ladies and gentlemen – far removed from the

Vies des dames galantes of the Abbé de Brantôme. The opening books are not easily summed up, oscillating between contrasting modes and venturing into regions which a mere giant story cannot easily survey.

The *Pantagruel* of 1532, first to be published of the four books, is broadly vulgar in most of its contents, rarely erudite in tone, in spite of passages in which it is clear that Rabelais had various classical or modern authors in mind, alluded to or parodied with small respect. Medical and pharmaceutical material is brief and inconsequential, asking little of the reader. There are burlesque references to books of the profession in the library of Saint-Victor and to doctors of Montpellier, 'qui sentoyent les clistères comme vieux diables.' In another vein, the famous letter from Gargantua urges Pantagruel to revisit 'les livres des médecins grecs, arabes, et latins, sans contemner les Thalmudistes et caballistes,' and by 'fréquentes anatomies' to acquire a 'parfaicte cognoissance de l'autre monde, qui est l'homme.'

But on the whole, allusions to surgery and medicine in this book are satirical or merely comic. Epistemon, decapitated in conflict with the Dipsodes, is repaired by the deft hands of Panurge, treated with ointments and white wine, after which he tells of his adventures 'en enfer et par les Champs Elisées,' recounting the present state of the great men of the past. A little later, Pantagruel falls ill; the 'drogues lénitives et diuréticques' of his doctors are responsible for the numerous hot springs of France and Italy, while the congestion in his immense intestinal tract is cleared by the efforts of workmen swallowed in seventeen copper balls under the direction of a solitary lantern-bearer.

Like *Pantagruel, Gargantua* (1534 or 1535) follows the conventional pattern of a giant story: birth, infancy, and education are followed by the entrance of the hero into the warfare of his father's world. In this novel, however, there is a difference. Here the full development of the child is given us, attention is paid to his physical, moral, and intellectual growth, rather than to the broad context of the universities and the monastic library satirized in the earlier book. Evangelical religion, as practiced by advanced preachers of the time, is part of the boy's daily routine. Tutor and pupil are in contact at all times: Gargantua learns and exercises, thoroughly and at length, in emphatic opposition to traditional schooling. The program of education is an expression of the humanist ideals and interests which Rabelais shared with his patron, the Cardinal Jean du Bellay, who had been one of the sponsors of the Collège des lecteurs royaux (1530), which later became the Collège de France. The views implicit in *Gargantua* represent a complete reaction against the theology and disciplines of the Sorbonne and the other colleges of Paris, and the dominant position of the officers of the University of Paris in the management of public education.

In these ways, and later in the third and fourth books of the cycle, Rabelais takes a stand on questions of the day – on the power of Rome and the new ferment in the church, on European politics and war, satirized in the latter half of the book in the struggle against Picrochole. In general, he finds a middle path with Erasmus and the Erasmians, between Luther and Rome, between Henry VIII and the Papacy, a direction which was for a time that of the French monarchy. Now in the professional life of Lyon, a larger and more cosmopolitan centre than Montpellier, he becomes aware of new outlooks on life and the arts, of changes desirable in education, of humanist attitudes towards the learning of the schools and towards traditional commentaries on ancient thought and science.

Gargantua is an organic book, roughly Platonic in plan even as it uses the traditional epic hero as its protagonist. The ascent from the grotesque detail of the birth scene, through the natural filth of a rural infancy, the naïve simplicity of his nursemaids and rustic clerical teachers, leads at last to contact with the son of one of the local gentry, whose trained elocution and polite manners reduce the lubberly child to tears. Gargantua is sent to Paris, where the fuller wisdom and wide experience of his tutor Ponocrates give him what he needs: training in ancient science, the capacity to observe the stars and the world of nature and man and to discuss his findings. He exercises on a giant's scale, and he seeks direct contact with the divine by reading the Bible and in prayer; in these passages there is no reference to the Mass.

Among innumerable comments, direct and implicit, on the University of Paris, the most telling is the grotesquely hilarious episode in which the dean of the faculty of theology comes to request the return of the bells of Notre Dame stolen by Gargantua. Perhaps even more ironically effective is the silent omission of all contact between Gargantua and the innumerable monkish teachers in the forty-odd colleges on and around the Montagne Sainte-Geneviève. But satire and farce do not hide Rabelais' constructive educational thought; good books wisely read and directed observation of good men and God's world are essential elements in the education of the young. There is realism in this, a recognition that this is how adolescents can discover their world and themselves if they have the opportunity. The emphasis is on the health of Gargantua, on his well-being, in the way of whose progress and growth nothing is permitted to stand.

After *Gargantua* came another visit to Italy, including several months in Rome. Rabelais returned to Lyon in 1536, and acquired a canonry in the

Abbey of Saint-Maur, near Paris, through the good offices of his patron Cardinal. In February or March of 1537 he was present with Guillaume Budé, the poet Clément Marot, and seven other scholars and men of letters at a banquet given in Paris by Étienne Dolet, the learned printer burned a few years later for heresy; the host celebrated his dinner in a Latin poem in which he describes his guests, among them

> Franciscus Rabelaesus, honos et gloria certa
> Artis Paeoniae, qui vel de limine Ditis
> Extinctos revocare potest et reddere luci,

lines which with Renaissance exaggeration associate Rabelais with Aesculapius and Hippocrates, the founders of the medical arts. In May 1537 Rabelais received his doctorate; now 42, perhaps older, he was able to acquit himself of the relatively heavy terminal expenses required by the traditions of Montpellier. He lectured in Lyon, performing anatomies; his skill was praised by contemporaries, for actual work was usually done by technicians. Later in the year he explicated the *Prognostics*, a Hippocratic text, in Montpellier. He seems to have been a successful teacher.

We now come to a problem of some importance in evaluating the medical career of Rabelais – the discussion of a surgical device, the Glossocomion, which some have said he invented.

For the use of surgeons to whom Greek and Latin were unknown, publishers had been providing French versions of classic texts, small duodecimos, cheap and convenient to carry. One of the most popular of these was Galen's *Methodus medendi*, the *Therapeutics*, which appeared in a series of volumes beginning about 1536. The translation was made in Lyon and attributed to one Philiatros, who may have been Jean Canappe, a colleague of Rabelais at the Grand Nosocomion, chief hospital of the city. Book 4 of this work had been published by François Juste, who had brought out *Pantagruel* and *Gargantua*; books 5 and 6 followed from the presses of Pierre de Sainte-Lucie, who had reprinted *Pantagruel* in 1535. Towards the end of book 6 is a crude woodcut (figure 3) representing an instrument described by Galen, not only in the *Methodus medendi*, but also in his commentary on the Hippocratic text *On Fractures*, and still more explicitly by Oribasius, *De machinamentis*. Galen refers regularly to the recent invention of the device, which would place its introduction to surgical practice at some time in the second century A.D.

What should have been puzzling is the attribution of its 'invention' to Rabelais. The date of the drawing is 1537; I have found no earlier attempt to

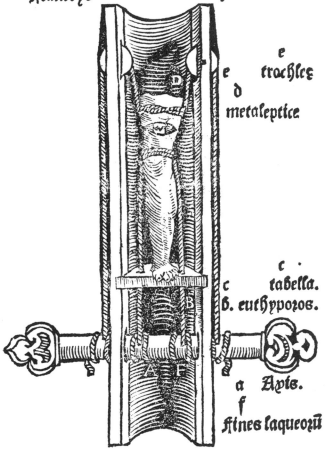

Glottocomon figure par l'inuention de M. francoys Rabelais docteur en medicine.

e
e trochleæ
d
metaleptice

c
c tabella.
b. euthyppozos.

a Axis.
f
fines laqueozū

FIGURE 3 Glossocomion or Glottocomon drawn by the art of Master François Rabelais, Doctor of Medicine. In this surgical instrument, the fractured leg was placed in a kind of trough, firmly attached by ropes which exerted tension by the winding of a single axis (*a*), to which all four ends of the two ropes (*f*) were fastened; *b* indicates the channel in which the tension is exerted, *c* a platform which keeps the patient's foot in position, *d* the reversed tension exerted on the upper part of the leg; and *e* the two pulleys by which the direction of the tension is reversed. This crude sketch based on Galen's description appears to be the first shown in a printed book; this earliest reference to Rabelais as a medical doctor is found in the only known copy of this edition of Galen's text in French translation (photo Bibl. nat., Paris).

represent the Glossocomion in a printed book, although such may have existed in Galenic manuscripts. And there seems to be no evidence that the instrument was used in hospitals for fractures of the femur. It had obvious disadvantages; cumbersome and demanding much force to operate, it had to be set firmly on a solid table, and even worse, it offered awkward and uncomfortable accommodation for the patient. Traction had to be applied by hand through the use of two cranks; the powerful men who performed this necessary function would undoubtedly be very much in the way of the surgeon working on the fracture and trying to achieve, without anaesthetics, of course, as perfect a setting of the bones as possible. The present writer has been told – by Sir Geoffrey Keynes – that the patient could be accommodated in the box face down, which is a position that the old illustrations never suggest. In contrast with the elaborate operating table of Guy de Chauliac (1300-68), the Glossocomion could be carried about, even if it resembled an instrument of torture. But as men with badly set fractured thighs were condemned to incurable lameness and painful walking, the device offered some hope for mobility, until the introduction of anaesthetics allowed the surgeon to work with relaxed muscles and give nature time to mend a broken femur in its original conformation.

However, on the basis of a hasty examination of this crude sketch, Arthur Heulhard of Nevers wrote a small book, *Rabelais Chirurgien* (1885), crediting Rabelais with the invention of the device, as well as of a kind of probe useful in hernia operations.

Unfortunately for Heulhard's thesis, too often quoted in the literature on Rabelais, the word *invention* used in connection with an old print or drawing refers simply to the effort of putting the sketch on paper, from which the print is reproduced. A second edition of the sixth book of the *Methodus medendi* replaces the ill-drawn handiwork of Rabelais with a better woodcut, no artist being named. In the ornamented initial capitals of the *Fabrica* of Vesalius, the device is shown in use on the lower leg, with no reference to a modern inventor; it was redrawn for Guido Guidi's *Chirurgia* of 1544, in two positions. These last drawings were made by Primaticcio; the Glossocomion here seems even less practical than before, because of the bad angle of traction through the upper pulleys. Even Ambroise Paré's *Chirurgie* makes no reference to contemporary uses of the box, a fact suggesting that active surgeons had other ways of dealing with a fracture of the femur. In short, the device could be used on the tibia, and it was fairly well known in erudite circles as it was to Rabelais, who had made the rough drawing for Pierre de Sainte-Lucie and who wrote the Latin word at the appropriate place in the margin of his folio Galen, of which the five handsome volumes from the Aldine Press are now in the library of the University of Sheffield. Theoretically practicable, the Glossocomion may have been tried, but in spite of ancient authority it was of doubtful utility in view of the disadvantages outlined above.

Something, however, was to be learned from this excursion, and it is not what Heulhard thought it was. One does not have to invent a device in order to profit from a lesson it may teach, nor does one have to be an expert draftsman to see a principle involved in the mechanics of the device one has drawn. Consideration of the text of such medical classics as those by Galen – in which there is continuous reference from the signs of trouble in the body to the available means of rectification – leads easily and quickly to a sense that man has a capacity to achieve power over natural process, that indeed man's life depends on the extent to which his understanding of nature can lead to a degree of management of the physical world for his own purposes. If this is true in matters of daily life, in the winning of shelter and food, for instance, it is even more certain that in conflict with natural effects, in injuries and disease, man must use nature against herself, reducing the tension of the muscles in order to set a broken bone.

And so collaboration with Canappe and the printers in the popularization of a classic text, in an attempt to supplement the armamentarium of contemporary surgeons by the portrayal of instruments described in those texts, and producing not a method by which an operation was performed but a picture of the instrument used in that operation, brings Rabelais to a new level in his thought, in which mechanical principles are placed in realistic contrast with an ideal system in which immanent goodness struggled with evil, in the hope that victory could be won by words and thoughts alone.

Up to this point, Rabelais' thought, so far as it was defined, had been largely Platonic, assuming that the true, the beautiful, and the good would ultimately triumph, in humanistic independence of the machinery devised by mankind. There was, and still is, a kind of thought that asks that the doctor step out of nature's way to let her do her own healing, inevitable if the vital principle in the patient cooperates and if external influences do not oppose. The coeducational Abbaye de Thélème described near the end of *Gargantua* had been an expression of an extreme form of this ideal; it was to be a source of health, both moral and physical, the birthplace of a more perfect mankind, even though certain cynics have feared it as a haven of immorality. It had no dogma, no doctrine except that of *fais ce que voudras*, which may be read *Do what thou wilt*, or perhaps *Do what Thou wilt*, 'Thy will be done,' if one seeks a teaching from the New Testament in it. Thélème had no discipline except that of self-control and communal freedom, and no disease. Its *vis medicatrix naturae*, the healing power of nature, worked within man, favoring life, the chief aid to the Hippocratic outlook. The physician's duty was to see that nothing interfered with the healing process.

Within this range of ideas, the natural tension of the muscles in major fractures was a rugged inconsistency. The surgeon's task was complicated by the necessity of overcoming the muscular force that nature herself interposed to thwart the reconstruction of the original form of the limb. Nature did not cooperate; her powers acted blindly to reject the surgeon's art. The bones could not be set without great and painful effort, and even when they were in position, only a most unnatural appliance could re-establish the normal limb. It was clear that Platonic optimism did not account for the facts.

Such thinking about causes and effects was corroborated by Rabelais' experience during two or three years in Piedmont as secretary and companion of Guillaume du Bellay, elder brother of Jean the Cardinal, and a leader of the French forces occupying the duchy of Savoie. Guillaume became governor of the province for a few months late in 1542, fell ill, and set out over the mountains for France. He died in January of 1543 at Saint Symphorien de Lay, between Lyon and Roanne; his body was embalmed by Rabelais and an associate, Master Gabriele Taffini of Savigliano, and taken to Le Mans for burial in the cathedral there. As governor of Savoie, Guillaume had been a much more enlightened administrator than occupied territories have usually enjoyed. When the harvest of 1541 had failed, du Bellay had imported wheat from the Rhône valley at his own expense for the use of the people of Turin, and similarly, when it was found necessary to billet cavalry there, he assigned them to the suburbs, where food and lodging for man and beast were more readily available than in the crowded city. Judicious intervention countervailed against the crude forces of natural law, and the value of human ingenuity was demonstrated. For Rabelais, the large-hearted leader remained a personal hero. Guillaume du Bellay's wisdom, his search for a middle path, his willingness to compromise in order to obtain religious peace in Europe, a design which coincided for a time with the policies of Francis I, expressed an ideal towards which Rabelais' thought had tended, and which now found even greater justification.

From such kernels sprang the *Tiers Livre*, the third book of 1546. The narrative pattern of the earlier books is abandoned as the development of ideas imposes a new design. The chief characters, Pantagruel, who derives many traits from du Bellay, and his companion, Panurge, now talk at leisure about topics uppermost in their creator's mind. It was not Rabelais' way to present ideas baldly, analyzed with subtle logic in the manner of Socrates and Plato. He uses rather the model of Lucian, of the *Colloquies* of Erasmus, of the farces and the *sermons joyeux* heard in the streets of Paris, in which the talk goes all around the subject, which is never entirely forgotten but never entirely visible either. The method is oblique, using a kind of symbolism, in comic tone, in which a character, in this instance Panurge, reveals his anxieties with tedious reiteration, at the same time making it clear that obviously he does not know himself. Other personages from the first two books reappear in the suite of Pantagruel, with some of their traits and qualities emphasized, their typical names justifying their presence and their actions. Epistemon, the wise, the prudent man, the scientist, accompanies Panurge on most of his quests for an answer to his problem. Working with material largely new in popular French literature, Rabelais displays consummate skill in planning the enquiry and the debate so that interest does not flag and monotony is avoided. Scene follows scene with variety in tone and color, always with the main thread of the argument in view.

Since the second book of the cycle, *Pantagruel*, had dealt at length with the war in which the forces of Gargantua and his son had conquered the Dipsodes, Rabelais finds a starting point for his third book in the political and demographic arrangements by which the newly acquired territory was to be governed. To Panurge Pantagruel assigns the wealthy fief of Salmiguondin, whose annual revenue amounts to the unimaginable sum of 6789106789 *royaulx*, large even in terms familiar in international economics today. Here, for the first time in a major work of literature, the exceptional freedom possible through the use of the Indo-Arabic numerals is exploited by an author; previously, large sums introduced by Rabelais or his predecessors had only rarely exceeded tens or at most hundreds of thousands, and these were written out in words, expressed in Roman numerals, or on occasion in a combination of the two, e.g. *xvij cens*.[2]

The new governor succeeds in spending three years' revenue in two weeks, and now has to face the reproachful eye of his ruler, justifying his behavior if he can. To do this he enters on a long and highly rhetorical praise of debts, the very basis of the universe, because they create it from nothing. Interpreting the cardinal virtues – Prudence, Justice, Fortitude, and Temperance – in a perverse defense of his greed, Panurge goes on to praise a society founded on credit, in which men pray for the welfare of their debtors, and a continuing free flow of cash: 'Créditeurs sont (je le maintiens jusques au feu exclusivement) créatures belles et bonnes. Qui rien ne preste est créature laide et mauvaise.' The verbal flux increases in its ornate intensity, and Pantagruel is

---

2 A curious example of the way in which Roman numerals were sometimes written may be found in the fifteenth chapter of Marcel Françon, ed., *Les Croniques admirables du puissant Roy Gargantua* (Rochecorbon, Éditions Charles Gay 1956) p. 38 in which the *chausses bouffées* require *taffectas* measuring 'iiiixx, xvii aulnes un quart.' No doubt this must be read as 'quatre vingt dix-sept aunes un quart.'

asked to imagine a world without debts; if there were no regular orbits for the planets, all would be in perturbation, for Jupiter would displace Saturn, Saturn would seek an alliance with Mars, Mercury would no longer serve the Gods, and there would be no more veneration for Venus. The moon would be dark without illumination from the Sun, the earth would cease to yield its exhalations, and men would no longer help each other. Faith, Hope, and Charity would be banished from society.

On the other hand, he continues, with a world in universal debt, the whole cosmos produces all its fruits, the stars give light and influence events, they enjoy their regular movements, the elements are sympathetic, there is no strife in the world, for man gives and receives, lends and borrows, according to the qualities given him by nature:

Je me pers en cette contemplation. Entre les humains paix, amour, dilection, fidelité, repous, banquetz, festins, joye, liesse, or, argent, menue monnaie, chaisnes, bagues, marchandises troteront de main en main. Nul proces, nulle guerre, nul débat, nul n'y sera usurier, nul leschart, nul chichart, nul refusant. Vray Dieu, ne sera ce l'aage d'or, le règne de Saturne, l'idée des regions Olympicques, es quelles toutes autres vertus cessent, charité seule regne, regente, domine, triumphe?

From the consideration of the cosmos and society Panurge now turns to 'nostre microcosme, *id est* petit monde, c'est l'homme,' and expounds in detail the principles of anatomy and physiology current among doctors of his time, still another analogy for his philosophy justifying massive indebtedness. Discussing the *Tiers Livre*, M.A. Screech points out[3] that the comic effect of this chapter arises from the effrontery of Panurge in adapting this traditional outlook to his particular needs and desires:

Vertus guoy je me naye, je me pers, je m'esguare, quand je entre on profond abisme de ce monde ainsi prestant, ainsi doibvant! Croyez que chose divine est prester: debvoir est vertus Heroïque.

Nevertheless it would be unlike Rabelais to accept the entire complex structure of Hippocratic physiology without reservations; there is little in his

---

3 *Le Tiers Livre: édition critique commentée par M.A. Screech*, Textes littéraires français (Geneva and Paris, Librairie Droz 1964) p. xvi: 'Ce n'est pas la théorie médicale que Rabelais trouve en ridicule ... la satire est réservée au seul Panurge'; and, p. 48: 'La comédie naît surtout de l'effronterie de Panurge, qui fait un mauvais usage de cette matière divine.' However, elsewhere (*The Rabelaisian Marriage* [Edward Arnold, London 1958] p. 153), Professor Screech writes that the *Tiers Livre* 'seeks the Mean by flirting at various times with various opinions.'

book to suggest that his critical sense became dormant in the face of a system so elaborately organized as that set forth in this fourth chapter. Panurge makes too many statements that have no basis in clinical experience, and uses too much finalist theory for Rabelais to take his physiology at face value. Even if the comic author is presenting the usual teachings of the schools of 1546, it remains difficult to believe that Rabelais himself was as fully committed to the pattern as his creature Panurge, who is consistently presented as a moral and philosophic foil to the increasing wisdom of Pantagruel.

Although the structure of academic medicine was not seriously threatened before the mid-seventeenth century when doctors were confronted by the findings of William Harvey and Jean Pecquet, there was already in Rabelais' time a ferment of scientific doubt evidenced by the work of innovators like Michael Servetus, Sylvius, Girolamo Fracastoro, and Guido Guidi, not to mention the great Vesalius. While these and others could not yet offer a comprehensive alternative to the system set forth by Panurge, still there were enough experimental indications to suggest new questions about the verbalistic explanations accepted in the schools. Pantagruel was no Béralde, nor was Panurge a Diafoirus, to mount a battle over the conventional attitudes of the past; and Rabelais was not a Molière writing in the atmosphere of the scientific revolution in opposition to the conservative Faculté de médecine of the University of Paris. Yet both author and his character are immersed in the climate of the Renaissance, in which questions were becoming as familiar as dogma, and a new philosophy was to set all in doubt before many decades had passed.

Thus when Panurge comes at long last to the particular private urge that motivates almost all of the rest of the book, his argument appropriately ends on a pun. The purpose of the internal structure of man, he says, is 'pour conserver et perpétuer le genre humain. Se faict le tout par prests et debtes de l'un à l'autre: dont est dict le debvoir de mariage.' And the chapter closes with a vivid and keenly felt contrast of the state of mind of those who accept their impulses with the unhappiness of those who do not: 'Poine par nature est au refusant interminée avec vexation parmy les membres et furie parmy les sens; au prestant loyer consigné, plaisir, alaigresse et volupté.' The response of Pantagruel to this, in the opening lines of chapter five, 'j'entends ... et me semblez bon topicqueur et bien affecté à vostre cause,' dissociates the giant completely from Panurge's sophistry.

The point of the long prelude is now clear: Panurge must marry, not because he has chosen a wife, but because he has need of conjugal company. Typically he hesitates, because he cannot be sure a wife will be faithful to him, and the question is posed: shall he marry and find himself cuckolded, or shall he be wise and remain single? A man usually answers this question for himself, but Panurge, who was decisive enough when he first appeared before the young Pantagruel, now must have guidance. This he seeks through the long range of chapters 9 to 46, asking his question of Vergil by means of dice, consulting dreams, dying poets, a witch, a deaf mute, a quartet of learned men (a theologian, a doctor, a philosopher, and an ancient jurist), and finally a court fool. The answers are mostly negative, but Panurge is not satisfied, and the conclusion of the book points to an expedition to the shrine of the holy bottle, where Panurge hopes his doubts will be resolved.

This book as a whole has been said to be a contribution to the much discussed *Querelle des femmes*, which offered authors of the Renaissance material for literary composition if they did not have much of importance to write about; at least they could be sure of some popularity by taking sides on the moot question of woman's place in society, as well as on their mental and moral powers. Rabelais knew that a book about women, especially if it was somewhat naughty, would appeal to many readers; however, Screech has shown pretty clearly that Rabelais was no misogynist,[4] and that in fact women, even if they are scarcely found in the pages of his book, come off there rather better than do men.

If this third book is an investigation of the means by which man may discover the answers to questions concerning his future and the mainsprings of his actions, it may offer a clue to Rabelais' understanding of nature and the powers of man himself. After finally rejecting the sources of rural wisdom in the Chinonais, the heart of Gargantua's little kingdom, Pantagruel and his company decide to sail to the new world in the west, there to seek the answer to Panurge's question. At the port of Thalasse, 'près Sammalo,' they assemble a fleet of twelve ships, to be piloted by Xenomanes, the lover of foreign things and the *traverseur des voyes périlleuses*. The ships are loaded with supplies for a long and hazardous voyage, and Rabelais notes also, with a great store of the herb Pantagruelion, 'tant verde et crude que conficte et praeparée.'

The four chapters in which this strange herb is discussed have been much debated, and it must be admitted that from some points of view they are unintelligible. They have slight comic value, they are pedantic in their review of the botanical aspects of the plant, and this long digression seems to have little relevance to what has gone before, and still less to what is to follow. Some have found in this discussion a religious significance, a symbol of Pantagruel's faith. Others have cited sources, in Pliny, Dioscorides, and Theophrastus or others, and have worked out carefully the ways in which

4 *The Rabelaisian Marriage, passim*

such plants as cannabis have been made to serve mankind, as hemp and flax to make linen and canvas, paper and books, red tape and legal documents, as well as in pharmacy.

Perhaps the sense of these chapters may be found if the *Tiers Livre* is looked at as a whole. The first pages of the book present a *dizain*:

FRANÇOIS RABELAIS A L'ESPRIT DE LA ROYNE DE NAVARRE

> Esprit abstraict, ravy, et ecstatic
> Qui frequentant les cieux, ton origine,
> As delaissé ton hoste et domestic,
> Ton corps concords, qui tant se morigine
> A tes edictz, en vie peregrine
> Sans sentement, et comme en Apathie:
> Vouldrois tu poinct faire quelque sortie
> De ton manoir divin, perpetuel?
> Et ça bas veoir une tierce partie
> Des faictz joyeux du bon Pantagruel?

These lines evoke the rapt and idealistic spirit of Marguerite d'Angoulême, Queen of Navarre, haunting the heavens whence she came, a divine eternal dwelling place, as she deserts her harmonious mortal self, the apathetic servant of her decrees, in contrast with the mundane realm and joyful deeds of good Pantagruel. In its obscure way, this epigraph, cast in a form much used by poets of the time including Marguerite herself, sets a pattern for the book. The world of ideas, of Platonic archetypes, is placed in opposition to the world of things, the doctor's realities of life and death, the statesman's necessities of decision in practical affairs, the maintenance of bodily health and public welfare – in short, the demands posed by existence in present exigencies while casting a prudent and imaginative eye to an unpredictable future.

If this book, then, is an inconclusive debate between a philosophically skeptical and pragmatic Pantagruel and a Panurge who demonstrably exhibits qualities diametrically opposed, – sophisticated credulity, thriftlessness to the point of folly, – then one may legitimately suggest that the Pantagruelion chapters, charged with reference to the useful arts and human skills, form a conscious and purposeful pendant to the fantastic kyrielle of occult sympathies expounded by Panurge at the beginning of the book. All of Rabelais' powers of eloquent expression had been exhibited in the three chapters of specious apologia, and generations of readers and critics have been led to think that this farrago of sympathies and antipathies was what the doctor from Montpellier believed. In contrast, the quiet and relatively factual account of Pantagruelion was merely irrelevant, a wanton offense to the reader, a prosaic passage inevitably deleted by every anthologist of 'les meilleures pages' of Rabelais.

But considered soberly, in the light of the great surge of technological invention, leading to radical changes in society and even in political relations, which the later middle ages had seen, it is by no means clear that Rabelais had any such intent. These chapters are composed with care, organized to proceed to a celestial climax in which the Olympian gods assembled see their realms invaded, and man achieving divine rank by means of his inventive use of a very humble plant. Three chapters, 49, 50, and 51, bring us to this conclusion. The first is limited to botany, with elaborate descriptions and many comparisons. The second records the preparation of flax for use – something Rabelais could see on property owned by his family in the neighborhood of Chinon. The last chapter develops the innumerable uses of the fibres derived from the plant, in sails, ropes, windmill vanes, cloth for beds, tables, windows, and garments; from linen rags in turn, paper in all its uses for communication and records, pledging property, transferring wealth; and finally the use of cannabis as a drug. Much is doubtless taken uncritically from Pliny, and some is fantastic extrapolation, but in the light of our present reading of Rabelais, it seems clear that he is asking us to return to the facts of human ingenuity and skill, and to recognize that our greatest good is achieved when we cooperate with nature, sometimes even forcing her to do our will.

Corroboration of this view may be found in the outburst on Olympus when man is seen to master the oceans, joining Taprobrana and Lapland, Java and Scythia; Icelanders and Greenlanders will drink of the Euphrates, Boreas will visit Auster, as Eurus will call on the west,

De mode que les Intelligences celestes, les Dieux, tant marins que terrestres, en ont esté tous effrayez, voyans par l'usaige de cestuy benedict Pantagruelion les peuples Arcticques en plein aspect des Antarcticques franchir la mer Athlanticque, passer les deux Tropicques, volter sous la Zone torride, mesurer tout le Zodiacque, s'esbatre soubs l'Æquinoctial, avoir l'un et l'autre Pole en veue à fleur de leur orizon.

This leads the Olympian gods to declare 'en pareil effroy' that the offspring of · Pantagruel may invent

herbe de semblable energie, moyenant laquelle pourront les humains visiter les sources des gresles, les bondes des pluyes, et l'officine des fouldres, pourront envahir les regions de la Lune, entrer le territoire des signes celestes et là prendre logis, les uns à l'Aigle d'or, les aultres au Mouton, les aultres à la Couronne, les aultres à la Herpe, les aultres au Lion d'argent, s'asseoir à table avecques nous, et nos déesses prendre à femmes, qui sont les seulx moyens d'estre deifiez.

With this danger in mind, the gods 'enfin ont mis le remede de y obvier en deliberation et au conseil.' Rabelais does not record the result of this committee meeting.

A final chapter brings us back to the realms of symbolic fantasy in which Rabelais so often moved. Pantagruelion is now equated with the mysterious asbestos, and with certain larches of antiquity of which it was said towers could be built for use in war that would resist the burning pitch and fagots of besieged cities. Indeed, the strange herb is now said to be superior to such substances, which suggests that we are not dealing with a common plant at all, but with some mysterious energy possessed by man.[5]

Thus Rabelais remains true to his profession; he depends on material aids to health, on surgical devices, on linen and cordage and medicines, on the product of art and skills, and not on words and formulae. He has come far from the easy trust in human nature of the Abbey of Thélème. Life is strenuous and demands intelligence and enterprise, and the full use of the muscles of the body as well as of the unlimited resources men of the Renaissance could see in the immense world opening around them. The seaman, the machinist, the miner, the wagoner, the tradesman, the hangman, and the surgeon all depend on rope and hemp and cloth in the pursuit of their professions. Like once stone and later bronze and iron, hemp and flax have now inaugurated a new level of civilization, an age to add to the anthropologist's horizons as he writes his own version of man's history. Human community is now built around treaties and charters, promissory notes and letters of credit, ledgers of account and minutes of councils of state, inscribed on paper made of linen rags. As ideas circulate in widening networks of correspondents, becoming printed books in the process, we can see that

5 The philosophical intent of this passage might well be compared with that of the 'Fabula de homine' which Juan Luis Vives composed about 1518, in which he presented the ascent of man to moral and intellectual equality with the gods in the form of a scenic pageant organized by Jupiter for the entertainment of his Olympian guests. In humanist fashion, Vives concerns himself largely with qualities of mind and judgment, very little with manual skills and the use of tools and materials. Rabelais' Pantagruelion may be said to mark an advance in the long passage leading to the scientific revolution of the following century.

thought and taste, philosophy – which in that century was science – and literature advance together and change the face and structure of man's world. The future lies in the new directions which the men of the fourteenth and fifteenth centuries had been exploring, in the use of techniques of their own invention or introduced by increased trade with the orient. The wit of Rabelais points towards the scientific revolution, the advancement of science and technology, the application of new understanding of nature to processes of manufacture and use – towards applied science. His original use of the Hindu-Arabic system of numbering in the early chapters of this very rich *Tiers Livre* shows that he glimpsed the power of arithmetic to increase the leverage man had gained with simple devices in skilful hands.

The last of the four authentic books of Rabelais, the *Quart Livre*, published complete in 1552, is the most complex and perhaps the most difficult of all. Its contents resist summary; ostensibly a voyage of discovery, it is in truth a further excursion into mythology and fantasy, derived in part from antiquity, in part from the incredible tales brought home by travelers in new-found lands. An imaginative distillation of the varieties of experience available to mankind, this fourth book is poetic and moral rather than philosophical and realistic. Unconvinced of the value of dissertations and scholarly commentary as means of communication, Rabelais uses comedy, in extended dialogues or dramatic scenes, hilarious with the Papimanes, full of pathos at the Isle of the Macreons, where Pantagruel meditates aloud and at length on the death of heroes, on Guillaume du Bellay, and on the ancient legend of Pan, whose death is put in the context of the Crucifixion:

Pantagruel, ce propous finy, resta en silence et profonde contemplation. Peu de temps apres, nous vismes les larmes decouller de ses oeilz grosses comme oeufs de austruche. Je me donne à Dieu, si j'en mens d'un seul mot.

While much of this fourth book is a sequel to the long confrontation of Pantagruel and the vacillating Panurge, certain sections stand out for their narrative quality: the grim farce of the sheep of the merchant of Taillebourg drowned by the malice of Panurge, the account of the great tempest in five chapters full of noise and turbulence and the blubbering cowardice of Panurge, and the imaginative color of the episode of the Frozen Words. There are a few references to technology and science: Messer Gaster, Lord Belly, master of all the useful arts, brings back the Pantagruelion theme in a new mode, while the Isle of Winds is inspired by a half-remembered Hippocratic text, *On Airs, Waters, and Places.* Although it lacks the overall structure and the consistent intellectual pattern of the third book, this final product of Rabelais' creative art ranks by itself as perhaps the finest flight of imagination in all of French literature.

The first doctor to write a great work of imaginative literature, as a creator of character and milieu Rabelais is beyond comparison with Robert Burton and Sir Thomas Browne. Ranked by Sir William Osler 'among the kings and queens of literature,' he owes much to his medical background and his clinical experience of human suffering. He knew and understood the humiliating denial of moral and ethical stature that is forced on man by radical disease and major surgery; the optimistic theory that all will always be well if nature is allowed to take its course without ingenious and sometimes drastic intervention he rejects as simply contrary to the facts. His ideal of health is clear in all his writings, emphatically at the end of the cycle when Panurge is reduced to shuddering filth as the guns of the fleet are fired before the Isle of Thieves. Sanity, moral discipline, sound hygiene – these ideals consistently underlie the fabric of the novels, particularly from the writing of *Gargantua* (1534 or 1535) through the third and fourth books. Rabelais took no delight in the abnormal or monstrous, though he had a talent for describing such phenomena. Intoxication was poisonous to him, and squalor the attribute of animals.

He cannot be read and interpreted intelligibly if the doctor and his outlook are omitted from analysis. The medical contribution must be recognized for what it is, and particularly for what it was in the French Renaissance. The opposition of health and unhealth appears everywhere in his book, sometimes in surprising circumstances. Health may be found in the clear vision of the dying Guillaume du Bellay, in the mad argument of Judge Bridoye, in the fooleries of Seigny Jean; unhealth in the aggressive fury of Picrochole, the sordid madness of the Sibylle de Panzoust, the tyranny of Quaresmeprenant, the bigotry of Homenaz, and above all in the person of Panurge himself. While conventional thinking is good, it is not the only good, for a shrewder insight may put accepted theories to rout and events may incomprehensibly justify perceptions from a source beyond professional routine. The expert knows the limitations of his tools, the shortcomings of his own powers, and the wisdom that will come when intuition extends his sense of concrete fact. Pantagruelism, 'une certaine gayeté d'esprit conficte en mespris des choses fortuites,' derived from ancient doctors and modern experience, makes for mental health and physical well-being. While Rabelais may not be an essential figure in the history of medicine, the outlook of the doctor, of his day as of ours, is essential to the understanding of his books and of himself.

This chapter is a revised version of an article published in *Annals of Science* 27 (1971): 117-34. Based on prolonged reading of *Gargantua and Pantagruel* rather than on the massive critical and biographical writing concerning Rabelais, it has profited from discussion with other *Rabelaisants*, in and out of seminars. An interpretation of the Pantagruelion episode by Professor Abraham Keller (*PMLA*, March 1951, pp. 235-43) is in some respects kin to my own.

The fifth book, published about ten years after the disappearance and presumed death of Rabelais, is at best only partially authentic, and does not figure in the present discussion, as there is no way of determining when Rabelais may have written the few chapters attributed to him or how they would have fitted into his general plan. To take the *Cinquième Livre* into consideration in establishing a pattern in his work would be to admit a contaminated source.

CHAPTER THREE

Science and
the *Pensées* of Pascal

SINCE THE seventeenth century it has occasionally been said that the French contribution to the advancement of science was systematic, discursive, argumentative, and rationalist, while that of the British was Baconian and empirical, seeking experimental evidence and rejecting verbal authority and deductive proofs; that, in short, the scientific revolution was in many ways an English phenomenon, the influence of which formed a basis for the radical thinking of Voltaire and others of his generation. At one time, broad inferences of this sort had their uses; now, however, they are more often heard in the classroom than found in the history of ideas. Seizing on a contrast of this nature, such as that between the temperaments of Francis Bacon and René Descartes, an expository mind discovers that he can use the well-known differences between two highly individual men as a basis for characterizing nations as a whole, at the same time neglecting the possibility of nuances, and even the probability that the inductive, experimental attitude could be found widely spread among the artisans and skilled craftsmen in France as well as in Britain, and indeed in Europe generally, in a higher degree than is suggested by the pedagogic stereotype.

Description of French amateurs of science as dogmatic and rationalist could hardly have been made before alternative criteria had been generally accepted as the basis for science, before the objectives and methods of the new scientists had been defined and recognized, not only by isolated individuals like William Harvey and Jean Rey, but also by the nascent academies, in Florence, London, and Paris. Thus it was about 1660 that the Dutch physicist Christiaan Huygens and the French mathematician Ismaël Boulliau agreed in criticizing certain members of the Montmor academy[1] because they preferred discussion in the manner of pedagogues to demonstration by well-planned experiment. Meetings, in private houses as well as in public assemblies, led to even more frequent occasions for the observation of cultural differences among scientists and amateurs, so that about 1670 one is not surprised to find the Frenchman Henry Justel writing that his compatriots do not possess the gift of scientific invention, that their role is to perfect and develop the ideas of others, ornamenting innovations with artistic detail or subjecting them to theoretical explanations and critical commentary. Eighty years later, in a chapter on the useful arts in *Le Siècle de Louis XIV*, Voltaire would remark that the mechanical and inventive superiority of the English had been so marked that the age could well have been described as *le siècle des Anglais*.

If differences there were between science in France and in England, they may have sprung from native temperament or they may have been cultural, a product of local circumstance, tradition, and education. René Taton, in his books of 1951 on the geometricians Girard Desargues (1591-1661) and Gaspard Monge (1746-1818),[2] noticed that the respect for ancient science and its methods that prevailed through most of the seventeenth century in France had been accompanied by a distaste for the mechanical aspects of the arts and crafts, for technology and the materials of the artisan. Desargues and, later, Monge were in a minority that did not share these prejudices; their work ran counter to the temper of their times, and their outlook, in particular that of Desargues, was absorbed slowly or not at all, so strong were the habits of the trades and the routines of the classroom.

As portrayed by Taton, Desargues was a notable example of the transition from a period in which the technical arts were divorced from theory to an age in which it came to be taken for granted that craft and organized knowledge would benefit equally from communication. The geometrician began to contribute to the simplifying and generalizing of unrelated principles as used by different craftsmen rather than to the abstract mathematics taught in contemporary schools. Desargues thought of perspective not as something invented and utilized by painters to create the illusion of space, or as empirical

1 Henri Louis Habert de Montmor, a wealthy *maître des requêtes* in the Parlement de Paris, entertained scientists and amateurs in weekly meetings in his house from the mid-1650s until about 1664; foreign visitors with kindred interests were welcomed. See Harcourt Brown, *Scientific Organizations in Seventeenth-Century France* (Baltimore, Williams and Wilkins for the History of Science Society 1934; New York, Russell and Russell 1967) pp. 64-134.
2 René Taton, *L'Œuvre mathématique de Girard Desargues* (Paris, Presses universitaires 1951). For relations of Pascal and Desargues see pp. 33-6.

rules for the production of a three-dimensional image on the flat area of wood or canvas, but rather as an opportunity for the translation by mathematical language of a visible object into lines and areas precisely placed and proportioned on the empty surface before him. Recognizing that the relationship between the lines from the observer's eye to the outlines and angles of the subject could be described in geometric terms and transferred to the artist's canvas, thus creating illusion, he achieved two results: first, a rational simplification of the painter's art, and furthermore, the discovery of a new and fruitful method of projective geometry. This attitude towards his work is summed up in a note appended to Abraham Bosse's *Manière universelle de Mr Desargues pour pratiquer la perspective*,[3] in which the geometrician admits that he had never had any taste for

l'estude ou recherche ny de la Physique ny de la Géométrie sinon en tant qu'elles peuvent servir à l'esprit d'un moyen d'arriver à quelque-sorte de connoissance des causes prochaines des effets des choses qui se puissent réduire en acte effectif au bien et commodité de la vie qui soit en usage pour l'entretien ou conservation de la santé, soit en leur application pour la pratique de quelque art ...

Desargues adds that much of the practice of the graphic arts is founded on the assured basis of geometric principles.

Invading the practical arts still further, Desargues considers how the dressing of stones for arches and vaults could be aided by the use of similar principles, thus extending the capacity of the often unlettered stonemason or builder by establishing a system of axioms to replace traditional rules of thumb. Mathematical calculations would allow him to progress from his usual simple problems to undertake more and more complex structures. Unfortunately, this theoretic approach appealed to very few disciples – those listed in his *Brouillon project d'exemple ... touchant la practique du trait à preuves pour la coupe des pierres en l'architecture* (1640) – and as a result Desargues' influence on the builder's art is difficult to evaluate. He is known to have designed at least one town house, several staircases, perrons, and other structures in Paris. His advice was sought in 1646 by the *prévôts* of the city of Lyon in connection with plans for a new hôtel de ville. Artists consulted him in matters of perspective, in particular the engraver Abraham

---

3 Abraham Bosse, *Manière universelle de Mr Desargues pour pratiquer la perspective par petit-pied comme le géométral: ensemble les plans et proportions des fortes et faibles touches, teintes et couleurs* (Paris 1648) (title from Taton, *L'Œuvre mathématique*, p.25)

Bosse and the painter Philippe de Champaigne, who was commissioned to portray a Crucifixion on the flat ceiling of a Carmelite church. The problem was to draw the Cross and two figures on a horizontal surface so that they would appear erect when viewed from below.

While Desargues was the geometrician, in search of a sounder approach to a limited area of practice, his contemporary, René Descartes (1590-1650), sought a universal method, useful in the problems of any discipline. Although he left no trace on the buildings of Paris and offered no advice to painters seeking to create the illusion of perpendicularity on a flat ceiling, Descartes could not resist the urge to put his newly found ideas to use. In the sixth section of the *Discours de la méthode* (1637) he writes that, after developing certain general ideas in physics and testing them in various special difficulties,

j'ai remarqué jusques où elles peuvent conduire, et combien elles diffèrent des principes dont on s'est servi jusques à présent, [et] j'ai cru que je ne pouvais les tenir cachées, sans pécher grandement contre la loi qui nous oblige à procurer, autant qu'il est en nous, le bien général de tous les hommes. Car elles m'ont fait voir qu'il est possible de parvenir à des connaissances qui soient fort utiles à la vie, et qu'au lieu de cette philosophie spéculative qu'on enseigne dans les écoles, on en peut trouver une pratique, par laquelle connaissant la force et les actions du feu, de l'eau, de l'air, des astres, des cieux et de tous les autres corps qui nous environnent, aussi distinctement que nous connaissons les divers métiers de nos artisans, nous les pourrions employer en même façon à tous les usages auxquels ils sont propres, et ainsi nous rendre comme maîtres et possesseurs de la nature.[4]

Desirable not only for the discovery of 'une infinité d'artifices' which would allow mankind to enjoy freely the fruits of the earth, this program would also aid in the preservation of health, 'laquelle est sans doute le premier bien et le fondement de tous les autres biens de cette vie,' for, he adds,

l'esprit dépend si fort du tempérament et de la disposition des organes du corps, que s'il est possible de trouver quelque moyen qui rende communément les hommes plus sages et plus habiles qu'ils n'ont été jusques ici, je crois que c'est dans la médecine qu'on doit le chercher.

And this is precisely the field in which even doctors confess that

tout ce qu'on y sait n'est presque rien à comparaison de ce qui reste à savoir, et qu'on se pourrait exempter d'une infinité de maladies, tant du corps que de l'esprit, et même

4 Descartes, *Discours de la méthode*, É. Gilson, ed. (Paris, Vrin 1920) pp. 121-2

aussi peut-être de l'affaiblissement de la vieillesse, si on avait assez de connaissance de leurs causes, et de tous les remèdes dont la nature nous a pourvus.

To this search for useful knowledge in all fields Descartes now plans to devote himself, hoping to persuade men of intelligence to proceed beyond his own conclusions, so that their joint efforts would permit greater success than any one man could achieve. Étienne Gilson suggests that this passage may have been written under the influence of Francis Bacon; whether or not that is so, it is clear that Descartes the theorist was not without a conception of the practical needs of the contemporary world.

Descartes' assertion of the value of systematic doubt went beyond the limited skepticism of Desargues, and had some influence on the conversational aspects of French science in the later years of the century. He was, however, no pyrrhonist; his questioning was ordered, and limited to the establishment of truths which could not be denied in the logic of common sense; 'clear and distinct ideas' were his ultimate goals. The Cartesianism of the vortices, *les tourbillons*, does not represent his thought as a whole, nor does it give a sense of the importance of the four phases of his method or of the criterion of truth which came to be accepted generally by thinkers in the exact sciences.

The Minorite father Marin Mersenne (1588-1648) was the chief link between Descartes and the world of techniques and the descriptive sciences. Mersenne's earliest scientific work was concerned with music and the mathematics of harmony, which led him to see with increasing clarity the thick tangle of error that had accumulated as opinions and conjectures had been passed without question from one generation to another. His personal views were formulated in a passage in the preface to the second book of his *Traité de l'harmonie universelle* (1627) in which he asks of men of learning and musicians

qu'ils ne croyent à nulle histoire de celles que les Anciens rapportent des effets de la musique ou de la manière qu'elle a été inventée, etc., qu'ils n'en ayent premièrement fait l'expérience ou qu'ils n'y soient forcez par la démonstration. Car c'est chose étrange que nous embrassons si facilement les opinions erronées de nos ancestres, encore qu'ils n'ayent eu nulle puissance, ny mesme le plus souvent nulle volonté de nous obliger à suivre ce qu'ils ont dit et ce qu'ils ont écrit. Je désire donc qu'on se tire de la captivité qui a accoustumé de lier les hommes et qu'on ne s'assujettisse plus à la tyrannie des opinions.[5]

5 For Mersenne see the *Correspondance du Père Marin Mersenne*, Mme Paul Tannery and C. De Waard, eds. (Paris, Beauchesne 1932–); the quotation from the *Harmonie universelle* has been taken from 1: xxix, note 3.

This was the mood of thinkers of the age, and the rising generation, of which Blaise Pascal was one, grew up in a circle in which Desargues, Descartes, and Mersenne were familiar figures. The world was opening up its secrets, and traditional modes of thought no longer offered adequate explanations of phenomena or useful guides to direct man in the natural world. Science was in a revolutionary state that would be clarified, described, and defined much later; if few men of the first half of the seventeenth century saw all its implications, at least many could see what had to be done in areas of their special competence. The progress made by individuals may have been slow, the changes achieved imperceptible, but the accumulated effect was great, and when the variety of the sciences of the century had been reviewed, men would appear who would put the whole vast circle in a single focus, and announce the arrival of what another century would call *la saine philosophie*.

The science of France in this period cannot be reduced and bound by simple formulae. Its nature was too complex, its outlook too much influenced by the increasing variety of the contemporary world. The personal documents which survive reflect this complexity; the correspondence of a man like Mersenne shows that the theologian does not neglect the value of plants and animals for the use and convenience of man, nor the importance of advances in technology for their contribution to theory and to the creation of new skills and trades. The problems man is most likely to solve are those whose solution will bring new conveniences, new comforts, new satisfactions, and the reduction of pain and stress in the course of his labor and travel. When these results have been achieved, new theorems, new principles, and new tools (material as well as intellectual) are at hand, which in turn permit the attack on still other problems of comfort and convenience, and the progression continues, *ad infinitum*.

In many ways, Blaise Pascal (1623-62) is typical of the new generation of scientists. Recognized as gifted in mathematics, he was put to work in the accounting office of his father, who was newly charged with the collection of taxes in Rouen; here he devised a means of escaping the drudgery of endless additions, producing with the aid of a clockmaker a workable adding-machine, geared to the livres, sous, and deniers in current use. Interesting to amateurs of curiosities, the invention would have found acceptance among book keepers if the metallurgy of the day had been able to produce racks and pinions hard enough to permit a speed of operation greater than that attainable in an accountant's head. The device was sound, but it remained undeveloped until the nineteenth century invented materials and the tooling necessary for accuracy and rapid response. The work of Galileo on water-pumps led Pascal to turn his attention to atmospheric pressure and hydraulics, and then to the problem of the vacuum in the barometric tube. In each area he displayed as much interest in the human context as in the purely scientific content.

He was as concerned as Desargues and Mersenne, and more so than Descartes, with the operations of the natural world and their relation to human perception and convenience. Separating natural philosophy from theology, he explicitly denies the value of natural objects in teaching the ways of God:

Et quoi, ne dites-vous pas vous-même que le ciel et les oiseaux prouvent Dieu?–Non. – Et votre religion, ne le dit-elle pas?–Non; car encore que cela est vrai en un sens pour quelques âmes à qui Dieu donna cette lumière, néanmoins cela est faux à l'égard de la plupart.(3)*

And again, in a different context, 'Le Dieu des Chrétiens ne consiste pas en un Dieu simplement auteur des vérités géométriques et de l'ordre des éléments; c'est la part des païens et des épicuriens' (447). Pascal concludes, at least tentatively, that those who seek God apart from Jesus Christ and who content themselves with Nature, either 'ne trouvent aucune lumière qui les satisfasse,' or find a means of knowing God and serving him without a mediator, thus falling into atheism or deism, which are two things Christianity abhors almost equally.

Consistent with this view of the separation of disciplines, Pascal's scientific interest lay in the autonomous realm of applied mathematics and mechanics rather than in generalized theory, and much of his activity was devoted, in a manner typical of his age, to the solution of problems of immediate concern, an outlook which carried over into his thinking about men and women. His gift for observing material things led to his observation of human behavior; there is a vast fund of objective comment on how people act and react in the *Pensées*. His concern with manners and morals, with ethics and politics, always a matter of concern in a legal family, led naturally to the analysis of character, the interpretation of tradition and custom, of the interplay of law and authority, of justice and brute force. His great design for a book to lead men to Christian teachings was strengthened by its foundation in a penetrating study of the demands of human nature and the circumstances of institutions and habits. Undoubtedly the extensive annotations on how men and women actually behave delayed the writing of his book, so that his illness and death prevented its completion, yet those very observations on the ways of mankind, the product of a scientist's scrupulous desire to collect and analyze instances before reaching conclusions, have made his book in all its disarray

* Numbers in the text refer to the *Pensées* in the Cluny edition, for which see note 1, p. 3 above.

one of the richest and most rewarding products of the French seventeenth century.

The *Pensées*, therefore, cannot easily be taken as a whole or read in linear fashion. There are too many visible bypaths and contrary directions: the *Apologie de la religion chrétienne*, which may have been the dominant interest of the last years of his life, is in constant disharmony with an objective scientific mood which appears whenever Pascal turns to the analysis of human behavior – psychology we could call it, although that word had not yet been invented. This scientific direction shows itself also when he thinks of the problems of persuasion, the difficulty of producing convincing arguments when the minds of his reading public are unreceptive or openly hostile; the pure doctrine of his gospel is modified and diluted in such passages as that dealing with the Wager, in which the powers of self-interest and the calculus of probabilities are introduced as a means to conversion without the intervention of divine grace. The book is full of instances collected in the Baconian spirit of induction; they do not all point in one direction, and Pascal makes no effort to interpret them in a single sense. In the long run, one surrenders to the wandering charm of the *Pensées*, delighting in the frequent passages where the expressive quality of the writing penetrates the critical spirit induced by the whole book, and the reader realizes that much of the seventeenth century is in these pages: its puritanism, its relentless pursuit of human nature, its scale of values and the recognition of the social perspective, and, finally, its unswerving quest for complete lucidity and truth in facts rather than in words – a quest which was a central element of the revolution in science in which Pascal played an important part. Pascal here appears as a man of a very real world, struggling to understand himself, and, beyond himself, humanity and its problems in the light of a Christian tradition with the essential aid of a consciously scientific method.

While the *Pensées* have been read and remembered chiefly as a monument of French literature, appreciated by many, loved by some, analyzed for their expressive and aesthetic qualities and their revelation of a unique and complex spirit, their value as a document for their times has not been forgotten. In addition to comments on the society and institutions of the period of the Fronde and Mazarin, numerous fragments in which we read Pascal's personal philosophy throw light on the opinions heard around him, on policies and prejudices as well as on the doctrines of theology and current ethics. Taken with our knowledge of Pascal as a public figure and in his family, all this offers insight into the special circumstances of his time, a historical understanding of the age, its changing ideas and developing taste. Some have gone so far as to seek a consistent metaphysics in the *Pensées*, hoping, a little vainly, to find a pattern of positions on ethics and government, on epistemology and logic.

Apart from the small circle of physicists and mathematicians who understood his scientific work, and the admiring Jansenists who listened to his conversation and tried to put his nearly indecipherable writings into the mould of an *Apologie de la religion chrétienne*, his contemporaries knew Pascal as a member of a conservative legal family, a man who dabbled in experiments with glass tubes and mercury, proposed and solved abstruse problems concerning curves, and remained with all that something of a recluse. He cannot be counted among the spiritual fathers of the Enlightenment and the *philosophes*; he had nothing of a Pierre Bayle about him, nor yet of a Fontenelle. He did not confront the establishment with a dissenting periodical and a *Dictionnaire critique et historique*, nor did he write an account of the natural philosophy of his day. Pascal has been grouped with the moralists of his era, with La Bruyère and La Rochefoucauld, men innocent of the sciences, yet perceptive critics of the manners and customs of the time. The author of the *Lettres provinciales* and the *Pensées* was a typical product of the late Renaissance, the years of Louis XIII, rather than of the classic era of Louis XIV. His work was incompletely known until much later; indeed the *Pensées* have not yet revealed all they hold, in spite of the strides made since 1842, when Victor Cousin opened the eyes of scholars to something of what could be found in the manuscripts.

Yet it may be said that from those years which preceded the painful disorder in which the *Pensées* were written sprang a number of phenomena, curious parallels and perhaps origins of some of the more typical aspects of the following century. There was a questioning of the bases of the thought and customs of the time; the monarchy and its institutions and the church and its conduct of its affairs were scrutinized and sometimes condemned. The fundamental postulates of the science and philosophy taught in the schools were criticized and new formulations proposed. Apparent in Pascal's writing, these preoccupations demonstrate a persistent mood of doubt and critical reappraisal, noticeably different from the conformist acceptance of authority often regarded as the dominant tone of the reign of Louis XIV. In his insistence on the importance of research and observation, characteristic of his early thinking and extending into the *Pensées*, even in their religious moments, there is a rejection, often explicit, of any demand for the acceptance of the unquestioned importance of traditional doctrines. A particular belief might be desirable and necessary; the underlying reason for it could still be questioned and restated.

Of course, from their first appearance in print in 1670, the *Pensées* have had an aura of holiness, with an overtone of tragedy intensified by the personal situation of the author and his Jansenist associates, and by the unfinished state of his book. There has not been much recognition of the way in which these intricately developed fragments are marked by so many different habits of mind. Comment, as always, tends to be selective, in accord with the interests and purposes of the commentator; it is difficult to be truly comprehensive in writing about this incredibly complex book, for no critic today can be as complicated, intellectually, emotionally, spiritually, as Pascal, or possess all his eminent qualities as physicist, mathematician, and practical inventor, with his rich legal background and his contacts with the upper and middle levels of seventeenth-century society. One cannot read these pages without uneasiness; there are too many discordant elements, too many passages of skeptical tendency, too many places where there is a spontaneous rejection of familiar Christian positions. From the thousand apophthegms and embryonic treatises the reader selects according to his taste or prejudice: 'Ce n'est pas dans Pascal mais dans moi que je trouve tout ce que j'y vois' (738 emended). Thus the books about him from 1670 to yesterday reflect a double image – Pascal, more or less faintly, and the modern critic, according to his objectivity and good sense. But at least one can ask that the critic observe Pascal's own maxim, 'Qui veut donner le sens de l'Écriture et ne le prend point de l'Écriture est ennemi de l'Écriture,' (248), and that a discussion of the *Pensées* be based on the written words of Pascal. The following remark (249), that there are two errors, to interpret everything literally or to take everything spiritually, refers no doubt to reading of the Bible, but it is, like others of Pascal's thoughts, a general warning about the interpretation of books, and may be applied to the reading of the *Pensées*.

Blaise Pascal shared with his contemporary Molière an exceptional awareness of the temper of his age, a sense of its rationality, its liking for facts and plain logical argument. A man of what Whitehead describes as the 'century of genius,' sharing its skepticism, its rejection of what was not plain common sense, he was not content to carry on scientific investigation and the invention of useful gadgets without consideration of the implications of what he was doing. His experiments with the column of mercury led to speculation about the nature of the apparently empty space at the top of the closed tube, and then to discussion of the validity of his analysis of the recorded phenomena. The immediate result was to have been a treatise on vacuum, a project which, like others, he never completed. We can surmise what that essay would have contained, but no surmise could have given us the relic of this work, the fragment of a preface for this treatise, written apparently about 1651, and published in 1779 by the Abbé Bossut. Telling us very little about vacuum, this document says much about Pascal and his conception of the methods of science.[6]

These disconnected paragraphs divide the criteria of truth into two groups, the authority of established texts and, opposed to that, the authority of observed fact in the natural world. The first shows the lawyer's background in written law and his respect for theology, history, and recorded geography; the second recognizes the significance of facts and reason, manifest in geometry, music, arithmetic, physics, medicine, and architecture. In this category one hears the echo of Desargues, Mersenne, and Descartes. A modern scholar, accustomed to refer the written record to archaeological, anthropological, or physiographical data, does not accept a classification of history or geography as a study in which tradition or authority must be accepted as ultimate proof. It is clear that here Pascal has derived his distinctions between the authority of books and that of objective experience from contemporary practice. A child of a notable legal family, surrounded by much used books of history, law, and doctrine, he knew that, as texts verify texts, so empirical facts must inform us of the character and processes of the natural world.

Thus, quite apart from a much noticed statement of the idea of progress, this essay throws valuable light on the nature and circumstances of Pascal's early studies. Drafted from the nascent experimentalist's point of view, it already defines qualities typical of the scientific disciplines – their cumulativeness, their cooperativeness, the repeatability of experiments, and the scientist's freedom with regard to previous conclusions and interpretations – at the same time that it emphasizes the subtlety and uniformity of nature. For Pascal, as for any scientist, science must necessarily be forever incomplete because of the vastness and variety of the physical universe; it must seek perfection in detail, as demanded by the geometric spirit; and it must remain skeptical of the traditional reasons for things and events. On the other hand, authoritarian studies attach great importance to an achieved or easily envisaged completeness; in contrast with the sciences, they are more concerned with an imposing and large-scale consistency than with accuracy in observing and recording detail.

From this point of view, in which Pascal approaches an understanding of the outlook of the humanist scholar, such complex phenomena as historical

---

6 The 'Préface sur le traité du vide' has been reprinted under various titles. See Blaise Pascal, *Opuscules et lettres*, L.Lafuma, ed. (Paris, Aubier 1955) pp. 49-56, and *Pensées et opuscules*, L. Brunschvicg ed. (Paris, Hachette 1900) pp. 74-83. Brunschvicg dates this text 'vers la fin de 1647.'

events, each with its unique causal chain, or human institutions, created by and composed of distinct individuals, possess an exceptional status, for which the discoverable laws of science cannot account. Explanation and description of such events and institutions depend in the long run on the respect for texts, on the authority of the language in which the circumstances happen to be described.

The simplicity of this antithesis between science and humanistic learning could not long suffice Pascal. As time passed, the distinctions between the authority of written tradition and natural philosophy, science, were refined as he observed more and more closely the processes by which knowledge from different disciplines was acquired and applied. In his short life – barely twenty years separate the beginning of his work on the column of mercury and the final interruption of the *Pensées* – what began as a gradual change became a revolution, and the completeness of his retreat from absorption and achievement in the sciences to submerge himself in religion remains a matter of wonder to his readers. In the preface to a projected textbook on geometry, we can see stages of this transformation of his thought. Analysis of movement, spaces, numbers, and times, he writes, shows that magnitudes can never reach absolute limits; one can always conceive a greater or a smaller, yet these concepts, which logic cannot prove, are the basis of geometry. Hence,

la géométrie ne peut définir les objets ni prouver les principes; mais par cette seule et avantageuse raison, que les uns et les autres sont dans une extrême clarté naturelle, qui convainc la raison plus puissamment que le discours ... Il n'y a point de connaissance naturelle dans l'homme qui précède celles-là, et qui les surpasse en clarté. Néanmoins, afin qu'il y ait exemple de tout, on trouve des esprits, excellents en toutes autres choses, que ces infinités choquent, et qui n'y peuvent en aucune sorte consentir.[7]

The discovery that there are at least two kinds of mind, those capable of abstractions and those that are not, leads Pascal to the further distinction between two means of obtaining persuasion,

deux entrées par où les opinions sont reçues dans l'âme, qui sont ses deux principales puissances, l'entendement et la volonté. La plus naturelle est celle de l'entendement, car on ne devrait jamais consentir qu'aux vérités démontrées; mais la plus ordinaire, quoique contre la nature, est celle de la volonté; car tout ce qu'il y a d'hommes sont presque toujours emportés à croire non pas par la preuve, mais par l'agrément.[8]

7 *Opuscules et lettres*, p. 131
8 Ibid p. 139

Throughout this passage on the art of persuasion ('De l'Art de persuader') Pascal is perplexed by the ease with which demonstrable truths such as those of geometry may be taught with little or no effect on the deeper regions of belief, at the same time that the will is persuaded by specious promises which in turn affect the critical judgment. Two things alone are certain: a proposition that offers neither logic nor irrational satisfactions is entirely incommunicable; where logical demonstration is possible when no satisfaction is in view, the art of persuasion, difficult as it may be, must be used to the full.

Thus, in the mind of Pascal, eloquence is determined by the combination of easily recognized qualitative reactions, positive or negative, capable of mathematical expression in simple equations. The left-hand side of each equation would present the sum of two components, the logical value and factual basis of the demonstration plus its acceptability to the hearer, the person to be persuaded, while the right-hand side would record the success of the operation, the degree of its eloquence and its persuasive power. If either component on the left is a minus quantity, the persuader finds himself in difficulty. In other words, more particularly when it is a case of a demonstrable proposition the hearer is unlikely to accept, Pascal has to face the necessity of adding art to argument. Now he has to analyze the nature of true propositions that may be argued only while it is recognized that they conflict with the interests and satisfactions of the hearer.

One recalls that these words were written for the introduction of a textbook designed to teach geometry in schools. Other passages show that Pascal was fully aware of the fact that the demonstration of truth is rarely equal to its acceptability,

puisqu'il faudrait ... connaître tout ce qui se passe dans le plus intérieur de l'homme, que l'homme même ne connaît presque jamais.

Il paraît de là, que quoi que ce soit qu'on veuille persuader, il faut avoir égard à la personne à qui on en veut, dont il faut connaître l'esprit et le cœur, quels principes il accorde, quelles choses il aime; et ensuite remarquer, dans la chose dont il s'agit, quels rapports elle a avec les principes avoués, ou avec les objets délicieux par les charmes qu'on lui donne.

De sorte que l'art de persuader consiste autant en celui d'agréer qu'en celui de convaincre, tant les hommes se gouvernent plus par caprice que par raison![9]

Pascal was by now fully aware of the need to distinguish between the objective truth which pure reason fully accepts and the agreed conventions which command assent among people in general, whether philosophically

9 Ibid p. 142

inclined or not. Naturally he felt himself better equipped for persuasion on the level of scientific understanding, but it is clear that even in this predominantly mathematical treatise he was interested by the task of achieving persuasion, 'éloquence' as he will call it in the *Pensées*, against the forces of self-interest.

With the first *Lettre écrite à un provincial par un de ses amis* in January of 1656, Pascal takes an important step away from the rigorously reasonable presentation of scientific propositions. Because 'le monde devient méfiant, et ne croit les choses que quand il les voit,' his purpose is to create vision, to illuminate a difficult subject-matter by the use of all the devices that he can muster – irony concerning those whose teachings he attacks, flattery of the reader, careful restatement of the arguments he opposes, and, on occasion, satiric comedy worthy of a Molière. In his attempt to persuade the general public he finds that the simple calculations and demonstrations of the geometric spirit will not suffice; assent must be won by a mingled resort to common sense and to the emotions, fears, and sympathies of the reader. These eighteen letters may perhaps be the most brilliantly unfair pamphlets ever written.

The literary limitations of the early Pascal, his laborious presentation of a balanced and discursive argument without appeal to what he described as the will, were yielding to the developing gifts of the polemicist. The persuasive powers of the sober qualities of science were submerged in a new view of human nature in which the *esprit de finesse*, the rapid intuitive power that sees things as a whole and resolves problems of conduct, emerged as dominant in the majority of mankind, speeding the process of philosophical understanding and the comprehension of theories just as it solved intimate personal and social dilemmas. The success, in a literary sense, of the *Lettres provinciales* had shown that persuasion, eloquence, included not only logical argument but also the art of pleasing by subtle devices close to the irrational. Pascal's study of the Christian tradition showed further that the inquiring reason was usually forced to play a minor role in the attainment of belief, and that acceptance of the central dogmas of Christianity depended on grace, or, in his favored word, on *charité*, taken in its original Greek sense – a gift reaching men by way of the suprarational pathway he describes as the heart. Perhaps it should be remarked that the doctrine that the heart was an organ of fine perception bore no relation to current physiological thinking. The linguistic usage was Aristotelian, justified by its occurrence in Lucretius, and it afforded Pascal a term needed in a case for which the precise and limited literary diction of his day did not allow. It was a term that everyone would understand, that went back to Homer and persists today, in English as in French.

The shift from the exact sciences to the study of man is well described in *pensée 736*. Contact with polite society, with the Chevalier de Méré, as well as his reading of Montaigne, had led Pascal to see that the sciences, already specialized in purpose and method, were not widely understood or highly valued in seventeenth-century Paris, and that they offered little occasion for intellectual contact with one's fellows:

J'avais passé longtemps dans l'étude des sciences abstraites; et le peu de communication qu'on en peut avoir m'en avait dégoûté. Quand j'ai commencé l'étude de l'homme, j'ai vu que ces sciences abstraites ne sont pas propres à l'homme, et que je m'égarais plus de ma condition en y pénétrant que les autres en l'ignorant; j'ai pardonné aux autres d'y peu savoir. Mais j'ai cru trouver au moins bien des compagnons en l'étude de l'homme, et que c'est le vrai étude qui lui est propre. J'ai été trompé: il y a encore moins qui l'étudient que la géométrie. Ce n'est que manque de savoir étudier cela qu'on cherche le reste. Mais n'est-ce pas que ce n'est pas encore là la science que l'homme doit avoir? et qu'il lui est meilleur de s'ignorer pour être heureux?

The irony is striking, but the tone of this reflection reveals much concerning Pascal's lonely search for the highest level of knowledge. Elsewhere, and perhaps later, he writes: 'La science des choses extérieures ne me consolera pas de l'ignorance de la morale, au temps de l'affliction; mais la science des mœurs me consolera toujours de l'ignorance des sciences extérieures' (22).

For the most part written on loose sheets of paper, the *Pensées* were partially classified by Pascal, who grouped some three hundred and eighty under headings presumably destined for the chapters of his book. About six hundred others remained unsorted, of which some cannot be fitted into the plan of the *Apologie*; a remnant is left whose purpose is undetermined. The collection as a whole continues to offer a challenge to scholars, who seek in various ways to produce a readable book, representative of Pascal's mature thought. That it has been impossible to produce such a book, an adequate portrayal of the subtleties of his mind, is due as much to the complexity of the man as to the intellectual distance that separates him from his critics. He tells us much about *l'intérieur de l'homme Pascal*, but we know much less about him as a public, social being, his daily ways, the chronology of his ideas, the superficial self, the way in which he would have accounted for the internal contradictions, the hesitations, and the sudden forward leaps that characterize his book. There was an inner dialogue in him: what were the roles of the interlocutors, the skeptic, the man of faith, the scientist, the satirist, the meticulous seeker of the *mot juste*? The reader can do little more than follow strands of his thought, one or two at a time, in the hope that some day the whole story will be told, the whole Pascal glimpsed in the variety of aspects under which he has been seen.

Various passages suggest that by a characteristic development of antitheses Pascal worked out a theory of levels of knowledge and action, each bound up with specific functions in life, and marked by a particular kind of insight. In the fragmentary preface on vacuum he had contrasted the life of reason with the activity of the animal mind, in which an instinct responds mechanically to various needs of daily life; the example he offers is the hexagonal shape of the cells in a honey comb. Study had shown him that while geometry could be taught on the level of pure reason, resistance to it in a mind unaccustomed to the concept of measured angles, lines, and areas could greatly reduce the possibility of useful communication. There were minds, indeed, quick, lively, delicate in apprehension, capable of subtle and refined perceptions, for whom chains of mathematical reasoning were not only distasteful and cumbersome, but distressing and impossible. Intuitive to a high degree himself, Pascal shows an acute sympathy with this type of mind; while he could work with lengthy sequences of argument, his mind leaped rapidly over elaborate calculations to reach correct results long before the appropriate ciphering could be done on paper. That he did not believe that this gift was necessarily an aspect of the mathematical reason itself is suggested by his remark in the essay on the art of persuasion, that 'on peut aisément être très habile homme et mauvais géomètre.'

In this way he reached a point at which he could group the intuitive processes of the mind, no matter how applied, whether in the arts, in insight into processes and methods, or in personal crises, and oppose them collectively to the pedestrian devices of argument, the syllogisms which lead step by step to logical conviction. This upper level where immediate perception occurs – upper, because Pascal always refers to this in terms of ascent and descent, head and brain over body, ruler over subjects, heaven over earth – being more noble than what is below, offers a third way of knowing, remote from the instinct and habit typical of animal or insect life, from which it is separated by a middle realm of the systematized sciences, physics, geometry, and astronomy, the area of logic, of deliberate reasoning on a basis of observed fact and operational measurement. 'Notre âme,' he writes, 'est jetée dans le corps, où elle trouve nombre, temps, dimensions; elle raisonne là-dessus et appelle cela nature, nécessité, et ne peut croire autre chose' (418).

There seems to be no precise and unchanging number of these gradations in Pascal's intention. Each level of the three noted here seems to be capable of subdivision as new distinctions appear. It is not surprising that at the heart of the discussion of the Wager (418) we should find a further distinction between the intuitional *esprit de finesse*, already described as useful in many spheres of daily life, and the *esprit de charité*, acting in the heart with altogether special intensity. Various *pensées* show his desire to develop the nuances:

La dernière démarche de la raison est de reconnaître qu'il y a une infinité de choses qui la surpassent. – Elle n'est que faible, si elle ne va jusqu'à connaître cela.
   Que si les choses naturelles la surpassent, que dira-t-on des surnaturelles? (186)

   C'est le cœur qui sent Dieu, et non la raison. Voilà ce que c'est que la Foi: Dieu sensible au cœur, non à la raison. (422)

   Le cœur a ses raisons que la raison ne connaît point; on le sait en mille choses.
   Je dis que le cœur aime l'être universel naturellement, et soi-même naturellement, selon qu'il s'y adonne; et il se durcit contre l'un ou l'autre, à son choix. Vous avez rejeté l'un et conservé l'autre. Est-ce par raison que vous vous aimez? (424)

A long and intricate *pensée* (305) develops the detail of these perceptions; as it illustrates the theory of levels fully worked out, it is worth quoting at some length:

La distance infinie des corps aux esprits figure la distance infiniment plus infinie des esprits à la charité, car elle est surnaturelle.
   Tout l'éclat des grandeurs n'a point de lustre pour les gens qui sont dans les recherches de l'esprit.
   La grandeur des gens d'esprit est invisible aux rois, aux riches, aux capitaines et à tous ces grands de chair.
   La grandeur de la sagesse, qui n'est nulle, sinon de Dieu, est invisible aux charnels et aux gens d'esprit; ce sont trois ordres différents de genre.
   Les grands génies ont leur empire, leur éclat, leur grandeur, leur victoire et leur lustre, et n'ont nul besoin des grandeurs charnelles, où elles n'ont pas de rapport. Ils sont vus non des yeux, mais des esprits; c'est assez.
   Les saints ont leur empire, leur éclat, leur victoire, leur lustre, et n'ont nul besoin ni rapport des grandeurs charnelles ou spirituelles, où elles n'ont nul rapport; car elles n'y ajoutent ni ôtent. Ils sont vus de Dieu et des anges, et non des corps ni des esprits curieux; Dieu leur suffit.
   Archimède sans éclat serait en même vénération. – Il n'a pas donné des batailles pour les yeux; mais il a fourni à tous les esprits ses inventions ...
   Jésus-Christ, sans biens et sans aucune production au dehors de science, est dans son ordre de sainteté. Il n'a point donné d'inventions, il n'a point régné; mais il a été

humble, patient, saint, saint, saint, saint à Dieu, terrible aux démons, sans aucun péché. Oh! qu'il est venu en grande pompe et en une prodigieuse magnificence aux yeux du cœur et qui voient la sagesse!

Here Pascal's orders of perception are completely externalized; differences are no longer subjective, they exist in a world with its own particular reality, summed up in eloquent peroration:

Tous les corps, le firmament, les étoiles, la terre et ses royaumes, ne valent pas le moindre des esprits; car il connaît tout cela, et soi; et les corps rien.

Tous les corps ensemble et tous les esprits ensemble et toutes leurs productions ne valent pas le moindre mouvement de charité; cela est d'un ordre infiniment plus élevé.

De tous les corps ensemble, on ne saurait en faire réussir une petite pensée; cela est impossible et d'un autre ordre. De tous les corps et esprits, on n'en saurait tirer un mouvement de vraie charité; cela est impossible ... d'un autre ordre, surnaturel.

The assertion of the limitations of the world revealed by science could hardly go farther.

The clear distinction between the world of nature, of *les connaissances naturelles*, understanding of which depends on the unhampered operations of the *esprit géométrique*, and the world of grace or *charité* underlies the argument of the Wager. Here the logic turns on the advantage to be gained by betting that God exists, a statement that positive knowledge, given by *les lumières naturelles*, does not permit us to make with assurance. In the circumstances, it is prudent to act as if he did exist; if he does not, we cannot suffer for our presumption, while if he does we may clearly gain. Pascal points out that on the one hand if we act as atheists, there is an even chance that we shall lose heavily, and that therefore it is the mathematical probability of preponderant loss – on which point Pascal was a recognized expert – that justifies wagering on God and the anticipation of the life to come. Like it or not, the wager is forced on us; we cannot remake the situation we find ourselves in, and we have a stake in the outcome of our conduct and beliefs. The fact that God, who has neither parts nor limits, is infinitely incomprehensible to us, is of no consequence; man can prove nothing about him, but we are committed, even from the atheist's point of view, to a life whose ultimate nature we do not know, whose essence is a subject of our speculation. This argument, which every Pascalian will recognize is merely sketched here, represents Pascal's most considerable effort to base his *Apologia* on grounds of geometrical thinking, *les lumières naturelles*.

Perhaps a final illustration of the meaning of this word *naturel* as Pascal uses it in these contexts may be found in the extensive *pensée*, 447, already quoted, which is devoted to a defense of Christianity as a mystery involving a Redeemer who unites in himself two natures, divine and human, which cannot be reconciled without Christian faith.

On ne peut connaître Jésus-Christ sans connaître tout ensemble et Dieu et sa misère.

Et c'est pourquoi je n'entreprendrai pas ici de prouver par des raisons naturelles, ou l'existence de Dieu, ou la Trinité, ou l'immortalité de l'âme, ni aucune des choses de cette nature, non seulement parce que je ne me sentirais pas assez fort pour trouver dans la Nature de quoi convaincre des athées endurcis, mais encore parce que cette connaissance, sans Jésus-Christ, est inutile et stérile. Quand un homme serait persuadé que les proportions des nombres sont des vérités immatérielles, éternelles et dépendantes d'une première vérité en qui elles subsistent et qu'on appelle Dieu, je ne le trouverais pas beaucoup avancé pour son salut.

Consideration of these *pensées* and others strengthens the impression that it is impossible to follow Pascal's thought if we do not accept with him the view that differences in the quality of knowledge and evidence separate natural philosophy, physics and geometry for example, from matters of faith on the one hand, and from instinct, the habits and passions of the body, on the other. Commentators, perhaps influenced by seventeenth-century discussions of innate ideas, have tended to see such entities at all levels of the Pascalian scheme, and have thus confused many insights that originally were quite clear. On the contrary, the adjective *naturel*, used with such words as *connaissances, lumières*, or *raison*, refers to knowledge and insights gained from direct experience of objects, perceptible to the bodily senses and available to the *esprit géométrique*, as opposed to instinct on the level of animal cunning, to the *esprit de finesse*, roughly the equivalent of the modern word intuition, or finally to the *esprit de charité*, the action of the grace of God. Each of these three forms of the general *esprit* is different from and higher than anything found in animals, and it seems quite certain that Pascal regards the information these different faculties communicate as data provided through experience, and not in any way innate, occult, or obscure. The word *naturel*, in short, implies the use of the clear light of reason, the *sens commun* of Descartes, a faculty which all men share, and which refers to an area of thought and experience in which communication is easiest and surest. For that very reason, it fails to convey the subtler insights and more complex revelations of religious experience.

Pascal was not a successful publicist like Voltaire, nor yet a facile writer. His thought, in the *Pensées* at least, evolved slowly from the sudden rapid insights of his *esprit de finesse* by means of scrupulous corrections and elaborations until a conclusion – if one can describe the accepted form of any of these fragments as conclusive – either reinforces, or on occasion reverses, the first impulsive thrust of his expression. Much of this sometimes tortuous path towards clarity may be followed in the edition produced by Zacharie Tourneur and Didier Anzieu from which we quote.

The process of transformation is apparent in *pensée* 865, which begins as a comment on human nature, with relevant illustrations, and is finally revised with the tenets of the *Apologie* in view. The first writing of the fragment reads as follows:

Car il ne faut pas se méconnaître, l'instrument par lequel la persuasion se fait n'est pas démonstration. Combien y a il de chose[s] démontrées! la coutume fait nos preuves les plus fortes et les plus crues. Qui a démontré qu'il sera demain jour et que nous mourrons? Et qu'y a il de plus cru? C'est donc la coutume qui nous en persuade; c'est elle qui fait tant de chrétiens, c'est elle qui fait les Turcs, les païens, les métiers, les soldats, etc. Enfin il faut avoir recours à elle, quand une fois nous avons vu où est la vérité afin de nous abreuver et nous teindre de cette créance, qui nous échappe à tout heure; car d'en avoir toujours les preuves présentes, c'est trop d'affaire. Il faut acquérir une créance plus facile, qui est celle de l'habitude, qui sans violence, sans art, sans argument, nous incline toutes nos puissances à cette croyance, en sorte que notre âme y tombe naturellement. Quand on ne croit que par la force de la conviction, et que l'automate est incliné à croire le contraire, ce n'est pas assez. Il faut donc faire croire nos deux pièces: l'esprit, démonstration par les raisons qu'il suffit d'avoir vues une fois en sa vie; et l'automate, par la coutume, et en ne lui permettant pas de s'incliner.

'Inclina cor meum, Deus!'

La raison agit avec lenteur et avec tant de vues, sur tant de principes, lesquels il faut qu'ils soient toujours présents, qu'à toute heure elle s'assoupit ou s'égare, manque d'avoir tous ses principes présents. Le sentiment n'agit pas ainsi: il agit en un instant et toujours est prêt à agir. Il faut donc mettre notre foi dans le sentiment; autrement elle sera toujours vacillante.

This *pensée* falls naturally into two parts: first, an observation on human nature, that geometrical demonstration does not necessarily persuade, and secondly, that belief arises from the cooperation of custom and habit with the truth as seen by the mind, the *esprit*. Such notions as belief in the recurrence of night and day do not carry logical proof, for the assurance we have in such matters is conjectural and probable only, even though generally accepted. Developing the argument that custom can and does persuade us of truth, creating belief, Pascal adds that it is therefore custom that creates religious, professional, and national loyalties. Hence, he concludes, truth once glimp-sed must be reinforced by custom and habitual behavior, so that we may be imbued with belief, for a truth can escape us at any moment since it is too much to expect that any man could have all truths continually in mind: 'Il faut acquérir une créance plus facile ... en sorte que notre âme y tombe naturelle-ment.' A final brief paragraph is less original, with its remark on the differ-ence between *la raison*, the geometric spirit, and the *esprit de finesse*, a Pascalian phrase which remains impossible to render in English, here linked to another of his characteristic expressions, *le sentiment*. It may be noted that this word, *sentiment*, common enough in the seventeenth century, is used with precision by Pascal to refer to the immediate perception, the image, sound, sensation, or other datum of consciousness. It does not indicate a 'feeling,' or an associated quality of emotional tone apart from the observed event in the experience of the senses.

The latter half of the *pensée*, perhaps a later addition, for it lacks erasures and interlineal and marginal revisions, bears more relation to the final form of the whole fragment than to the primitive wording of the opening phrases, conceived before the addition of the language by which this shrewd note on the ways of human nature was given its Christian tinge and thus made suitable for inclusion in the *Apologie*. The dichotomy *automate-esprit* is now woven back into the text as far as the first sentence: 'Car il ne faut pas se méconnaître, nous sommes automate autant qu'esprit,' the last six words added to strengthen the Christian direction imposed on this secular and objective comment on mankind. With half a dozen other alterations, these revisions change the *pensée* from an observation on persuasion (*éloquence*) into a contribution to the Pascalian view of the means of promoting belief by the use of his characteristic distinction of levels of perception and intelligence.

The chief difference, however, between the text as we have read it so far and the form in which it appears in the usual editions[10] lies in a sentence which Pascal added just after the observation that it is custom which makes 'tant de chrétiens ... les Turcs, les païens, les métiers, les soldats,' a remark which in its original clarity undoes much of the purpose of the *Apologie*. Realizing that he has blundered into doctrinal error, he produces a revealing insertion: 'Il y a la foi reçue dans le baptême de plus aux Chrétiens qu'aux païens.' In short, the evidence of the manuscript is that Pascal began this reflection on human nature, observed in and for itself, without dogmatic

10 This *pensée* is numbered 252 by Brunschvicg. L. Lafuma places it at no. 7 in the edition published by J. Delmas et Cie in 1960, and no. 821 in the revision published by the Éditions du Seuil in 1962.

preconceptions. If this is representative, we have in him a man whose work for the promotion of Christianity carried over and utilized much of the method and outlook of the scientist in the empirical seventeenth-century mould.

This impression deepens as one reads the earlier chapters of the *Pensées*, the fragments classified by Pascal himself and placed by the editors of the *Copie*, probably Antoine Arnauld and Pierre Nicole, at the threshold of their arrangement of the collection.[11] Here, after a preliminary section, 'Ordre,' concerned chiefly with the general shape of the book, come Pascal's sections, 'Vanité,' 'Misère,' 'Ennui,' 'Raison des effets,' up to and including the tenth, 'Le Souverain Bien,' presenting a series of wide-ranging comments on mankind which have quite as much interest for the moralist and uncommitted amateur of human nature as for the pious Christian. On the basis of a count as nearly objective as mortal frailty permits, the 134 fragments grouped by Pascal in these nine sections are preponderantly secular and untendentious; in some ways they are as unrelievedly pessimistic about human nature as any of the *Maxims* of La Rochefoucauld. There is little Christian charity here: man is vain, inconstant, fickle, selfish, stupid, tyrannized over by institutions of his own creating, the victim of his imagination and self-esteem, with no firm base in the world, no hope for improvement in the face of a universe he cannot understand, which offers no evidence for a deity. The general tone of these chapters is such that one finds no great difficulty in envisaging Pascal as the author *in propria persona* of the desperately agnostic or even atheistic passages which have troubled many of his editors, such as two paragraphs in the heart of 429 and the whole of 430, summed up in the familiar 'le silence éternel de ces espaces infinis m'effraie' (194).

Such passages as these have frequently been interpreted as products of Pascal's efforts to express the thoughts of those 'qui cherchent en gémissant,' atheists seeking refuge from their godless universe. There are few passages so frankly desperate as those referred to above, and these are heavily outnumbered by others in which Christian teachings are eloquently and vigorously set forth. We have seen, however, enough ambivalence in Pascal's thought to justify the proposition that he was fully aware of the agnostic outlook, and at moments shared it. The earliest editors of the *Pensées* knew that the texts they had to work with were not uniformly orthodox and pious; they were quite conscious of the explosive nature of his thinking. The persistent assumption

11 The first attempt to bring order into the disarray in which the *Pensées* were found was made by Pascal's family and friends soon after his death in 1662. The result was the first *Copie*, now MS fonds français 9203 in the Bibliothèque nationale. Cf. the introduction to the Cluny edition, 1: lxi-lxiv.

that this complex book is directed towards only one goal demands our question. Emotionally, Pascal was committed to the Christian point of view; he could never have accepted Bertrand Russell's view that the state of human knowledge is such that 'either to assert or to deny the universal reign of law is a mark of prejudice; the rational man will regard the question as open.' That the question was not entirely closed in Pascal's mind makes his book the more interesting; there is dramatic value in the tension perceptible on almost every page.

This dual outlook, the pessimism, the agnosticism, the note of ineluctable doubt, in contrast with Pascal's special kind of Jansenist piety, produces a dialogue whose alternations possess a certain charm. The scientist's method, his assumption that the world of nature has its autonomy, its built-in structure and its impetus, its self-contained regularities extending even to the behavior of men and women, his clear and disillusioned vision of a universe complete and self-sustaining, conflicts with his other view, to which he held with equal firmness, that the universe is unreal in comparison with the divine element in the heart of man himself. The resulting struggle can be resolved only by an act of will, a creation of unity 'en mettant l'esprit et l'automate ensemble,' a state consecrated by custom and habit.

Nowhere is this state of tension more apparent than in the famous 'Disproportion de l'homme' (Cluny 197, Brunschvicg 72). The introduction is remarkable, some ten or twelve lines which break off in the middle of a sentence, canceled probably because Pascal felt he could not hope to keep his reader with him, plunging far too quickly into the middle of an argument that in a very real sense sums up his life and work:

Voilà où nous mènent les connaissances naturelles.

Si celles-là ne sont véritables, il n'y a point de vérité dans l'homme, et si elles le sont, l'homme y trouve un grand sujet d'humiliation, forcé à s'abaisser d'une ou d'autre manière.

Et, puisqu'il ne peut subsister sans les croire, je souhaite, avant que de passer outre et d'entrer dans les plus grandes recherches de la Nature, qu'il la considère une fois sérieusement et à loisir, qu'il se regarde aussi soi-même et qu'il juge s'il a quelque proportion avec elle, par la comparaison qu'il fera de ces deux objets et connaissant quelle proportion il y a ...

Canceled by Pascal, these opening lines strike the note heard throughout the long *pensée*, developing his generalized view of the natural world and man's place in it. From the first words, 'This is where natural knowledge brings us,' language which indicates unmistakably the conclusion of an extended interior debate, through to the uncompleted diminuendo which terminates the whole argument ('pour consommer la preuve de notre faiblesse je finirai par ces deux considérations ... '), the curve of his thought turns on the implications of the new sciences, their extension into new areas of investigation, and the outlook their view of the natural world imposes on the present and the immediate future of the mind of man. Pascal speaks here of science, not of instinctive knowledge or innate ideas, as some current translations would have us believe.

The *pensée* begins with dimensions of magnitude, looking in turn at the macrocosm and the infinitely small, reflecting on the humble position of man, his senses baffled by the concepts of size made available by new instruments, the telescope and the microscope. The direction shifts; the infinitely small is now the *principe*, the seed, and the huge universe is the end, *la fin des choses*. The analogy satisfies neither us nor Pascal, and he is on another tack; after a page on man's presumption, he turns to discuss man's intelligence, whose limitations are the tolerances of our senses in a dozen different dimensions: hearing, sight, perception of distance, brevity and length of discourse; *trop de vérité nous étonne*; then pleasure, harmony, good deeds, heat and cold, excess of any quality, age or youth, finally *trop et trop peu d'instruction*. In short, extremes are to us as if they did not exist, and as if we did not exist for them: *elles nous échappent ou nous à elles*.

Any account of the topics discussed in this long essay must omit much detail, passing over many passages elaborated with consummate care. Pascal's thought gradually finds itself through a maze of words crossed out, recommenced, replaced, until at last a form has been reached to approximate his sense of what he has to say. The extremes which 'escape us or from which we escape' lead into one of the most memorable paragraphs of the whole book:

Voilà notre état véritable. C'est ce qui nous rend incapables de savoir certainement et d'ignorer absolument. Nous voguons sur un milieu vaste, toujours incertains et flottants, poussés d'un bout vers l'autre; quelque terme où nous pensions nous attacher et nous affermir, il branle et nous quitte, et si nous le suivons, il échappe à nos prises, nous glisse et fuit d'une fuite éternelle. Rien ne s'arrête pour nous. C'est l'état qui nous est naturel et toutefois le plus contraire à notre inclination; nous brûlons de désir de trouver une assiette ferme, et une dernière base constante pour y édifier une tour que s'élève à l'infini; mais tout notre fondement craque, et la terre s'ouvre jusqu'aux abîmes.[12]

12 Cluny 1; 149 and 151; 152

There have been many attempts to account for this remarkable passage. Pascal may be indulging in reverie, a dream state, in which he presents a series of images describing the human condition in a huge universe, 'une sphère infinie, dont le centre est partout, la circonférence nulle part.' But the words he finds for this have a magic of their own; he cannot stop on static verbs, he must use verbs of action and movement. 'Nous voguons' replaces 'nous sommes,' transforming the *milieu* from a silent, motionless universe into a great sea or stream, giving life to the previously vague *flottants*, and arousing a sequence of shifting sensations which suggest a vessel moving through mist or fog, passing buoys which escape the grasp of the drifting traveler. To this reader, the passage compares the fog-bound philosopher with a passenger on the *coche d'eau* which carried wayfarers on the wide reaches of the Loire; after the traveler from Paris left the highway at Orléans, he found relief from the discomfort of springless wagons on rough and dusty roads in the comfortable boats which plied the frequently misty river in either direction, down stream to the châteaux, Tours, Nantes, and the ocean, or up to his native Auvergne.[13]

In any case, this is a vivid interlude in the philosophizing of this long *pensée*. Seeking confidence in the principles of natural philosophy, the mind is frustrated as it watches its points of reference disappear in a white ambience in which nothing can stay fixed. These sentences raise the level of Pascal's thought to poetry: the finites cannot be grasped, there is no holding the infinity of the universe. Man cannot build his tower of Babel or seek sure knowledge of this world: 'La seule comparaison que nous faisons de nous au fini nous fait peine.'

But with one of his astounding transitions, Pascal rebounds, and is off on a program for scientific investigation that will take mankind a century to realize.

Si l'homme s'étudiait le premier, il verrait combien il est incapable de passer outre. Comment se pourrait-il qu'une partie connût le tout? Mais il aspirera peut-être à connaître au moins les parties avec lesquelles il a de la proportion? Mais les parties du monde ont toutes un tel rapport et un tel enchaînement l'une avec l'autre, que je crois impossible de connaître l'une sans l'autre et sans le tout.

The transition is clear: from frustration at the difficulty of freeing himself from the human predicament, Pascal turns to the possibility of discovering

13 Cf. Pascal's letter to Fermat from Bienassis, 10 August 1660: 'Je suis engagé d'aller [de Bourbon] en Poitou par eau jusqu'à Saumur ... je passerai par Orléans en allant à Saumur par la rivière' (*Opuscules et lettres*, pp. 218-19).

the parts of the universe with which man bears a direct relationship; from that advance in knowledge man can proceed to the study of relationships within the natural world, leading to an understanding of the whole. Theological skepticism about science disappears as the scientist is revived in Pascal; one after another the sciences of the time, whether well developed already or merely glimpsed as new kinds of problems come to light, are passed in review: 'L'homme a rapport à tout ce qu'il connaît.'

Man needs space to contain him, which suggests geometry, even in three dimensions for a better calculation of positions in a stellar universe; his existence in time demands a keener analysis of that concept. He moves in order to live, and we know little enough about the movement of the bones and muscles, although there has been some experimentation and thinking about problems of that order. Man is composed of elements, and, with many others, Pascal is aware that alchemy, in spite of some practical knowledge, is in a poor state as far as scientific theory is concerned; the crude elemental basis of hot and cold, moist and dry, may satisfy a literary mode in verbal terms, but is of little use in a laboratory or a sick-room. Why does man need heat to live? How does he utilize his food? What values for life does he draw from the air? Pascal's questions were in the intellectual climate of the day; these matters are already interesting his contemporaries, Jean Pecquet, Giovanni Alfonso Borelli, Nils Steensen (or Steno), Marcello Malpighi, Robert Boyle, Richard Lower, John Mayow, and Thomas Sydenham, not to mention such predecessors as William Harvey, and the three French scientists, Desargues, Descartes, and Mersenne, whom he had known in Paris, as well as a spirit to whom he seems to have been specially kin, Pierre Gassendi.

From the particular, Pascal passes to the general question of man in the natural world:

Il voit la lumière; il sent les corps; enfin tout tombe sous son alliance. Il faut donc, pour connaître l'homme, savoir d'où vient qu'il a besoin d'air pour subsister; et, pour connaître l'air, savoir par où il a ce rapport à la vie de l'homme, etc. ...

La flamme ne subsiste point sans l'air; donc, pour connaître l'un, il faut connaître l'autre.

If science begins by asking the right questions, then rarely are the *Pensées* more scientific than right here. The mood of resignation to be ignorant which characterized some of the opening paragraphs of this *pensée* is forgotten. Pascal now returns to his assertion of progress in knowledge, repeating that it is impossible 'de connaître les parties sans connaître le tout, non plus que de connaître le tout sans connaître particulièrement les parties.'

This review of urgent questions leads to a discussion of method in understanding nature and man himself. Things are simple; man is complex, dual in nature, 'composé de deux natures opposées et de divers genres: d'âme et de corps.' It is impossible, he adds,

que la partie qui raisonne en nous soit autre que spirituelle: et quand on prétendrait que nous serions simplement corporels, cela nous exclurait bien davantage de la connaissance des choses, n'y ayant rien de si inconcevable que de dire que la matière se connaît soi-même; il ne nous est pas possible de connaître comment elle se connaîtrait.

Hence, he concludes, if we are simply material beings, we can know nothing at all; and if we are composed of mind and matter, we cannot know simple things, 'spirituelles ou corporelles.'

This is why philosophers confuse the ideas of things, speaking of corporeal things in terms of spirits, and of things of the spirit in terms of the body,

car ils disent hardiment que les corps tendent en bas, qu'ils aspirent à leur centre, qu'ils fuient leur destruction, qu'ils craignent le vide, qu'ils ont des inclinations, des sympathies, des antipathies, qui sont toutes choses qui n'appartiennent qu'aux esprits; et en parlant des esprits, ils les considèrent comme en un lieu et leur attribue le mouvement d'une place à une autre, qui sont choses qui n'appartiennent qu'aux corps.[14]

The verbal nonsense referred to in these lines, the misapplication of terms, is a frequent theme in Pascal. Much of his work in physics had to meet the incomprehension of men whose thought was cast in the conventional terms of ancient physics; the debate over vacuum and the *horreur du vide* was only the most striking example of the semantic problem he faced. One of the chief tasks of the new scientists was literary in nature; it was important to attain clarification and general understanding of the terminology coming into use, and of the point of view from which the natural world was to be viewed.

Quite appropriately, this long fragment has been much discussed. Its sources have been studied, and they have their interest; Pascal's work was based on much reading of older authors, as he recognized when he wrote, in the preface to his treatise on vacuum, that

les premières connaissances que [les anciens] nous ont données ont servi de degrés aux nôtres et que dans ces avantages nous leur sommes redevables de l'ascendant que nous avons sur eux; parce que, s'étant élevés jusqu'à un certain degré où ils nous ont portés, le moindre effort nous fait monter plus haut, et avec moins de peine et moins de gloire nous nous trouvons au-dessus d'eux.[15]

What is important is the use Pascal has made of his literary and scientific sources, and the massive and complex unity in which he has cast this imaginative résumé of his thinking about the natural world and man's place in it. Taken as a whole, and allowing for the fact that in its incompletely revised state it is not as Pascal would have sent it to the printer, it is a noble piece of prose, colorful, with movement and imagery, and, in spite of one or two awkward transitions, it possesses a rhythm which holds the reader throughout. Its liveliest moments are those in which the dynamism of the scientific vision has seized Pascal, taking his thought through familiar and much-traveled channels. Mathematician and physicist, with astronomers among his friends, Pascal grasped the concept of a universe much larger than the telescopes could show, and the contrasting potentialities of complex structures made visible by the microscope. Analogy leads him far afield, and as he turns from speculation to speculation, his reader follows a prospect opening far beyond the projects of the academies of the time and the achievements of the virtuosi.

At one point in the writing of the *pensée* on disproportion, Pascal composed a conclusion which set the natural world in contrast with man. After a sentence which sums up much of the long fragment ('Voilà une partie des causes qui rendent l'homme si imbécile à connaître la Nature'), he begins again:

Elle est infinie en deux manières, il est fini et limité; elle dure et se maintient perpétuellement en son être, il passe et est mortel; les choses en particulier se corrompent et se changent à chaque instant, il ne les voit qu'en passant; elles ont leur principe et leur fin, il ne conçoit ni l'un ni l'autre; elles sont simples, et il est composé de deux natures différentes; et pour consommer la preuve de notre faiblesse, je finirai par cette réflexion sur l'état de notre nature ... [16]

Canceled by Pascal, this inconclusive paragraph has been omitted by many editors, printed as a footnote by Brunschvicg, and preserved in the sequence by the editors of Cluny. On reflection, Pascal may have realized that its emphasis on the permanence of Nature, on the autonomy and simplicity of natural processes, and on the limitations of mankind, was out of harmony

15 *Opuscules et lettres*, p. 53
16 Cluny I: 158

with the Christian teachings of the *Apologie*. So the sentences were dropped, and Pascal comes rapidly to the unsatisfactory conclusion of his long discourse. The lines immediately preceding the paragraph omitted had been based on a passage in the *City of God*, 'Modus quo corporibus adhaerent spiritus comprehendi non potest, et hoc tamen homo est,' which he describes as 'le comble de ses difficultés, et cependant c'est son propre être.' This final statement of the quandary of man expresses the problem of Pascal himself, unresolved as the *pensée* reaches its end: 'Enfin, pour consommer la preuve de notre faiblesse, je finirai par ces deux considérations ... ' – considerations which are never stated, but which recall the double alternatives set forth in the second of the *pensées* as themes for the book's two parts:

> Misère de l'homme sans Dieu;
> Félicité de l'homme avec Dieu;
> AUTREMENT
> Que la Nature est corrompue;
> Qu'il y a un réparateur.

More consonant with the conscious purpose of the *Apologie* is another *pensée* (111), which read originally as follows:

Ce n'est point de l'espace que je dois chercher ma dignité, mais c'est de la pensée. Je n'aurai point d'avantage en possédant des terres. L'univers me comprend et m'engloutit comme un point; par la pensée je le comprends.

And yet Pascal's sense of man's physical unimportance in the vast universe, in which concepts of order and impersonal law were emerging, is unrelieved by any prolonged confidence in the power of the scientific mind to grasp the meaning of the whole. Silence is eternal, space is infinite, and together the two are awesome.

Thus he could not believe that progress in science, no matter how assured, was truly significant, for he could not conceive of the emergence of principles which would lend purpose to what seemed destined to remain forever a vast machine. He may have turned from science through reading Jansenius, as Sainte-Beuve suggests,[17] or he may have lost confidence because of the necessity of tolerating insights which he rejected because they could not be reconciled with the fundamentals of faith. Temperamentally he rejected the cooperative requirements on whose values he had once insisted. Now he

17 Sainte-Beuve, *Port-Royal*, III, iv (Paris, Hachette 1888) 2: 478-81

sought isolation and avoided contacts, natural enough in the state of his health, but also a trait of character as time passed.

His pessimism may have hardened with the years, but it became more influential as his later work was revealed and absorbed in the body of modern literature. Perhaps largely against his own intent, Pascal has come at last to offer a model and an inspiration to generations of anti-rationalists, a model whose imaginative power bears slight relation to the significance and validity of his thought as a scientist or to his insights as an observer of mankind. In himself he illustrates very clearly the tensions of French thought in his own age. The place of science was precisely delimited, bounded by the area of humanist interest in man and his needs, aesthetic, moral, and social, and set apart, at the end of his life, as it had been at the beginning, from history, geography, law, and theology. Apart from these, there was the area of belief and action in which man follows the *esprit de finesse*, in particular the realm of faith, where one may be given *la charité*, divine grace, in which the heart is the percipient organ. At the highest level, this is the final cognitive faculty, intuitive and comprehensive, seeing the object of its thought in all its aspects, aware of persons, objects, actions, and events rather than of mathematical constructs, of a personal involvement in the universe rather than of an impersonal scheme of mindless vortices in an imagined *plenum*.[18]

Sections of this chapter have been revised from two articles, 'Pascal and *les connaissances naturelles*' in *Explorations V* (Toronto 1955) pp. 146-55, and 'Pascal *philosophe*,' read at the Second Congress on the Enlightenment, St Andrews, 1967, and published in *Studies on Voltaire and the Eighteenth Century* 55 (1967): pp. 309-20.

18 For a modern view of man and science not unlike that of Pascal, see S.I. Dockx, 'La Connaissance scientifique' in *Actualités scientifiques et industrielles* 1153, XIX Congrès internationale de philosophie des sciences V, Physique (Paris, Herman 1951) p. 27: 'Mais d'autre part la science ne peut prétendre étendre à tout ce qui est le procédé de la connaissance mathématique, car au-dessus du mesurable et du mathématique il y a: l'homme, être essentiellement métaphysique.'

And for a penetrating view of Pascal's outlook on the material universe see the writings of A.W.S. Baird, especially his wide-ranging article, 'Pascal's idea of nature' in *Isis* 61 (1970): 297-320, of which the last sentences read: 'Instead of trying to classify things by explaining one property in terms of another, we must accept nature as we find it, with the various phenomena enjoying separate existence. To interpret it otherwise is to falsify nature, and Pascal's censure would fall with equal severity on an *a priori* scheme into which everything is fitted willy nilly and on one which simply ignores recalcitrant elements. The continuity which runs all through its productions does not prevent Pascal from seeing nature as always saying something new, as growing ever more complex before man's gaze.'

CHAPTER FOUR

History, science, and
the *Journal des sçavans*

WHETHER HE should record the development of intelligence and the achievements of the arts and sciences or devote his efforts to the description of the play of irrational forces – pride, ambition, superstition and intolerance, xenophobia and chauvinism, and the like – is a question that has faced the historian ever since communal memories began. A chronicler turns with difficulty from the narration of the rivalries of dynasties to the less rousing tale of the gradual comprehension of the natural world through the invention of methods and techniques, the acquisition of accurate knowledge, the creation of works of beauty, and the development of mathematical theory. The practical solution that Voltaire found in his *Siècle de Louis XIV*, a concentration of the history of ideas and the arts and sciences in separate and terminal chapters of a relatively large book, has become a normal – and somewhat unsatisfactory – pattern, even in narratives limited to a single century or country.

The problem of how inclusive historiography should be became more acute as skeptics turned from the classicism of the Renaissance and towards science and ultimately the Enlightenment. One historian conscious of the change in outlook imposed by new disciplines in physics and astronomy was François Eudes de Mézeray (1610-83), whose *Histoire de France depuis Pharamond* had begun to appear in 1643, to be completed in further volumes in 1646 and 1651. Attempting to rework his massive folios into manageable dimensions for an *Abrégé chronologique* (1668), he found that contemporary emphasis on the sciences demanded attention, and that an account of the recent past required consideration of innovations in thought, stemming from the invention of the telescope, the application of mathematical method by Galileo and Descartes, and the descriptive sciences since Francis Bacon. In this new perspective, the succession of events bore no relation to the traditional epochs based on kings and dynasties. To contemporary eyes, the age before the introduction of printing and artillery and the opening of new worlds overseas by mariners equipped with the magnetic compass was clouded over by a special kind of darkness, an ignorance that appeared deeper as the years rolled by and as new knowledge, new speculation, and new devices cast more light on the universe and man's place in it.

Mézeray was a fairly typical man of the late Renaissance. He was born in the small Norman village from which he finally took the name by which he was to be known. His father was, according to the *Dictionnaire historique* of Louis Moreri, 'un homme d'esprit, et assez accommodé des biens de la fortune.' There were two brothers in the Eudes family, to whom their father gave a particularly careful education; the second son, Jean, became a priest and wrote works of devotion. At Caen, where they studied, François went from ancient history to history in general. Later, in Paris, he worked for a time for Jean Baudoin (1590?-1650?), translator of Francis Bacon, Tasso, and others, who was planning a history of the Merovingian monarchs, a project which Mézeray later expanded into his general history of France. During these years he came into the favor of the chancellor, Pierre Séguier, received a pension, and was given the title of *historiographe du Roi*. Moreri remarks of him that he was recognized as one of the most faithful historians that had so far appeared in France.

Mézeray was a late appointment to the committee set up to supervise the *Gazette*, a news weekly founded in 1631 by Théophraste Renaudot (1586-1653).His elder colleagues included the genealogist Pierre de la Garde d'Hozier (1592-1660), the poet Vincent Voiture (1597-1648), and the wit and diplomat Guillaume Bautru (1586-1665). With Mézeray there served his contemporary, the novelist La Calprenède (1614-63). The presence of such a committee of supervision suggests Colbert's desire to maintain a diversity of minds in the management of the periodical, to prevent the development of a specialized professional outlook prejudicial to the official objectives of the enterprise. The *Gazette* had been a publisher's success, useful in a highly centralized state as a means of controlling the news, a ploy of which few at that time were conscious. It reported current events from far and near, in that order; as a printed weekly brochure it supplanted the cumbersome and often irregular *nouvelles à la main*, hand-written sheets which had been the usual medium for the circulation of fact and comment on political events, enlivened with such items of special human interest as the individual correspondent could discover. These laboriously produced and limited means of communication were now supplemented, and soon replaced, by the circulation of multiple standardized copies in print, and Renaudot's Bureau d'adresse became the principal centre in France for the dissemination of news.[1]

It was an easy and obvious step from a gazette spreading information concerning public affairs to a journal recording events of intellectual interest and describing recent books, and Mézeray soon saw that a general literary journal would fill a need among scholars and scientists, the savants and the amateurs, of most of Europe. Among his papers in the Bibliothèque nationale[2] is the draft of a *privilège* for a *journal littéraire général*, describing in detail what such a periodical should be, and what it should contain. Attention to this document was first drawn in 1853 by the critic Sainte-Beuve, in a *causerie du lundi* on Mézeray as a historian, referring to its scope in passing, and dating it on circumstantial grounds from 1663. Incomplete and unsigned, the text bears nothing to indicate a precise date, and Sainte-Beuve associated it vaguely with the *Journal des sçavans* of 1665. Mézeray's draft belongs obviously to the first years of the ministry of Colbert; its close resemblance to the terms of the twenty year *privilège* accorded those who produced the journal, as well as to the contents and outlook of that periodical, suggests that the events of these months should be looked at more closely.

Mézeray's project arose from a desire to record inventions and discoveries in the various arts and sciences, which he regarded as no less important than the successes of war and politics, although difficult to insert in the narrative stream. Hence such matters must be collected separately and an account of them published as they occur, preferably weekly. Because they bring prestige to a great state like France, which excels in intelligence as well as in valor, and because regular and continuing publication demands financial resources, the historian is to be permitted to gather and record new knowledge, theoretical as well as practical, with the aid of personal assistants as well as foreign correspondents whose work must be paid for. Such knowledge will be found in various sciences, physics, mathematics, astronomy, medicine, anatomy

---

1 For Renaudot see Howard M. Solomon, *Public Welfare, Science, and Propaganda in Seventeenth Century France: the Innovations of Théophraste Renaudot* (Princeton, Princeton University Press 1972). The *conférences* held by Renaudot are discussed in Brown, *Scientific Organizations*, pp. 18-30.
2 For Mézeray see W.H. Evans, *L'Historien Mézeray et la conception de l'histoire en France au 17e siècle* (Paris 1930). His project for a *privilège* is in the Bibliothèque nationale, fonds français 20792, between ff. 112 and 113. Found and published by C.-A. Sainte-Beuve in a *feuilleton* dated 30 May 1853, then in his *Causeries du lundi* 8: 183-4, it was printed in more correct text by Evans, pp. 63-4.

and surgery, pharmacy and chemistry, as well as in the arts, fine and useful, painting, architecture, navigation, agriculture, textiles and dyes, the manufacture of useful articles, and generally in all the skills and techniques, liberal as well as mechanical. Furthermore, the editor will collect and announce the discovery of documents, objects, and monuments of every sort, large and small, which may contribute to historical knowledge, as well as the titles of books and other publications from the whole of Europe. All of these activities will be permitted under the terms of the proposed *privilège*, subject to the usual restriction that there is to be no judgment or reflection on ethics, religion, or politics, in any way which may concern the interests of France or of other Christian princes.

Such a document is the work of a humanist and scholar, concerned with the project's comprehensive range and intellectual integrity rather than with the means by which such a periodical is to find or create a public of readers who will contribute to its support. The breadth of the program is typical of the period. In the 1660s the sciences were assuming priority in many minds; their novelty stirred the imagination and stimulated speculation. The arts, on the other hand, changed slowly in familiar patterns, and in Mézeray's view their news value was clearly secondary. Again, typically also, no attention was paid to the established disciplines taught and protected in the schools: theology, the history of church and state, and canon law were not expected to produce anything of interest for a journalist of 1665.

It was no coincidence, therefore, that when Denis de Sallo (1626-69) began to edit the *Journal des sçavans* it should follow closely in time and pattern the project outlined by Mézeray. De Sallo lived in the same house as the older historian in the rue Montorgueil; they shared interests in history, with emphasis on legal problems. Committed scholars, with strong Gallican leanings, they were accustomed to freedom of expression in conversation as well as in their writings. As a *conseiller* in the Parlement de Paris, de Sallo had been a colleague of the printer Jean Cusson before the latter gave up his legal practice on inheriting the *librairie* which was to be his chief interest, a business which was to produce a series of scientific books and pamphlets over a period of several years.[3]

The *Journal des sçavans* appeared as a quarto pamphlet of twelve pages, on Monday, 5 January 1665, 'A Paris, chez Jean Cusson, rue S. Jacques, à l'image de S. Jean Baptiste, avec privilège du Roy.' An introductory editorial, 'L'Imprimeur au lecteur,' took up many of the themes that had interested

---

3 Jean Cusson is mentioned briefly in Brown, *Scientific Organizations*, pp. 206-7; some of his publications are listed on pp. 295-6 of that book.

Mézeray, with different emphasis and in different order. Instead of news of inventions, theoretical ideas, and practical knowledge of trades and professions, the business-like bookseller knew his public wanted literary news; he knew that facts might be interesting but a reading public was anxious to know what books were available in the shops of the rue St Jacques. Entertained by novelty, savoring irony, and appreciative of good writing, men and women of the day were not averse to controversy.

This foreword may have been written by either de Sallo or Cusson; no doubt it was satisfactory to both. It clarifies what the new journal will do – primarily inform the reader of 'ce qui se passe de nouveau dans la République de Lettres' – words which indicate at once an international outlook. It will list important books printed in several countries of Europe, giving information concerning their content and potential utility; all through de Sallo's editorship the emphasis is on the value of books to the reader. Eminent scholars who die will be memorialized in brief biographies, and their works catalogued. Experiments in physics and chemistry, discoveries in the arts and sciences, new machines, curious or useful inventions, astronomical observations, advances in anatomy and medicine – all such matters will be included. There will also be some account of the chief decisions of secular and ecclesiastical courts, French and foreign. Thus an effort will be made to record events worthy of the curiosity of men of letters, so that the new journal may be truly comprehensive.

Several paragraphs follow in which the *imprimeur* sets forth the uses of this notable innovation. The working scholar will find in it an opportunity to establish contact with others, claiming priority or asking for assistance; the amateur without literary ambition will be able to communicate his observations and reflections informally. The collector of books will discover what is new and available, and those who do not buy will have a means of acquiring 'une connaissance générale' concerning what others are reading.

After some debate, the editors have decided on weekly publication,

parce que les choses vieilleroient trop, si on différoit d'en parler pendant l'espace d'un an ou d'un mois. Outre que plusieurs personnes de qualité ont tesmoigné que ce Journal venant de temps en temps, leur seroit agréable, et leur serviroit de divertissement; qu'au contraire ils seroient fatiguez de la lecture d'un Volume entier de ces sortes de choses, qui auroient perdu la grâce de la nouveauté.

This indication of the editors' desire to produce a periodical pleasing to men of taste as well as learning is followed by a warning: the reader must not be surprised to discover opinions which differ from his own, for the editor will take no responsibility for the views of authors discussed, nor guarantee their validity. And finally, the style of the journal will not be uniform, since several persons will contribute to it; the less pleasing aspects of this diversity will be removed by the Sieur de Hédouville, who has been asked to adjust the articles which come from different hands in such a way as to achieve a measure of regularity, concerning matters of style only. He is to take no sides, as this is to be 'un ouvrage qui ne doit pas être moins libre de toute sorte de préjugé qu'exempt de passion et de partialité.'

Unknown to fame, the 'Sieur de Hédouville' has generally been taken to refer to the first literary journalist, Denis de Sallo himself, who is said to have had a valet from this Norman hamlet. De Sallo was born in Paris, although his family came originally from Poitou; he was educated in the usual classical disciplines, and admitted to the Paris Bar in 1652. Devoted to scholarship rather than to the practice of law, he wrote much on legal and historical points for the private information of noble patrons. The generally useful old biographical dictionary of Louis Moreri tells us that de Sallo's continual attachment to books led to a disease that deprived him of the capacity to walk, so that he had to be carried from his house to his carriage: a medical colleague suggests the presence of a diabetic condition, even though Henri Justel wrote to Henry Oldenburg that de Sallo 'has the gout.'

De Sallo had maintained contact with other scholars, perhaps particularly with Mézeray. We know that he had been in Germany in 1657 and 1658, in company with the humanist Eméric Bigot, when the two witnessed the election of the Emperor Leopold I, in succession to Ferdinand III.[4] This was an occasion of peculiar interest to the French, as Leopold's chief rival was Louis XIV. Both candidates were young, and the political stakes were high. But perhaps because of deteriorating health, de Sallo has left little record of his activities in the last ten years of his life, a period in which he is known only as the editor of the journal, a role which still has its obscurities. When his correspondence with Oldenburg, secretary of the Royal Society of London, came to an end, Justel offered the excuse that de Sallo's 'grandes occupations' were making heavy demands on his time – a phrase which may well be a euphemism for his declining health. When he died in the summer of 1669, he left a library of nearly four thousand volumes, and some two hundred manuscripts.

As the earliest periodical directed specifically to the learned public, the *virtuosi* and the *curiosi*, professionals and amateurs of erudition and science,

4 L.E. Doucette, *Emery Bigot, Seventeenth-Century French Humanist* (Toronto, University of Toronto Press 1970) p. 11

the intellectual orientation of de Sallo's periodical deserves an attention it has not always received. After the first number of 5 January 1665, twelve others appeared weekly up to the end of March, when publication ceased without warning. Various causes for this abrupt interruption have been suggested, none of them quite adequate. While the reading public was not accustomed to serious critical commentary on current topics in periodical form, and some in particular who had written stupid books could not bear to have that pointed out, such factors do not explain the sudden demise of what was apparently a commercial success. On the contrary, familiarity with the ways of official-dom under the *Grand Monarque* indicates police action, taken by authority because of the generally Gallican and anti-Vatican slant visible in many of the brief notices on new books in almost every number.

It was not widely known who was responsible for the contents of the journal, and various guesses, more or less educated, were offered. The opin-ion of Gui Patin (1601-72), better known for his lively and caustic letters than for his capacity as a professor in the Paris Faculté de médicine, attributing the journal to the Abbé Bourzeis, de Sallo, the novelist Gomberville, the poet and critic Jean Chapelain, and others, has been repeated uncritically down to the present day, even in the pages of the *Journal des savants* of 1965, although no corroborating evidence has been forthcoming for Gomberville, and few circumstantial clues for Bourzeis. Perhaps more precise documentation con-cerning the journal and its cessation in March of 1665 may be found some day. In the meantime we may be content with a letter of Francesco Marucelli, the bibliophile *residente* of the Grand Dukes of Tuscany, who reported to Prince Leopold of the Medici on 1 May 1665 that the officers of the king had claimed that the journal was being published without their prior approval, and that De Sallo, who had assumed the editorial labor and expense while leaving the profit to the printer, preferred to give up the effort rather than submit to censorship. Marucelli's letter adds that others, who had been assisting de Sallo, give some hope that the periodical will be resumed in the future.[5]

There were various ways of controlling publication in seventeenth-century Paris. A normal means was by insisting that every publication be submitted in page proof before the issuance of the *privilège*. This text was read by a committee more or less competent in the field of interest involved, and after approval the book could go through the final stages, receive its title page with the magic words, 'avec privilège du Roy,' and be sold freely in the shops. This procedure could lead to interminable delays and prohibitions, and, in the case

5 Marucelli to Leopold of Tuscany, 1 May 1665; Biblioteca nazionale, Florence, Galileiani Posteriori, tomo 18, f. 173

of a big book, like Richard Simon's *Histoire critique du vieux testament,* of which a proof copy exists in the library of Brown University, could be extremely expensive to the printer and publisher. For the publisher of a weekly periodical which attempted to discuss current issues in church or state or to comment on ecclesiastical policy, it could be disastrous. Pamphlets and ephemeral literature could be printed and sold without much trouble, but the accumulating weekly numbers were mounting into a substantial book, and in spite of declared impartiality, certain points of view were becoming quite clear to all readers.

The first number was innocuous enough. Its ten articles ranged from reviews of recent editions of early historians of the African church to an account of a monstrous birth near Oxford, contributed by Henry Oldenburg, and from a short notice on Henry Spelman's glossary of late Latin to a comment on Giuseppe Campani's *Ragguaglio di nuove osservationi* concerning his new lenses and telescopes. The tone is factual and concise; sometimes, as in discussing a new edition of Martin Schoock's *De sternutatione,* a question is raised, in this case of the relation of the opinion that sneezing is of strictly nasal origin to an older view that in some way the brain is involved, because certain odors can cause headaches, and therefore the olfactory nerves must serve some purpose. A comment on Descartes' *De l'Homme,* edited in 1664 by Clerselier, gives a brief statement of the mechanical view of man, distinguishing the activity of the organs of the body from those which originate in the soul, raising no questions and expressing no doubts. Another discipline is represented when someone, the editor himself or perhaps even Mézeray, writes about James Howell's *Dissertatio de praecedentia regum Galliae, Hispaniae et Angliae* (London 1664); in this case, Howell's argument that the evidence of various historians, each on behalf of the rights of his respective sovereign, cancels out, and that therefore all sovereigns are equal, is contradicted by the statement that Henry III of England would never seat himself above Louis IX of France. Of seven books noticed in this number, two were published in London, two in Amsterdam, and one each in Paris, Dijon, and Rome. Five were in Latin, one in French, and one, Campani's, in Italian. The broad base, intellectual as well as international, is visible at once.

Of more than eighty books reviewed in the thirteen numbers of 1665, three were in Italian, one in Spanish, and the balance equally divided between French and Latin. Some half-dozen have retained their importance: Descartes' *De l'Homme*; Thomas Willis' *Cerebri anatome*; La Rochefoucauld's *Reflexions, ou Sentences et Maximes morales* (the review was at least approved if not written by the susceptible author himself); Nicolas Stensen's *De musculis et glandulis*; Thomas Stanley's important edition of Aeschylus (comment: 'elle doit être mise dans toutes les bibliothèques, les autres n'y pouvant faire figure'); and finally, the first of the *Philosophical Transactions*, edited by Henry Oldenburg, secretary of the Royal Society of London, from March of 1665. This last entry is not a review; rather it records the success of the newly founded monthly journal and thus of the innovation of the learned periodical as shown by international acceptance, and translations in Italy and Germany:

Mais on a fait plus en Angleterre. Car comme la belle Philosophie y fleurit plus qu'en aucun autre lieu du monde; on a pris soin d'y faire un Journal en Anglais sous le titre de *Philosophical Transactions*, pour faire sçavoir à tout le monde ce qui se découvre de nouveau dans la Philosophie. C'est de là qu'il faut attendre une infinité de belles choses. Car il y a une Société de Physiciens, qui s'appliquent incessamment à la recherche de la nature ... Cette compagnie produit tous les jours une infinité de beaux Ouvrages. Mais parce qu'ils sont la pluspart écrits en langue Angloise, on n'a pu jusques à présent en rendre compte dans ce Journal. Mais on a enfin trouvé un interprète Anglois, par le moyen duquel on pourra à l'avenir l'enrichir de tout ce qui se fera de beau en Angleterre.

This is the last word in the first year of the *Journal des sçavans*, 1665.

Not all the titles discussed were significant; occasionally the editors have a little ironic play with the inevitable bad book, pretentious and trivial, or absurdly outmoded in its science. They keep a balance between history, theology, and the new sciences, and offer a few comments on works of literary interest, plays by Pierre Corneille and Quinault, *contes* by La Fontaine, translations from Plutarch by François Tallement and Tanneguy Le Fèvre, Sorel's *Bibliothèque françoise*, as well as René Rapin's Latin poem on gardens, which enjoyed a continental reputation through the rest of the century.

Erudite without pedantry or jargon, occasionally witty, even lightly malicious when the occasion justified it, allusive and deriving from the learning and science of the day, the reviews which fill the pages of these weekly brochures are still worth reading as one attempts to recapture the temper and climate of the age. These thirteen numbers achieved much of what the editors hoped for. From the outset, de Sallo maintained much independence of thought, as much freedom of expression as he dared. The break in publication at the end of March showed that he had overestimated the tolerance of the censors, and when Jean Gallois, a member of de Sallo's household and an assistant in the editorial work, brought out a new series in the first week of January of 1666, the more limited outlook of the journal reflected the closer controls under which he had to work. But the message of plain-spoken objectivity on which good journalism rests was clear, and twenty years later Pierre Bayle, the chief journalist of the century, could look back to these issues printed under de Sallo's leadership as a model when he began his work on the *Nouvelles de la république des lettres*.

In the long run, the journal's most important contribution was for the sciences, which depend more than other disciplines on regular and frequent means of publication. As a historian, Mézeray was probably not aware of the role a good periodical could play in this field; he had envisaged the preservation of a record of events, discoveries, inventions, theories, publications, and the like, so that future chroniclers might have a dated structure for their narratives. The *Journal des sçavans*, however, came into existence in a milieu in which natural philosophers were attracting more attention than had been usual in Paris. It was not long since experiments with Pascal's barometer had been performed on church towers and hills around the city; telescopes were visible in attic windows and sometimes in public squares; the comet of 1664-5 was drawing crowds to open spaces where it was visible, and there was talk of the need of an observatory. Doctors were debating Harvey's views on the circulation of the blood, as well as the use of chemical remedies such as antimony. Jean Pecquet, one of the scientists formerly patronized by the disgraced Surintendant Foucquet, had made a name for himself with his discoveries in the vascular system. But along with sound science, there was even more quackery in the air, and serious men were stimulated to put their work on a basis which would lend authority to recognized fact and sound theory as distinguished from uneducated superstition.

These circumstances opened a path for the new periodical which would be defined and charted in the decades that followed. There is evidence that scientific matters were important in the perspective of the founders from the first; Oldenburg and the Dutch physicist Christiaan Huygens were asked for their assistance before publication began, and three books on scientific topics were noticed in the first number. In proportion to the total contents, scientific material was substantial and informative. There were reviews of a dozen books on various aspects of medicine, astronomy, and related subjects, and nine communications of some interest to scientists, adding up to over a quarter of the total space of the thirteen numbers. In addition to the letter concerning the monstrous birth near Oxford, we find in the third number (19 January) an account, also from London, of William Petty's twin-hulled vessel *Experiment*; the next two issues offer a discussion of the comet, to which we return presently. The sixth issue, 9 February, ends with an *éloge* of the mathematician Pierre de Fermat, a clear and fair evaluation of his work, without technical details. From the eighth number on, the last pages of each are taken up with Huygens' pendulum clocks, primarily with their use for the determination of longitudes on long sea voyages. A letter of 5 February expresses Huygens' satisfaction over the results of Robert Holmes' Atlantic travels with the clocks, foreshadowing what was to be realized a century later with the chronometers of John Harrison, timekeepers of a very different type. The eleventh number, 16 March, describes the curious phenomenon of two clocks whose pendulums began to swing in unison, an effect which he sheepishly explains in his next letter as a result of the suspension of the two clocks from a single shelf.

It is clear that the editors felt that anything even marginally scientific could be printed in their pages, perhaps in the hope that a largely humanistically trained public could be led to read such matters with increasing acumen. They were obtaining cooperation from two of the chief scientific centres of the day – from London, where the Royal Society had assumed its role as a focus of experimental activity, and from the laboratory of Christiaan Huygens at the Hague. The best scientific writing in the journal of this year shows that there were good minds among its contributors, even though many notices were brief.

The most striking instance of the outlook and manner of de Sallo and his associates is the extensive article in the fourth number, of 26 January. Entitled 'De la Comète,' it begins with an account of a formal gathering on the topic of comets in general, held in the Collège des Jésuites before a distinguished group of nobility and others. Four set speeches were presented by the Jesuits Arrouis and Grandamy, the mathematician Roberval, professor in the Collège royal, and a Flemish doctor, Phelippeaux. Each of these expounded different views of the nature and behavior of comets, seeking their causes and effects; these examples of highly speculative thinking are set forth in some detail, without comment. After having given due place to the uneducated guesswork of the traditionalists, the editor of the periodical turns with obvious relief to 'quelque chose de particulier,' and relates at length the efforts of the leading French astronomer of the day, Adrien Auzout, to describe, not causes and effects, but the movement of comets, and that of the comet of this winter of 1664-5 especially. Careful observations had allowed Auzout to trace the course of the comet through the fixed stars, and to suggest the hypothesis of its movement in the plane of a circle, with calculable regularities as it moved towards and away from the sun. On this basis, he predicted where the comet would be in the course of the next few weeks, concluding that there is nothing more regular than the course of comets, 'contre le sentiment de tous les Astronomes qui ont précédé.' The article ends with details of observations made by Jacques Buot, 'cosmographe et ingénieur ordinaire du Roy,' indicating the path of the comet and explaining the different appearances of its tail. Finally the journalist concludes that those who had argued that there had been two comets in the sky this season were wrong, that the great length of its track through the heavens is not surprising, and that the movement of cômets is as regular as that of other celestial bodies. There is no need to underline the irony of this whole article, perhaps the most important in the numbers issued in this year; the four speakers at the Jesuit college were talking demonstrable nonsense, and the future of astronomy lay with accurate observations made with the best instruments and interpreted with mathematical skill. The distribution of these readable and intelligent pages among the *literati* of Europe would do more for the dissemination of the understanding of science among humanist scholars than the printing of a dozen isolated tracts on technical problems.

Clearly the writers for the *Journal des sçavans*, whoever they may have been, were writing on behalf of science and reason and in vigorous criticism of the remnants of scholasticism that still hung over intellectual activity in Paris. In these pages, the two great divisions of the learned world could be seen in contrast and opposition; the tradition of words and syllogism, the authority of the book, was confronted with the critical outlook, asking for facts, whether in history or in the study of languages or the sciences. Sometimes the two perspectives are contrasted without comment, by a witty juxtaposition of books – a serious contribution to knowledge placed next to a particularly stupid piece of pedantry. Mézeray's practice of objective statement without comment is continued here; another use of the typically ironic style familiar to readers of Pascal and Molière. The patently trivial does not have to be so labeled for the intelligent; for the rest, one may hope that further contact with sound and productive lines of thought will lead to a climate of opinion in which ideas may be permitted fulfilment in action.

What the French call *le sourire de la raison* appears in several of the journals of de Sallo's editorship, but nowhere more clearly than in the final essay of the number following the long article on comets. Characteristically in the age of French literary classicism, the question of the gender of the word *comète* arose; in the preceding number the feminine had been used, in line with common usage. Now the issue is raised seriously, with philological discussion of literary precedents and Greek etymology. Astronomers may theorize about comets; *le peuple* fears their effects and portent; and those who are not *assez éclairés* to discover their nature, nor yet superstitious enough to be afraid, debate over their gender. The classicist prefers the masculine, which has authority, while others who resist the tyranny of antiquity find that the French 'aimant sur tous les genres le féminin' could accept this metamorphosis as with other words, 'qui par le changement de genres ont, ce semble, acquis une grace particulière.' The conclusion is, after much citation of poets and others, for the feminine gender, for 'l'usage ... comme l'on sçait, est le tyran des langues vivantes, et ne rend jamais raison de ce qu'il veut.' One resists it in vain, for there is no way of upsetting 'ce qu'il a une fois estably; et que de mépriser ses loix, c'est s'exposer à se faire prendre ou pour un esprit foible, ou pour un factieux dans l'Empire des belles lettres.'

On another level, and in other contexts, where flippancy is objectionable, de Sallo and his colleagues make clear distinctions between the tradition that depends on the Bible and the Fathers of the Church, and the outlook of modern scientists. They make no effort to reach a compromise between the Christian view of man in the world and the evidence accumulating concerning the nature of the universe. In contrast with Pascal's distress, they are content to compartmentalize knowledge, and astronomers and physicists are not criticized for their disregard of theological considerations. The view of writers of conservative tendency, such as those of the Jesuit Grandamy expressed in his book *Le Cours de la comète*, dedicated to the Prince de Condé, are stated clearly enough for an alert reader to discern their unsatisfactory nature and their lack of relevance to current knowledge, yet in such a way as to avoid offending readers who may share the author's views. While there are polemical passages, on the whole the periodical of 1665 exhibits an effort to be discreet, although an initiate cannot miss the irony with which some topics are discussed, and the clarity with which some views are shown to be preposterous. Repeatedly it is suggested that the wisest course is suspension of judgment, which is in itself an indication of how much ground had been gained by the scientific outlook.

This point of view appears most clearly in a review in the last number of the year, 30 March, of J. Gonet's *Dissertatio theologica de probabilitate*, published in Bordeaux in 1664. The critic here finds that both Jansenists and Jesuits are refuted, adding frankly that judgment must be reserved until intentions and common sense are discovered, for these are 'les véritables loix par lesquelles ces questions se terminent.' In such matters one must choose as judge 'un homme qui ait plus de solidité que de subtilité, & qui s'arreste plus aux grandes maximes qu'aux subterfuges.' Among books one must choose the most disinterested: 'L'Évangile et les Pères sont les véritables & les uniques consultans, ausquels il faut avoir recours dans nos doutes & nos irresolutions;' and among the pagans, Cicero, who in his *De officiis* defends the maxims of Christianity better than many professing Christians. The general tone is best seen in a sentence in the middle of the review:

Mais ce qu'on estime le plus dans ce livre, après l'érudition qui y paroist, est la franchise avec laquelle celuy qui en est l'auteur reconnoist que les disputes et les contestations qui se forment pour résoudre la pluspart des cas de conscience sont le plus souvent vaines et inutiles.

Hardly anything could appear more dangerous in the eyes of the theologians who had a major voice in controlling the publication of the literature of science and erudition in these years.

The *Journal des sçavans* of 1665 represents a collective enterprise, in that several persons were recruited to assist the editor, not only in Paris and the French provinces, but in England, the Netherlands, and doubtless elsewhere, to report interesting events and news of books. It belongs to the general movement of the century towards freer discussion – a wide-ranging effort to collect the best thought of the time, and to bring the intellectual activity of the age into the focus that only a single periodical publication could achieve. If this thought could be seen in a single perspective, a kind of unity might be reached through an ironic survey of opposing views, in which all might see the necessity for better comprehension between men of different disciplines, different schools of theology and philosophy, using varying methods and criteria in their evaluation of observed and recorded fact and opinion. It was a realization of the method Montaigne had called *conférence*, achieved in a new medium, through which erudition and science could be seen in the light of a common standard of rationality, perceptible in the pages of a *journal littéraire général* as envisaged by Mézeray. From the pioneers of the *Journal des sçavans* Pierre Bayle derived encouragement for his independent monthly which conveyed news of the Republic of Letters, the international and ecumenical fellowship of savants whose interests and communications transcended boundaries and creedal differences. From them he also discovered that the weekly format demanded too much of an editor who was obliged to maintain variety of subject-matter and outlook while holding to solid scholarship and consistent criteria in appraising new books as they came to his desk. He learned the importance of close cooperation with an intelligent and courageous publisher, whose shop could ensure regular appearance of the numbers, carefully printed in uniform format so that ultimately the series could be bound as an ornament for any library.

In many ways the *Journal des sçavans*, through the innumerable imitations to which it gave rise, initiated a revolution in the world of letters and science. Now there was a forum for discussion, occasionally acrid and harsh, but with time becoming ironic and polite, a place where ideas could be submitted to the reading public without the inevitable prejudice that Pascal recognized in personal encounters, created by tone of voice, gesture, and facial expression.

There was also a developing sense of standards, criteria by which argument might be resolved and truth discovered, even if they were only pragmatic. New evidence could be applied to old preconceptions facing new kinds of criticism. The objective outsider, whom an article in the last of de Sallo's weeklies advocated as the referee for questions in which there was room for doubt, could be found in the readers of a periodical whose authors were unknown and unnamed. In short, the *Journal des sçavans* offered the model for debate on matters of doctrine and history which Colbert could not realize when he tried to found an academy in which historians, philologists, and others would meet for the advancement of learning. That effort, a counterpart to the Académie des sciences, then new and groping its way towards success, failed as violent controversy divided scholars whose different preconceptions prevented the discovery of truth through conference. Only the men who worked in the relatively new fields of mathematical physics and observational astronomy achieved useful sessions, and this was done by excluding those who held to strict doctrines, such as Cartesians and Jesuits. The motto of the Royal Society of London, *nullius in verba magistri*, was typical, not only of the empirical Englishmen and Scots who founded that organization, but of the new sciences in Europe generally.

Perhaps it is not unfair to see in this journalistic venture, characteristic of the skeptical mood of humanists and natural philosophers of the seventeenth century, one of the growing points from which came the secular encyclopedism of the next hundred years. In that age, Pierre Bayle, Ephraim Chambers, J.H. Zedler, Denis Diderot and others, men of learning and wide vision, could attempt to achieve a summation of contemporary knowledge in many fields, with the aid of competent and vigorous scholars and the cooperation of enterprising, if sometimes mercenary, publishers. In the eighteenth century, freedom of speech and writing would not yet be complete, but by then skeptical literature in bookstores and libraries had accumulated in so many forms and in such quantities that neither censorship nor thought control could ever again be universal and unchallenged. The learned journalists had made their point: the impersonal evaluation of objective fact now offered a basis for philosophy and action that intelligent men could not ultimately neglect.

An earlier form of this chapter appeared in the *Journal of the History of Ideas* 33 (1972): 365-78. The *Journal des sçavans* has been used in the Amsterdam reprint of 1679, references being made by date and number in the series. The present chapter does not appreciably duplicate the contents of chapter 9 of my *Scientific Organizations in Seventeenth-Century France* (see chapter 3, note 1). The assistance of Professor William F. Church and Dr Frederick W. Barnes Jr. of Brown University is gratefully acknowledged, as also is a suggestion by Professor Philip Wiener, executive editor of the *Journal of the History of Ideas*, who has given permission to use these pages.

CHAPTER FIVE

'Les gens de maintenant'

— Nous lisons des anciens, Mademoiselle, que leur coutume était d'enlever par force de la maison des pères les filles qu'on menait marier, afin qu'il ne semblât pas que ce fût de leur consentement qu'elles convolaient dans les bras d'un homme.
— Les anciens, Monsieur, sont les anciens, et nous sommes les gens de maintenant.

(*Le Malade imaginaire* II vi)

THE DOGMATISM of Thomas Diafoirus, the dim-witted son of a doctor high in the Faculté de médecine, and the admirable impertinence of Angélique, daughter of Argan, the *malade imaginaire*, sum up the issues of Molière's last comedy. Types they may be, but most of the characters of the play represent points of view in conflict in 1673 and there is much contemporary humanity involved. The spirit of youth, of adventure and delight in experience, new knowledge and an imagined future, confronts the stagnant dogmatism of the schools, the uncriticized legacy of the past. The Rabelaisian father-and-son doctors Diafoirus, grotesquely labeled with a name half-Greek, half-obscenely vulgar French, converse in consecrated nonsense about the couch of a man debilitated by their remedies, their uncouth verbiage a parody of the Galenisms of the Paris faculty. The thrust of the play is against the structure of a tradition ossified in language that once purported to explain the processes of nature by giving names to entities naïvely created by a theorizing mind.

The comedy of the imaginary invalid, then, poses the conflict between nature and theory, between a healthy body and a mind obsessed with the need for medical aid. Argan is not old, he has no recognizable illness; minor aches and twinges have given him into the hands of incompetent but enterprising charlatans, draped in the raiment of a medical degree, pompous and conceited, unable to diagnose an ailment, and equally incapable of decisive action to restore their patient to normal health of mind and body. This caricature of the profession of the time has its justification; while all around sensible men, doctors and laymen alike, were saying that far more remained to be learned concerning life and health than was already known, medical practitioners were still riding their traditional mules in elaborate costumes and imposing their dubious concoctions and dangerous diagnoses on a public ignorant of science and uncritically obedient to the dictates issuing from a façade of ancient learning. The wealthy and the aristocrat could afford to employ personal physicians from Montpellier and take advantage of a science more up to date, less doctrinaire; the poor lacked such luxuries. As the elder Diafoirus puts it, after complaining that 'notre métier auprès des grands ne m'a jamais paru agréable':

Le public est commode. Vous n'avez à répondre de vos actions à personne; et pourvu que l'on suive le courant des règles de l'art, on ne se met point en peine de tout ce qui peut arriver. Mais ce qu'il y a de fâcheux auprès des grands, c'est que, quand ils viennent à être malades, ils veulent absolument que leurs médecins les guérissent.

The deeper conflict of the play is kin to that visible in the *Pensées* of Pascal and in the pages of the *Journal des sçavans* — a struggle between the living and growing knowledge of a vital century and the misunderstood and therefore largely futile débris of the ancients. The conflict between past and present lines up the opposing forces: the girl Angélique, her ally the servant Toinette, and finally her uncle Béralde, Argan's sensible and skeptical brother, united to combat the mania of the hypochondriac, with his group of attendant physicians, Diafoirus father and son, Purgon, and the apothecary Fleurant (the word means 'smelly'), all of whom are enriching themselves at Argan's expense. Around them Béline, stepmother of Argan's daughters, and the shadowy Cléante, whom Angélique will finally marry, complete the organization of the play.

From the opening lines the theme is set: Argan is making up his accounts using counters on the table. He calls his servant Toinette, asks if his cathartics have been effective, and demands a broth to be taken with the next dose. The exchange between master and servant establishes the pace and tone of the play:

— Ce Monsieur Fleurant-là et ce Monsieur Purgon s'égayent bien sur votre corps; ils ont en vous une bonne vache à lait; et je voudrais bien leur demander quel mal vous avez, pour faire tant de remèdes.

—Taisez-vous, ignorante, ce n'est pas à vous à contrôler les ordonnances de la médecine.

Toinette's desire to know just what Argan suffers from is never satisfied; his malady is never explained. He has paid much for his medications; in his opening lines he has told us that in the current month he has been purged in one way or another some twenty times, in the month preceding, thirty-two; 'Je ne m'étonne pas si je ne me porte pas si bien ce mois-ci que l'autre.' Monsieur Purgon must be informed, and asked to increase the frequency of treatment. The complete lack of information about Argan's malady, the reckless use of laxatives and enemas, and the patient's neurotic dependence on medical help, which an incompetent faculty is only too willing to satisfy, give us the basis for what might well have been a scathing attack on contemporary medicine.

Yet it must be said that Molière handles the profession gently. No contemporary or subsequent commentator has been able to identify with certainty any doctor Molière may have had in mind. As Béralde will say (III iii) 'Ce ne sont pas les médecins qu'il joue, mais le ridicule de la médecine.' The play turns on Argan and his personal situation: his infatuation with medicine and his doctors, and finally the disarray into which his particular mania has thrown his household — recalling another play in which the protagonist was similarly infatuated with the fake pietist Tartuffe. But the intellectual integrity of Molière does not permit him to scamp the moral issue and avoid the debate about the fundamentals of contemporary medicine. The doctors are portrayed at nearly full length — types, of course, not persons — balanced by a critical Béralde who makes his points with telling logic. Skilled dramatist that he is, Molière remains well on the reasonable side of the Shavian comedy of ideas. Working in a theatre of limited size and comfort, for an audience mostly standing, whose physical endurance can take only so much argument and disquisition, but who appreciate a good debating point or a telling touch of satire, he must give them a mingling of romance and farce, and some relevance to contemporary society and its problems in the guise of a group of recognizable human traits.

And so this *Malade imaginaire* is not a *pièce à thèse*, written to prove a point in morals or social thinking, nor is it a philosophical dialogue. It is primarily comedy, a somewhat elevated farce 'dont le projet a été fait pour délasser [le Roi] de ses nobles travaux,' the campaigns of 1672 in the Low

Countries. With its ambiguous title and its characteristic mingling of thoughtful comedy and farce, its atmosphere of laughter ranging from an ironic smile to a roar that arises from below the diaphragm, the play echoes much of its author's earlier work, even the four great comedies in five acts of studied verse. If in the winter of 1673 Molière knew, as he most probably did, that he had not long to live,[1] the play hardly shows it, unless the defiant tone of Béralde's remark about 'vos grands médecins' ('Entendez les parler, les plus habiles du monde. Voyez les faire, les plus ignorants de tous les hommes') contains a trace of private despair about his own condition. The autobiographical note is unusual in the formal literature of the period; one notices in passing however, that in Chrysale of *Les Femmes savantes* (1672) and now in Argan Molière writes parts that tax his physical powers much less than did Harpagon (*L'Avare*, 1668) and Scapin (1671).

If the autobiographical note is rare, the undercurrent of intelligent comment on contemporary life is frequent enough. In many of his plays much is made of what we now call the generation gap, always perceptible in a period of rapid ideological change, expressed in the failure of the older members of a group to understand what is going all round. Here, as in earlier comedies, there is the conflict of youth with age, of the young with authority, of the flexible with rigidity, of the joy of living and loving with the sense that safety and security can only be found in strict obedience to traditional rules. As a good comic author, Molière plays on the secret drive hidden in every playgoer, the thrust towards happiness, and he finds the happy ending which may prove very little about the intellectual content of the play, except that it represents the path to the future, human continuity as opposed to the finality which traditional legalism would impose.

There is little need to consider the plotting of the play, which has no strikingly novel features. More important is the use of moments in the action where the emphasis falls on opposing positions, that of traditional medicine on one hand, and the argument of the rational, naturalistic human being on the other. The elder Diafoirus speaks with pride of his great booby of a son, 'qui n'a jamais eu l'imagination bien vive, ce feu d'esprit qu'on remarque dans quelques-uns,' who could not read at nine or take part in boyish games. With

---

1 Grimarest, the earliest biographer of Molière, quotes remarks made by the comedian to his wife in the presence of the actor Baron on the morning of the final performance of the play, which indicate that Molière's last months had been much troubled: 'Tant que ma vie a été mêlée également de douleur et de plaisir, je me suis cru heureux; mais aujourd'hui que je suis accablé de peines sans pouvoir compter sur aucuns momens de satisfaction et douceur, je vois bien qu'il me faut quitter la partie; je ne puis plus tenir contre les douleurs et déplaisirs, qui ne me donnent pas un instant de relâche. Mais, ajouta-t-il en réfléchissant, qu'un homme souffre avant que de mourir! Cependant je sens bien que je finis' (*La Vie de M. de Molière* [1705] p. 179).

difficulty he had taken his degree, and now he makes much noise in the 'disputes de notre école':

Mais sur toute chose, ce qui me plaît en lui, et en quoi il suit mon exemple, c'est qu'il s'attache aveuglément aux opinions de nos anciens, et que jamais il n'a voulu comprendre ni écouter les raisons et les expériences des prétendues découvertes de notre siècle, touchant la circulation du sang et autres opinions de même farine.

It is a further comment on the doctors that the medical knowledge they display as they jointly examine Argan's pulse shows no understanding of the words they use. One adjective contradicts another, and the inference they draw any spectator must have found ridiculous. Unhappily it echoes the famous consultation of four of the leading doctors of Paris as they walked in the Bois de Vincennes after a visit to the deathbed of Mazarin.

Béralde, enlisted in the struggle to get Angélique married according to her desires, attacks the problem at its most sensitive point: Argan's wish to have the uncouth Thomas Diafoirus for a son-in-law, and the alternative proposed by the shrewish second wife – the relegation of Angélique to a convent. So Béralde tackles the question of Argan's health: 'J'entends, mon frère, que je ne vois homme qui soit moins malade que vous, et que je ne demanderais point une meilleure constitution que la vôtre.' Argan replies that Purgon threatens him with death if he does not take his medicines regularly, asking if Béralde does not believe that medicine is 'véritable,' to which comes the ready answer, 'Bien loin de la tenir véritable, je la trouve, entre nous, une des plus grandes folies qui soit parmi les hommes; et à regarder les choses en philosophe ... je ne vois rien de plus ridicule qu'un homme qui se veut mêler d'en guérir un autre.'

The argument cannot be left with this paradox, and Argan's questions lead Béralde to outline his attitude in some detail. Men cannot cure others because 'les ressorts de notre machine sont des mystères jusques-ici, où les hommes ne voient goutte, et que la nature nous a mis au-devant des yeux des voiles trop épais pour y connaître quelque chose.' Doctors know for the most part 'de fort belles humanités, savent parler en beau latin, savent nommer en grec toutes les maladies, les définir et les diviser; mais pour tout ce qui est de les guérir, c'est ce qu'ils ne savent point du tout.' He comes to the point with his description of Monsieur Purgon, a portrait in detail in the manner of the ancient Theophrastus:

[Il] n'y sait point de finesse; c'est un homme tout médecin, depuis la tête jusqu'aux pieds; un homme qui croit à ses règles plus qu'à toutes les démonstrations des mathématiques, et qui croirait du crime à les vouloir examiner; qui ne voit rien d'obscur dans la médecine, rien de douteux, rien de difficile, et qui, avec une impétuosité de prévention, une raideur de confiance, une brutalité de sens commun et de raison, donne au travers des purgations et des saignées, et ne balance aucune chose.

The case against the doctors is summed up:

Lorsqu'un médecin vous parle d'aider, de secourir, de soulager la nature, de lui ôter ce qui lui nuit, et de lui donner ce qui lui manque, de la rétablir et de la remettre dans une pleine facilité de ses fonctions; lorsqu'il vous parle de rectifier le sang, de tempérer les entrailles et le cerveau, de dégonfler la rate, de raccommoder la poitrine, de réparer le foie, de fortifier le cœur, de rétablir et conserver la chaleur naturelle, et d'avoir des secrets pour étendre la vie à de longues années: il vous dit justement le roman de la médecine. Mais quand vous en venez à la vérité et à l'expérience, vous ne trouvez rien de tout cela; et il en est comme de ces beaux songes qui ne vous laissent au réveil que le déplaisir de les avoir crus.

The picture of the charlatan is now complete; Molière knows that the science which lies behind these phrases does not exist, that they sound well but have no meaning.

The scene ends with Argan's bitter tirade against Molière for his attacks on doctors and their profession. Béralde has brought this on by suggesting he would have liked 'de pouvoir un peu vous tirer de l'erreur où vous êtes, et, pour vous divertir, vous mener voir sur ce chapitre, quelqu'une des comédies de Molière.'

There is really little need to analyze the presentation of doctors in Molière's early plays. From Le Médecin volant (1659) to Le Médecin malgré lui (1666) the doctor was usually Sganarelle in disguise, advancing the plot by the deception. Doctors in person were introduced in L'Amour médecin, another trifle of 1665; one member of the Faculté remarks that 'le plus grand faible des hommes, c'est l'amour qu'ils ont pour la vie; et nous en profitons nous autres par notre propre galimatias.' In a three-act play of 1669, two doctors appear, talking at some length about a régime to be followed by Monsieur de Pourceaugnac, in order to keep him from meeting Julie, whom he has come to Paris to marry. In each of these cases, the medical profession, real or false, is used as an element of the plot of the farce, and while the language of the doctor is parodied for comic effect, nothing more serious is attempted; there is no discussion of the principles of practice or the scientific foundation of the art.

Thus Le Malade imaginaire stands apart from the other plays in which doctors appear. The features of the traditional doctor of the Italian comedy are present, heightened in many respects. The pompous air and diction of the dialogue, the parody of the language of the schools, the explicit nature of the remedies used, the effect of Toinette's use of medical disguise to deceive Argan, all combine to accentuate the imbecility of Diafoirus father and son, and the extended parody of a ceremony of matriculation with which the performance ends carries the farcical impression to extremes which Molière had not so far attempted. What may easily be lost in the consideration of the comedy as comedy is the kind of content that is lost in purely aesthetic criticism of Rabelais – the fact that Molière here has something to say, that there is an intellectual integrity about the whole production, takes this play out of the rank of his comedies of situation and places it with *Tartuffe* and *Dom Juan*. Like those plays, it gives expression to ideas which break through the confines of the classic theatre to make contact with many aspects of seventeenth-century thought.

It has been said that Boileau once described Molière to Louis XIV as the most intelligent man of the age; much reading of the comedies offers ample confirmation of that statement. One moves from the best writers of his time to his pages with no sense of loss. Pascal, Racine, La Fontaine, La Rochefoucauld, Molière meets them all on an equal footing. Molière has as good a sense of the stage as Racine, and a more varied command of language; he is as sound on intellectual method as Pascal, as incisive a moralist as La Rochefoucauld. And he has his own special gift, apparent to every person who has tried to put his plays on the stage: a capacity to render character by suggesting stage movement and gesture within the spoken line that has rarely been equalled in any age.

From the present point of view, Molière had remarkable comprehension of what was afoot in the scientific thought of his time, not only on the level of the chattering *Femmes savantes*, but in Béralde's suggestion of the sense of mystery in the natural world that is apparent in the *Pensées*, and later in Isaac Newton ('finding a smoother pebble or a prettier shell than ordinary, while the great ocean of Truth lay all undiscovered before me'). It was not the mode to approach the sublime in comedy, and Béralde was no Newton; his creator had not done scientific work, but he understood something of what was going on among men of science, some of whom he knew personally, and his doctor, Jean-Armand de Mauvillain, *doyen* of the Faculté in 1666-8, was independent enough to give his patient a hint that all was not well inside the profession. It was well known that there had been solitary workers in anatomy: William Harvey in England, and Jean Pecquet, the Frenchman who was described as the only man in the country to make an advance to rival that of Harvey, and whose work was rejected by the Diafoiruses and the Guy

Patins of the medical schools. As the play opens, Argan counts his debts by methods long obsolete, and lives in a world that might have been up to date in 1450: his bookkeeping and his medications are equally outmoded. The doctor of tradition has become a national menace, and Molière knows it and says so. Whether his particular pungency is due to his inevitably declining health in 1672-3 or arises from the exceptional scientific activity of the preceding years, one cannot say. Mauvillain may be responsible for the sound skepticism of Béralde, but this likewise we shall never know. In any case, *Le Malade imaginaire* remains a substantial contribution to the popular scientific discussions of the day, chiefly for its attitude of relentless distrust of contemporary doctrines and practice, and for what it added to the really important part of the quarrel of the ancients and moderns – the place of the new sciences among the old masters.

Historians of science in seventeenth-century France are well aware of the justification of Molière's satire on the doctors of the Paris faculty. J. Lévy-Valensi, in his book, *La Médecine et les médecins français au dix-septième siècle* (Paris 1933), remarks (p. 2) that 'si Montpellier accueille le progrès, Paris qui n'apporte que peu de chose à l'œuvre commune se fait l'adversaire impitoyable de toute nouveauté.' In its scientific discussions with provincial doctors, with the surgeons or the apothecaries, he continues, 'la très salubre Faculté de médecine de Paris n'a pas le beau rôle,' adding (p. 11) that 'la Faculté de médecine ne veut rien admettre de ce qui n'est pas dans les anciens; alors que partout ailleurs les médecins se recommandent de l'observation et de l'expérience, elle ne veut connaître que la tradition.' As the general purpose of Lévy-Valensi's book is to present what is best in the Faculté as it was in the seventeenth century, these concessions to its critics must be accepted at face value.

The deep divisions in the medical profession in this period may be appropriately thought of as a phase of the *Querelle des anciens et des modernes*, most frequently discussed in its literary aspects, and even as late as 1690 a matter of acrimonious debate in the home of poets and critics, the Académie française, dividing its members between those who were devoted to the literature of Greece and Rome and those who were aware of the great differences between modern times and classical antiquity. In scientific circles this issue of the value of classic writings as models for imitation could hardly arise, because the pace of discovery and invention was so rapid that the manifestos of traditionalists lost their relevancy almost as fast as they were published. In the medical schools the debate turned on the question of the circulation of the blood, made actual by the publication and dissemination of William Harvey's radically original *De motu cordis* (1628), which has been soberly described as the greatest single book in the history of medicine. No earlier work had approached this area of speculation with the wealth of varied and meticulously careful experimentation that the English doctor had devised, nor had any physiologist applied the methods of mathematics and simple physics with such imaginative skill. The book is so remarkable an exposition of sound method that it deserves attention as a source of inspiration and ideas to the rising generation of scientists in many parts of Europe.

New in conception and in procedure, the book enters into a discussion of the motions of the heart with a minimum of reference to previous writers. As Harvey says in his dedication,

I had no purpose to swell this treatise into a large volume by quoting the names and writings of anatomists, or to make a parade of the strength of my memory, the extent of my reading, or the amount of my pains; because I profess both to learn and to teach anatomy, not from books but from dissections; not from the positions of philosophers but from the fabric of matter.[2]

When he follows this with a discussion of the inconsistencies he finds in Galen and in Fabricius of Acquapendente, in which traditional teachings on the heart are shown to be so self-contradictory as to be quite incredible, the dismay with which his book was received by the Faculté de médecine becomes comprehensible. After this introduction comes a brief chapter in which he outlines his motives for writing, first to correct certain misrepresentations of his views and, secondly, to put his work and conclusions in the hands of his friends. With the second chapter, Harvey is concerned with reporting his method of investigation and what it has demonstrated.

Derived from ingenious experimentation on live animals over several years, Harvey's findings were not easily understood by many of his readers; even though the concept of circular motion was familiar enough in the cosmos of the late Renaissance, it did not seem reasonable to apply it to the analysis of the anatomy of man. But the originality of the book was immediately apparent, and opinion was accordingly divided, some welcoming it as a breach in the mass of doctrine taught traditionally in the schools, others, schoolmen themselves, seeing in it nothing but one more wrong-headed attack on Galen, completely offensive to the Faculté. The concept of the heart as a muscular pump, forcing the blood outward through the arteries, then receiving its return from the veins, was altogether too contradictory to the

---

2 William Harvey, *De motu cordis et sanguinis*, translated by Robert Willis, MD, for the Sydenham Society, 1848, reprinted in *Circulation of the Blood and other Writings* (London, Everyman's Library 1907)

Galenic doctrine to be understood in Paris; too many hours had been spent in classes teaching the ebb and flow movement in the veins, the innate heat provided by the heart, the complex of spirits, vital, animal, and natural, that accompanied the blood as it nourished the muscles and organs of the body. All this ancient theoretical structure was demolished by Harvey's little book. His opening account of the dissection of living animals, especially as the heart 'begins to flag, to move more slowly, and, as it were, to die,' offered the first glimpse of the movements of the muscles of the heart, of which, when the fibres 'contract simultaneously, by an admirable adjustment, all the internal surfaces are drawn together as if with cords, and so is the charge of blood expelled with force.' From this point the author proceeds to the motion of the arteries and auricles, and a survey of the 'motion, action, and office' of the heart and the course of the blood from the vena cava into the right atrium of the heart and then into the pulmonary artery of the lungs. Now Harvey expounds his major paradox, proposing that there may be a 'motion as it were in a circle,' the arteries carrying the 'digested, perfect, peculiarly nutritive fluid,' while the veins bring back the 'cruder, effete blood rendered unfit for nutrition.' Next he calculates the amount of blood ejected in one beat, and then in the thousands of beats in one hour, showing that the whole mass of blood must necessarily pass through the system many times in one day so that the blood is in continuous motion. After discussing the valves in the veins and offering technical arguments in favor of his views, he concludes in chapter 14 'that the blood in an animal body is impelled in a circle, and is in a state of ceaseless motion; that this is the act or function which the heart performs by means of its pulse; and that this is the sole and only end of the motion and contraction of the heart.'[3]

3 In Harvey's *Prelectiones anatomiae universalis*, translated and edited by C.D. O'Malley, F.N.L. Poynter, and K.F. Russell in *Lectures on the Whole of Anatomy* (Berkeley and Los Angeles, University of California Press 1961) p. 190, there is a less formal expression of his views:
'From these things it appears that the action of the heart is in accordance with what is moved; blood is moved from the vena cava into the lungs through the pulmonary artery, and from the lungs through the pulmonary vein into the aorta. With the heart relaxed that blood first enters into the right ventricle from the vena cava and into the left atrium from the pulmonary vein.
'The heart having been extended and contracted, just as by a kind of force it propels from the right ventricle into the lungs from the left into the aorta, wherefore occurs the pulse of the arteries and much speculation by Galen regarding the pulses of the heart, especially of the internal rest and systole, although I believe never realized by touch.'
Harvey's irony towards Galen then turns against Aristotle's view of the nature of the heart and the motion of the blood: 'But for the sake of what thing? Aristotle. Of nothing but passion, as in boiling pottage.'

Based on the examination of innumerable different types of living beings – 'toads, frogs, serpents, small fishes, crabs, shrimps, snails and shell-fish,' as well as dogs and hogs – Harvey's book is a model of scientific method and presentation. His conclusion, that 'all these appearances ... seem clearly to illustrate and fully to confirm the truth contended for throughout these pages, and at the same time to stand in opposition to the vulgar opinion: for it would be very difficult to explain in any other way to what purpose all is constructed and arranged as we have seen it to be,' offered a direct challenge to those contemporaries who rejected his views.[4]

There were, of course, many who did just that, but in spite of their efforts the circulatory theory made its way in scientific and medical circles. The critics were neither silenced nor convinced, but like those who opposed Einstein or the quantum theory, they died off without heirs: 'Le combat cessa faute de combattants.' Much more important than the conservative Guy Patins and Jean Riolans of the Faculté de médecine were the investigators who understood the challenge of Harvey's work and faced the innumerable questions to which *De motu cordis* had led; in France the most important was Jean Pecquet (1622-74). In 1627 Gasparo Aselli announced the discovery of the lacteal vessels in a recently fed dog; in 1628 the patron of science and letters, Nicolas Claude Fabri de Peiresc, obtained the cadaver of an executed felon who had eaten copiously before death, and the lacteals were seen by a

---

4 Published in Frankfurt in 1628, the *Exercitatio anatomica de motu cordis et sanguinis* circulated freely across Europe; Pierre Gassendi read it and recommended it to Peiresc, who had already heard of it from a diplomat traveling in the south of France. The book was so fresh in its material that, even though he spoke in its praise, Gassendi could not accept the concept of an impermeable septum.

A comment on Harvey in the fifth part of the *Discours de la méthode* indicates that Descartes had read but had hardly understood *De motu cordis*. The careful experimental and mathematical evidence is neglected, as Descartes proposes the expansion of the blood on contact with the innate heat of the heart as the cause of the systolic expulsion of the blood into the arteries. Reading the several paragraphs devoted to this discussion, one understands the pungent comment of Pascal: 'Descartes inutile et incertain' (Cluny 914), especially when the elder mathematician had to meet the results of careful physiological research.

A further remark in Cluny 84 elaborates Pascal's view: 'Il faut dire en gros: "Cela se fait par figure et mouvement." Car cela est vrai. Mais de dire quelles et composer la machine, cela est ridicule; car cela est inutile et incertain et pénible.' Content to describe phenomena in terms of measuring form and motion, Pascal will make no hypothesis concerning cause or purpose. The lengthy section in which Descartes develops his views on the role of the heart and lungs in the functioning of the circulatory system through unverified analogies and unproven conclusions abundantly justifies the remark attributed to Pascal that 'la philosophie cartésienne' was 'le roman de la nature semblable à peu près à l'histoire de Don Quichot' (Cluny, appendix 2, ¶H).

surgeon of Aix en Provence for the first time in man. In 1634, J. Wesling of Venice described these vessels in the human subject, and in the next few years Thomas Bartholin of Copenhagen and Pecquet were both at work on the problems raised by this series of discoveries. In 1651 Pecquet published an account of the process by which the chyle reaches the circulatory system through the receptacle which for long bore his name at the base of the thoracic duct, the duct itself, and the sub-clavial vein.

On 22 August 1671, the bibliophile and intellectual *nouvelliste* Henry Justel wrote to Samuel de Fermat, the son of the mathematician Pierre, announcing among other things:

Il court un Arrest burlesque qui a esté faict à cause de la deffense d'enseigner la philosophie de Descartes par lequel apres avoir oui le rapport de Jacques de la Poterie on maintient Aristote dans la possession des Écoles et on faict deffense à la Raison de le troubler sur peine d'estre declarée heretique, enjoint au cœur d'estre le principe des nerfs et au chyle d'aller droict au foye sans plus passer par le cœur, et deffend au sang d'estre plus vagabond, errer, ny circuler dans le corps sur peine d'estre abandonné à la faculté de médecine [les identités et autres formules] sont remises en leur bonne fame et renommée et le feu dans la plus haute region de l'air. Il est enjoint aux Repetiteurs hybernois de leur prester main forte pour l'execution de cet Arrest et la Raison est bannie a perpetuité de l'Université.[5]

Failure to comment in one sense or another on this scholarly hoax indicates Justel's amused approval of its purport quite as much as his caution in discussing controversial matters in correspondence passing through the public postal service.

The letter refers to a pamphlet by a friend and disciple of Gassendi, a literate and progressive doctor from, as we might expect, Montpellier, François Bernier. His little book, entitled *Requeste des maistres ès arts, professeurs, et regens de l'Université de Paris présentée à la cour souveraine de Parnasse, ensemble l'arrest intervenu sur ladite requeste contre tous ceux qui prétendent faire enseigner ou croire de nouvelles découvertes qui ne sont pas dans Aristote*, bore the imprint 'A Delphe, par la Société des Imprimeurs ordinaires de la Cour de Parnasse.' It is a typical expression of the views of those who watched the final gasps of scholastic teaching with much satisfac-

---

5 Bibliothèque de Toulouse, MS 846, f. 126. The words in brackets are illegible in the manuscript and have been supplied from the text of the *Arrêt*. For Henry Justel (1620-93) see Harcourt Brown, *Scientific Organizations* (see chapter 3, note 1 above) pp. 161-84.

tion and a good deal of mirth, a parody of the formal language of the lawcourts, and a witty reversal of the methods by which teachings were kept under such control as public officials could maintain. In Bernier's time it was, of course, not possible to mount a direct attack on the ecclesiastical heart of power in the University of Paris. Views critical of orthodox doctrine or the authority of the hierarchy led to suppression or strict control, as the first editors of the *Journal des sçavans* had discovered, but it was possible to suggest opinions on secular matters, such as medicine and the physical sciences. Those who moved in circles beyond the reach of the faculty of theology had ways of avoiding the censor; satire and parody were generally appreciated. Rabelais was still read, by conservatives like Guy Patin and by moderns like Molière; *Pantagruel* was not approved, but the books were bought in editions published in the Netherlands by the Elzeviers and others. That book illustrated the ironic distance a satirist pamphleteer can maintain between his comic types and the meaning he may intend in his writings.

The *Arrêt burlesque* has been associated primarily with Boileau ever since it first appeared in his *Œuvres complètes,* and the chief source of information about its composition and significance has been the annotations in these editions; as they are said to be based on comments by Boileau himself, their accuracy is presumed. The account offered here derives from an edition of Amsterdam (1717) in four duodecimo volumes; the first footnote, somewhat abridged, tells us:

L'Université de Paris vouloit présenter requête au Parlement pour empêcher qu'on n'enseignât la Philosophie de Descartes. On en parla même a Mr le Premier Président de Lamoignon, qui dit un jour a Mr Despréaux ... qu'il ne pourroit se dispenser de donner un Arrêt conforme à la Requête de l'Université. Sur cela Mr Despréaux imagina cet Arrêt burlesque, et le composa avec le secours de Mr Bernier et de Mr Racine, qui fournirent chacun leurs pensées. Mr Dongois, neveu de l'auteur et Greffier de la Grand'Chambre, y eut aussi beaucoup de part, surtout pour le stile et les termes de pratique qu'il entendoit mieux qu'eux.[6]

A little later, Dongois presented the *Arrêt burlesque* to Lamoignon with other papers to be signed; Lamoignon noticed the subterfuge, attributed the document to Boileau at once, and was much amused: 'Il convenoit que cet Arrêt burlesque l'avoit empêché d'en donner un sérieux, qui auroit apprêté à rire à tout le monde.'

6 *Œuvres de Nicolas Boileau Despréaux, avec des éclaircissemens historiques donnés par lui-même* (Amsterdam 1717) 4: 55-62

These annotations tell us that Boileau's version appeared in 1674, under the title *Arrêt donné en faveur des Maîtres-ès-Arts, Médecins et Professeurs de l'Université pour le maintien de la doctrine d'Aristote*, and that a number of changes were made between the first publication and its incorporation in the collected *Œuvres* of 1701. It is apparent that Boileau reduced the contribution of his colleagues as the years passed, so that the work in its final form came to be very typically Boileau's own. As a result of this, respective contributions of the dramatist Jean Racine, François Bernier, and the nephew Dongois have never been established.

In Boileau's text the satire begins by reciting that the court has seen a *requête* presented by the regents, masters of arts, doctors and professors of the university, acting for themselves and as defenders of Aristotle, 'ancien professeur Roïal en grec dans le Collège du Lycée et Précepteur du feu Roi de querelleuse mémoire Alexandre dit le Grand,' showing that recently 'une inconnue nommée la Raison' has attempted to enter the schools of the university, and with the aid of 'certains Quidams factieux' – Gassendists, Cartesians, and others – has placed herself in a position to oust forcibly the said Aristotle, 'ancien et paisible possesseur desdites Écoles' against whom Reason and her associates have already published certain books in which Aristotle has been subjected to examination, which is 'directement opposé aux Lois, Us, et Coutumes de ladite Université.' Furthermore, Reason has changed various things in Nature, taking from the heart the prerogative of being the seat of the nervous system, now transferred to the brain; attributing to the heart the duty of receiving the chyle, formerly the function of the liver; and causing the blood to convey itself 'par tout le corps,' wandering and circulating through the veins and arteries. And for all these vexations there is no other justification than '*l'Expérience* dont le témoignage n'a jamais été reçu dans lesdites Écoles.' And the curing of fevers by such remedies as quinquina or cinchona bark, unknown to Hippocrates and Aristotle, without 'saignées, purgations, ni évacuations précédentes' is not only irregular but 'tortionnaire et abusif,' since Reason has not been admitted to the faculty and cannot be consulted by it.

Other offenses are listed; the court finally orders that Aristotle be maintained in possession of the schools, that he shall be taught and followed by the regents, doctors, masters of arts, and professors, who are not obliged to read him or to know his language. The heart is ordered to be the origin of the nerves, a doctrine which all must believe in spite of experiment to the contrary; the chyle is ordered to go directly to the liver without passing by the heart; and the blood is to cease wandering and circulating in the body. Reason is to cease and desist from the use of emetic wines, powders, cinchona bark, and other unapproved drugs, and finally doctors are to restore their patients to their former state of illness, and the familiar remedies are to be used once more.

Pamphlets such as this circulated freely and were widely read, and discussion was undoubtedly freer than some of the established institutions would have liked. Public opinion was influenced, and conservative authorities could no longer count on the quiet acceptance of dogmatic statements in matters where the general good was at stake, in questions of health, convenience, or safety. The printers could sell pamphlets like this over – or under – the counter, as Pascal and his associates had found with his *Lettres provinciales* and Jean Cusson with the *Journal des sçavans* and his numerous leaflets of a scientific nature.

Everyone who has participated in the life of a large institution knows that there are aspects of its affairs that concern for its public image will keep in discreet obscurity. Internal stresses deriving from disagreement on policy or its implementation may easily develop from personal loyalties or rational conviction; the impact of a new foundation or of a new direction given to a corporate body already strong and active can easily disturb the equilibrium and create tensions distorting the settled pattern of reactions and routine. Lévy-Valensi's book on seventeenth-century doctors places the Faculté de médecine at the centre of its interests; while he describes various aspects of its thought and outlook, the author's loyalty to his profession, even after more than two centuries have passed and the University of Paris and the Faculté have changed beyond recognition, prevents him from discussing its problems in depth or mentioning various episodes in which it was radically divided on important issues or behaved with less than scientific objectivity when its long-range interests were at stake. One has the sense that a book could be written on many matters that are merely mentioned in passing or barely hinted at. We need more histories in which science and scientific institutions are treated frankly and in reasonable detail, with appropriate attention to failures and mistakes, in which the private aspect is not sacrificed to the public image, and in which individuals who work independently are not regarded as of less importance than those who work within the framework of a large organization.

The Faculté de médecine was not universally beloved; surgeons and pharmacists rebelled against its hegemony, as did the Montpellier doctors. The members of the new Académie des sciences had no reason to fear it, but their outlook was scientific and not pedagogic, and they had little reason to think of it except as a keeper of ancient traditions and therefore a potential obstacle to certain lines of investigation; there were doctors who belonged to both organizations, promoting thereby understanding and sometimes compromise on controversial issues. Outside of the Académie and the Faculté there were a few whose work came into the purview of neither body except when their activities became a matter of the health, welfare, or rights of third parties. Among those of this last category are Jean Denis and the surgeon Paul Emerez, for their trial of transfusion of blood.[7]

Although it has long been known that animal blood was conveyed into human veins in Paris in 1667, modern commentators and historians have usually passed over the implications of these efforts to develop a new method of therapy based on recent advances in the understanding of the function of the blood. The innovators' lack of success has led to the burial of their work under the unfavorable comments of some contemporaries and the edicts of various persons of authority, in Paris, Rome, and elsewhere. Perhaps neglect of the episode is justified if one takes the view that the history of science is the story of a series of uninterrupted discoveries of truth through the use of impeccable method, and that failures and misconceptions have no interest. The perspective of the general historian is necessary here, for such an episode as this offers an opportunity to explore the climate of intelligence of a period in which science was attaining new prestige and better understanding because of the founding of institutions and journals whose purpose was the promotion of those very objectives.

From the height of modern knowledge of the nature and peculiarities of blood, the effort recorded in the numerous pamphlets and other documents produced as a result of these experiments seems to be premature. Denis and his associate Emerez have been regarded as rash and foolhardy triflers with

7 For a more complete discussion of the work of Jean Denis, the reader is referred to my article in *Isis* 39 (1948): 15-29, 'Jean Denis and transfusion of blood, Paris, 1667-1668,' from which several pages have been revised for the present context. The article offers a somewhat fuller bibliography, particularly of the pamphlets and periodical literature of the day. A volume in the printed books of the Bibliothèque nationale, Paris, Te[13].42, contains twenty-one publications concerning these tests, as well as two letters by Antoine de la Poterie published in full in *Isis*.

Research for this episode has been done in many places, in Paris and London, in the Boston Medical Library, the New York Academy of Medicine, and elsewhere. I am indebted to Sir Geoffrey Keynes, who first encouraged me to pursue the study of the writings concerning Denis, and to the late George Sarton, who urged me to publish after hearing a paper on this topic in its original form read before the Boston Medical History Club in November 1947. Dr. Bertram Bernheim of Baltimore, Maryland, and Dr I.W.M. Baxter of Parry Sound, Ontario, have shown courteous interest in this part of this chapter and have given me sound advice; they are, of course, in no wise responsible for opinions or conclusions I may have expressed.

the human body, callous to suffering, and careless of the interests of the profession. That the period in which these debates occurred was marked by rapid changes in thought and considerable advances in the understanding of natural process, accompanied by numerous false starts and bad guesses, is often forgotten. The men most closely concerned with these experimental procedures and the subsequent discussions recognized that the questions for which they were attempting to find answers could not be asked privately and in the dark. If their work were to be useful and their method valuable in therapy, the whole series of tests should be made in the presence of an enlightened public, with representatives of the medical profession as well as surgeons and educated laymen on hand to see just what went on. The truth that would prevail would be the conclusion most credible to an informed and skeptical private citizen, impressed by logical argument and demonstrated fact, after a fair examination of alternative opinions.

Interest in the possible use of intravenous injection began with the general acceptance of William Harvey's discovery and explanation of the function of the heart and the circulation of the blood. Irrational associations in these areas were gradually breaking down; the magical view of blood was yielding to knowledge of its relation to the vital processes and the function of the liver. Much speculation had led to suggestions of ways in which it might be possible to alter the characteristics of blood by infusing liquids with specific qualities designed to cure disease of mind or body. Christopher Wren experimented on a dog at Oxford in 1656, perhaps the first of many tests in different parts of Europe, some of them on human subjects. The first transfusion from one animal to another was made by Richard Lower in 1665, and another in 1666. His method was described in the *Philosophical Transactions* of the Royal Society of London in December of 1666, and reported in the *Journal des sçavans* of 31 January 1667.

French scientists soon discovered the interest of what was going on in England, and within a short time some of them were imitating experiments performed in London. The Académie des sciences set up a commission to investigate and test this method; its members were Louis Gayant (or Gayen) a surgeon, the astronomer Adrien Auzout, and the physician-turned-architect, Claude Perrault. Of these Gayant was to make the tests; Auzout, whose broad interests and general competence were widely recognized, presumably represented the point of view of method; while Perrault as a medical academician in the confidence of the ministry and a member of the Faculté de médecine, could report on the significance of the results.

Experiments began in the royal library, the usual meeting place of the Académie, on 22 January 1667, and continued on the 24th, 26th, and 28th;

the second and fourth tests, as well as three final trials, were made 'chez Gayant,' whose surgery was undoubtedly a more appropriate place. There were no public reports on these experiments and their outcome; unsatisfactory references occur in private correspondence, repeated in the *Philosophical Transactions* of June and October. The *Journal des sçavans* maintains a complete silence on the activities of the Académie in this field; that this was exceptional is shown by the appearance in the issue of April 4 of a letter concerning the examination of the thorax of a woman by a group which consisted of Gayant and Jean Pecquet, who seem to have done the work, again with Perrault as observer. Later in the year, on November 28, there is an account of the dissection of a large fish in the royal library, described in a letter to Cureau de la Chambre, a member of the Académie. A week later, there is a record of the dissection of a lion which had died in the royal menagerie. One may surmise that there was a desire to avoid public controversy about what was going on in the Académie, especially as the active debate in the pages of the *Journal des sçavans* and in the numerous pamphlets then appearing was producing some embarrassment among those who wanted to see reason and a sense of fact prevail.

A report of the experiments by Gayant and his colleagues was made for the Académie and kept in its files; this was the basis for a revised statement published in the final volume of a collection of *Essais de physique* by Claude Perrault.[8] The original version remained in manuscript and unpublished until 1963, when an English translation was presented by Hebbel E. Hoff and Roger Guillemin in the *Journal of the History of Medicine*; the document has had no influence on the literature of the subject, either technical or historical. It makes no reference to Auzout; and there is no use of the first person singular which would imply Perrault's participation. It might be pointed out that Auzout had been *persona non grata* to Perrault since his criticism of Perrault's imposing edition of Vitruvius, which seems to have led also to Auzout's exclusion from the Académie in the spring of 1668. Gayant had died on military service in 1673; as a surgeon he was of lower status, employed in manual operations only.

According to Perrault, the experiments in the Académie were carried out before 'a certain person' had performed others 'with an éclat and in a spirit entirely the opposite to the conduct of the investigators' who worked in the Académie; members of the Académie had no wish to take sides in the public debate, although their advice was asked for in the climactic scene in the courts. Perrault finally admits that those who had made the experiments in

8 Claude Perrault, *Essais de physique ou recueil de plusieurs traitez touchant les choses naturelles* (Paris 1688) 4 volumes, 12 mo.

the Académie were not all of one mind, and that there were some who were prejudiced by the authority of the foreigners who had expressed approval of transfusion. The limited number of participants makes it very easy to identify those who disagreed; doubtless there had been words between Adrien Auzout and Perrault, and one wonders a little why these two had been put on the one small commission.

To set the record straight, Perrault declares that Gayant worked with precision, using methods capable of giving a sure understanding of what was done. This, he says, could not be claimed for the experiments done abroad and in Paris, where there seems to have been no sure way of telling how much blood had passed from one animal to another. It should be noted that it was only in the seventh and final test that Gayant had worked out a method of comparing the weights of the dogs before and after the tests were performed; the method had been suggested by Robert Boyle to Dr Richard Lower and published in the *Philosophical Transactions* of February 1667, which could easily have been available in Paris before Gayant began his last group of three tests in March. One notes also that the *Journal des sçavans* for January 31 contained an 'Extrait du Journal d'Angleterre, contenant la manière de faire passer le sang d'un animal dans un autre'; this was taken from the *Transactions* of December 1666, where it appeared under the heading 'The method observed in transfusing the blood out of one animal into another' attributed to Richard Lower.

The chief interest in all this testing and discussion today lies in the light thrown on the habits and outlook of seventeenth-century scientists and the reading public. The wealthy Henri-Louis Habert de Montmor, whose house had been a principal centre of scientific activity for some twelve years preceding the establishment of the Académie des sciences in the last months of 1666, had retained his interest in these matters, even though officers of the realm had taken over the functions of maintaining the advancement of science. News of the considerable activity in England was available to all who read the *Journal des sçavans*, and there were leakages of information from the royal library, as apparently the bond of secrecy imposed on academicians was not complete. Such members as Adrien Auzout frequented circles where curiosity about matters of science was common. The trend of the time was toward communication and debate, for it was widely recognized that only by free circulation of ideas and conclusions could science be advanced. The spirit of secrecy which set the medieval and Renaissance craftsman apart from his seventeenth-century heir in the academies had largely disappeared.

The Faculté de médecine apparently took no part in any of this movement, although individual doctors found ways of making their different views public. The chief operators, Gayant in the Académie and Emerez working with Denis, were surgeons. Perrault was acting as a servant of the Crown and the Académie, and Jean Denis was out of faculty control as an independent, whose status in medicine still seems to be unsettled, although he has commonly been thought to be one of the Montpellier doctors. In the view of the Faculté it seemed doubtful if anything could be learned from animals, whose temperament – to use an old technical term – and humors, including blood, were so completely different from man's. Thus outside of the institutions there was room for the private investigator, and Robert Boyle, one of the leaders in the science of the time, as both experimentalist and animator, had made a lively plea for more workers in the field. As Lower's work progressed, Boyle had composed a long list of queries, fourteen of which had been published in the *Transactions* of February 1667, with a plea that others would take up Lower's work, corroborating his results and adding to the sum of knowledge in the area of investigation he had opened.

There was, therefore, a place for private research, and Habert de Montmor sponsored the enterprise of Denis and Emerez, no doubt looking after most of the expense as well as offering protection in the event of problems raised by agents of the state or city. In the atmosphere of the age, projects of many kinds were undertaken by many kinds of men: exploration, colonization, commercial and industrial enterprises, invention, privateering, and foreign military service, as well as more strictly scientific ventures such as that in question. The pioneering spirit shown by the surgeons was thus no very strange phenomenon; the really adventurous participants were the subjects, human and animal, who entered into this unprecedented struggle between their own body fluids, which were incompletely understood, and the still stranger substances, chemical or organic, introduced into their vascular systems. Still another motive for this particular venture might be mentioned. Pierre Gassendi, the philosopher, had spent his last years in the house of Montmor, where he died in 1655 after a short illness for which the prescribed therapy was bleeding. This was performed some twenty times by order of Guy Patin and Jean Riolan, regents of the Faculté, and Gassendi's system could not take it. In view of the great respect and love the scientists and amateurs of Paris had for Gassendi, it could be that Montmor had a valid reason for trying to find some remedy which would supplement the traditional phlebotomy, which Claude Perrault cites as a therapy 'which the experience of two thousand years has demonstrated to be capable of producing the greatest effects that can be expected in medicine.' In any case, Montmor's role as patron of the sciences and the arts stands high in the not very inspiring story of the uses to which great wealth was put in France of the *ancien régime*.

In spite of much discussion and controversy, the central figure in the present story remains somewhat mysterious. Jean Denis – in his later publications his name appears as Jean-Baptiste — was a product of the twilight zone between the end of the Renaissance and the age of the new kind of man, who grew up, as did Pascal and Isaac Newton, with the scientific revolution stirring all around him. He was born most probably about 1640, in Paris, where his father was a hydraulic engineer in the royal service. Although on the title page of one of his late publications he is described as *médecin*, and in biographical dictionaries he is said to be a doctor from Montpellier, no trace of him has been found in the archives of that famous school. He was an independent lecturer on scientific topics, with good social connections, and not regarded as dangerous or ill-equipped by a number of properly graduated doctors, not only of Montpellier but also of the Paris Faculté. The Saturday *conférences* held in his house on the Quai des Grands Augustins were well attended; there was a surprising vogue for these rather social gatherings, where a lecturer would speak of his special interests, with demonstrations, experiments, or curiosities to lend spice to his words. Various references indicate that the house of Denis was the meeting place of many persons well known in the society of the time, some of them remembered in the annals of literature.

So when under Montmor's sponsorship Denis began his series of tests of transfusion of blood from one animal to another, his work was followed with much interest. The first public session was made on 3 March 1667 using a small dog 'resembling a fox' and a spaniel bitch; while Lower had drawn all the blood from one animal, Denis tried from the first to manage the operation so as to save the lives of both. In detail his technique followed that used by Lower, except that he drew blood from the crural artery rather than from the carotid; this in the expectation that convulsions and the risk of death would be reduced. In his pamphlets, Denis writes of his experiments in a factual style, estimating the quantities of blood taken from the various donors. In his diary, 21 November 1667, Samuel Pepys is more explicit: he writes that the English experimenters 'propose to let in about twelve ounces; which, they compute, is what will be let in in a minute's time by the watch.' But even this reflects the difficulty of precision in measurement.

When a second test was made, on March 8, the operators prepared the animals to be used, and worked in a warm room. Blood was taken from the previous recipient and transferred to a third dog by means of an improved technique. Use of the crural artery was justified, and the experimenters had learned that the dogs make a better recovery with more post-operative care. The chief improvement was in the use of shorter and thinner tubes, less likely to produce coagulation and stoppage, and in the preservation of body heat. The operation was less dangerous than they had feared; the blood used had served three dogs in a very few days with inconvenience to none, each dog being now well, friendly, and strong. An unnamed physician present was much impressed, confessing frankly that he would not have thought the operation possible if he had not seen and examined the circumstances himself. Denis announced a further trial for March 19, in his public *conférence*, where all interested might come to see the blood of a healthy young dog transferred into a mangy old cur. In a private letter, Henry Justel told Pierre Daniel Huet that he had seen the operation described in the *Journal des sçavans*, and that Denis promised that still another trial would be performed for the Jesuit fathers in the Collège de Clermont on March 31.[9] There is little doubt that Denis and Emerez were thinking of the application of this operation to human patients, and acquiring the skills and knowledge necessary for that final step.

These experiments continued, and Denis soon began to try the effect of introducing the blood from calves into three dogs; the results were good – indeed one dog reduced by loss of blood on a previous day recovered his strength and now showed surprising liveliness. Emerez was now using a type of venesection which avoided the elaborate system of ligatures described by Lower. One learns that he kept his dogs under observation, watching for ill effects. In one letter at this time, he mentions that he has transfused some nineteen dogs, all of whom have survived and are in good health. He has paid attention to the preparation of donors as well as of recipients; he recommends that those who plan to employ this method to best advantage should feed their animals well, with more care than usual, since the blood of calves well fed on milk and yolks of eggs will be more pleasant than those fed otherwise.

Early in June 1667, Claude Tardy, a member of the Paris Faculté, brought out a pamphlet suggesting possibilities of transfusion from human donor to human patient, vein to vein, and limiting strictly the quantity of blood to be taken from the donor.[10] This would permit the rejuvenation of the elderly, and, to quote the editor of the *Journal des sçavans*, 'Il dit que cette opération est très utile pour la guérison des maladies qui viennent de l'acrimonie du sang, comme sont les ulcères, les Eresipèles, &c.' The usual medications do not reach these afflictions quickly, but 'un nouveau sang bien tempéré allant directement dans les parties malades par la transfusion, doit donner un soulagement beaucoup plus prompt et plus assuré.'

All this literature reminds the modern reader that the science of biochemistry is comparatively a recent development, and that analysis of the blood was

---

9 Justel's letters to P.D. Huet are in the Ashburnham collection of the Biblioteca Medicea-Laurenziana, Florence.
10 Claude Tardy, *Traité de l'écoulement du sang d'un homme dans les veines d'un autre et de ses utilitez* (Paris 1667) 15pp.

not yet possible. Doctors were still evaluating what they could see and feel in terms of familiar qualities, warm or cold to the touch, heavy or light as fluids, dark or bright in color, and variations in smell and taste. As instrumentation improved, shrewd observers could foresee tremendous possibilities once refinements were attained, and those who clung to the old tools and the traditional methods were more and more open to the critical comment of younger scientists.

The treatise by Claude Tardy may very well be the first published text seriously proposing a technique and specific function for transfusion between human subjects. Nothing in either of the two journals had suggested this logical outcome, although, according to Henry Oldenburg (October 1667), the English scientists 'had practiced it long ago upon Man, if they had not been so tender in hazarding the life of Man ... nor so scrupulous to incur the Penalties of the Law, which in England is more strict and nice in cases of this concernment, than those of many other Nations are.' Oldenburg adds that he himself had seen the instruments ready for this operation, and heard the method agreed on; in the same number of the *Transactions* he inserts a letter from Dr Edmund King, who says that 'we have been ready for this experiment these six months, and wait for nothing but good opportunities, and the removal of some considerations of a moral nature.'

But Denis and Emerez had already gone ahead, and the *Journal des sçavans* of 28 June 1667 reviews a new pamphlet in which they announce to Montmor that the transfusion of blood,

que quelques-uns croyoient impossible, que plusieurs jugeoient dangereux, et que la plupart estimoient au moins inutile, s'est heureusement faite sur deux hommes, et la première expérience qu'on en a faite a guéry une personne d'une maladie assez fâcheuse.

The reviewer omits reference to the debates in connection with this innovation, but lists the chief reasons why Denis believes the transfer of blood to a patient is not unnatural. It resembles the means by which a foetus is nourished in the womb; it is a direct means of feeding a patient suffering from loss of blood; and the blood is received in a form demanding no further digestion. He adds that this should bring agreement between doctors who have been arguing the advantages and disadvantages of bleeding, because transfusion replaces bad blood with good, thus leaving the patient's strength undiminished. Old ideas concerning the blood still persist uncriticized, for he goes on to argue that while human blood would be good, animal blood would be better, for the absence of passions among animals means that their blood is uncorrupted by the evils of the human soul. We drink milk and eat flesh from these animals, why should we not use their blood in our own systems? Furthermore, one can prepare animals as donors through proper feeding.

The account of two tests follows. The first subject, a boy of fifteen, by nature alert and lively, had been sick with a fever for about two months, and in spite of twenty bleedings had become so sleepy and lethargic that, even after sleeping ten hours at night, he drowsed all day, even at meals and in active pursuits. These symptoms suggested the utility of transfusion and Emerez opened a vein at the elbow, drew off about three ounces of blood which seemed thick and dark, then through the same vein inserted some blood drawn from the carotid artery of a lamb. The patient did not suffer during the operation, except to feel warm the full length of his arm; Denis states that he received about eleven ounces of blood in this way. The boy said that a pain in his side hurt him rather less; he had fallen from a ten-foot ladder the day before. Next morning he woke earlier than usual, was much gayer, and dined well without falling asleep. After a few irregular days, he seemed quite cured, and his lethargy had gone.

The second experiment was made more for curiosity than for therapy. A healthy man of about forty-five, a bearer of sedan-chairs, offered to undergo the operation for a small sum. The quantities drawn and transfused were increased, some twenty ounces of lamb's blood being introduced into his system. The patient was very cheerful during the operation and complained of nothing except considerable warmth in his arm. The porter then dressed the meat of the lamb whose blood he had received, and went to drink his fee with friends. Although he had been advised to rest, he went out to earn more money the next day, said he had never felt better, and returned to make sure that the operators would ask no one but him to serve as patient. These two cases are offered a proof of French priority in transfusion of human beings.

Meanwhile, tests on animals continued, and the printed records do not tell the whole story. Henry Justel, the Huguenot bibliophile and cosmopolitan friend of almost every amateur of science and erudition who came to Paris in the years 1663 to 1680 (including Leibniz, Wren, Pepys, Magalotti, and numerous younger men, some of whom became personages of importance in later days), was well acquainted with Jean Denis and followed his experiments with a somewhat skeptical interest. Early in June, he wrote to Huet that there were plans to transfuse the blood of a fox into a sheep; in July he writes again that the French claims to have been the first in field with their trials of transfusion are not justified, and that the English who first tested it had never been in France, and had no knowledge of talk about the method. In August he writes that the experiment has been tried on an old sick horse, who is now much better; Justel adds that 'il est à craindre que le changement qu'on remarque à ces animaux-là ne vienne du soin qu'on prend d'eux et de la nourriture qu'on leur donne.' He adds that if transfusion does no good at least it does no harm. In October, the operators have been offered several 'phrénétiques' for their experiments, but so far they have not wished to undertake anything inappropriate. They have put the blood of a lamb into a fox, 'mais le renard en est mort.'

The interest was kept up. On December 16, Justel tells Huet that the English have carried out a transfusion on a man, with success and very easily; the patient was not uncomfortable. This would be the strange Arthur Coga, who received a guinea for his services, fell among drinking companions, and was no credit to his surgeons. Pepys speaks of this case again in his diary on 30 November 1667; the experiment was done by Lower and Edmund King on the 23rd, six months after the first human transfusions had been done in France. Pepys tells of talking with Coga, who had been able to give a description of the operations to the Royal Society in Latin; the diary reports that Coga 'finds himself much better since, and as a new man, but he is cracked a little in the head, though he speaks reasonably and very well'; Coga had a second transfusion of which the results are not recorded, probably because they were somewhat obscured by drink.

Since transfusion had become an international enterprise, with results seeming to corroborate the view that the procedure was worth following up, it is not surprising to find Denis and his associate proceeding to a series of tests on men who were desperately in need of help, the usual nostrums being quite fruitless. The case of the Baron Bond may be passed over quickly; this Swedish nobleman was travelling on the Grand Tour, and fell ill in Paris. He was in a hopeless state before an appeal was made to Denis, who reluctantly consented to operate. The results were bad, the Baron died, and the report was, as Oldenburg wrote to Robert Boyle, that 'his intestines were all gangrened, so that it was not possible to have recovered him by any known natural means.'

The second of these patients, the mentally unbalanced Mauroy, usually known as Saint Amant, became the most important of all the cases treated by Denis. The fatal outcome led to a grotesquely complicated series of trials in the courts, and although these ended with exoneration for the operators, they put an effective stop to the short vogue of transfusion, not only in Paris, but in other centres where the method had been tried or envisaged. Denis transfused blood into other patients after Saint Amant, but none of them achieved the posthumous fame of the incendiary valet of Madame de Sévigné. The documents are fairly full, although hardly precise enough for a modern scientist. We can follow the early stages of the affair and recognize several of the persons involved. The fullest account comes from letters written by Antoine de la Poterie, an amateur of the sciences employed by Montmor, to Samuel de Sorbière, at this time attached to the embassy of the Duc de Chaulnes in Rome. Sorbière had been secretary of the Académie Montmor, and in 1663 he had been one of the first French visitors to the Royal Society of London; his visit gave him an opportunity to report on the scientific activity then achieving international repute. These letters led to publication in Italian of an account of the transfusion experiments; interest in the new procedure had spread to most of Europe.[11]

La Poterie's first letter, from Paris on 28 December 1667, is no casual item in a regularly friendly correspondence. A carefully prepared account, it was intended for circulation and perhaps reproduction in the press. The experiment described in it was made under the sponsorship of Montmor in the presence of 'Monsieur le Comte de Frontenac, Monsieur L'Abbé Bourdelot, de plusieurs sçavans médecins de cette ville et d'autres personnes considérables.' Frontenac, brother-in-law of Montmor, became governor of New France in 1672; Bourdelot was a member of the household of the Prince de Condé, and moderator of a weekly *conférence* on scientific topics held for several years from about 1665.

La Poterie describes Saint Amant as a man who had been 'fort adroit' and endowed with good sense until he had become insane about four years before, when he began to run about the streets, his actions and speech uncontrolled. Madame de Sévigné had been forced to dismiss him, as he had tried on different occasions to set the house on fire, had torn his clothing and run about naked. One cold night he had hidden himself in a pile of hay in an archway; the horses of the night watch began to eat the hay, which woke Saint Amant, who seized the horses by their tails, so that the watchmen fled thinking the devil was pursuing them.

Montmor was interested, and imagined that a transfusion of calf's blood might relieve the demented man and help him regain his senses. He consulted Madame de Sévigné and asked Denis and Emerez for their help; Saint Amant was sought and found, and brought to Montmor's house for observation. On 19 December 1667, about six in the evening, the operation began; about a quart of blood was taken from a vein in the arm, and a pint transferred from an artery of the calf by means of little silver tubes. Dr Noël Vallant preserved a drawing of the tubes (figure 4) which shows them to have been between two and three inches long, and slightly curved.

On the 21st the operation was begun again with another calf, as the patient had begun to 'extravaguer' as before. This time about a pint was taken from

11 The letters by La Poterie have been published in *Isis* 39, (1948): 21-3.

him, and about two quarts transfused. 'M. Emerez fit si bien que toute la compagnie en demeura satisfaite,' but the patient felt hot through his whole body, and suffered severe pain in his back while the doctors felt his agitated pulse. His doublet was unlaced as he was suffocating; he vomited, passed urine and faeces, and was put to bed where he slept peacefully with no sign of madness. In the morning he asked for his confessor, who heard him quietly, and said he deemed him capable of receiving the sacrament. He was drowsy all day Thursday, but various persons agreed he was in his right mind; he was bled again that evening, and on Friday night he slept well again and received an enema, so that on Saturday one of the local priests considered him capable of receiving communion, which was brought to him on the Sunday. He still complained of exhaustion and generalized pain, which was attributed to fatigue and exposure, regarded as evidence that he had regained his mental balance. Montmor was willing to spare nothing to see that this invention was perfected, so pleased was he to see that this man had confessed his sins and received the sacrament.

Sorbière's position in the embassy at Rome made him a desirable ally for Montmor and the two experimenters, particularly as the whole matter could easily be raised in ecclesiastical circles; support from Rome could be helpful in the case of conflict with the faculties of medicine and theology in Paris. The interest of the Faculté de médecine was already apparent; three members of the institution were among the 'sçavans médecins' present at the first operation on Saint Amant.

A few days later another letter was written by La Poterie to Sorbière, recording general satisfaction with the cure apparent in Saint Amant; his acceptance as a communicant by the church was as good a proof of his return to mental health as could be obtained in seventeenth-century Paris. Denis now publishes a fuller account of his patient, described as a man thirty-four years of age, whose troubles began some seven or eight years previously, brought on by an unhappy love affair. His mental lapses occurred at intervals and lasted some ten months each; it was difficult for him to find employment, for his tendency to arson kept those who associated with him in a state of fear. Denis claims that his advice to Montmor was that transfusion would not kill the man, that a cure could not be guaranteed, and that transfusion from a calf might allay the heat and ebullition of his blood. The man assigned to guard the patient was the porter on whom the trial had been made some seven months before. Saint Amant's wife had sought him in different towns and had now found him in Paris; she was surprised at his kindness to her, particularly at the full moon, when he had usually been most violent and had beaten her. Denis remarks on his calm mind, normal functions, good sleeping, and discreet behavior; he offers no conjectures or hypotheses to account for these

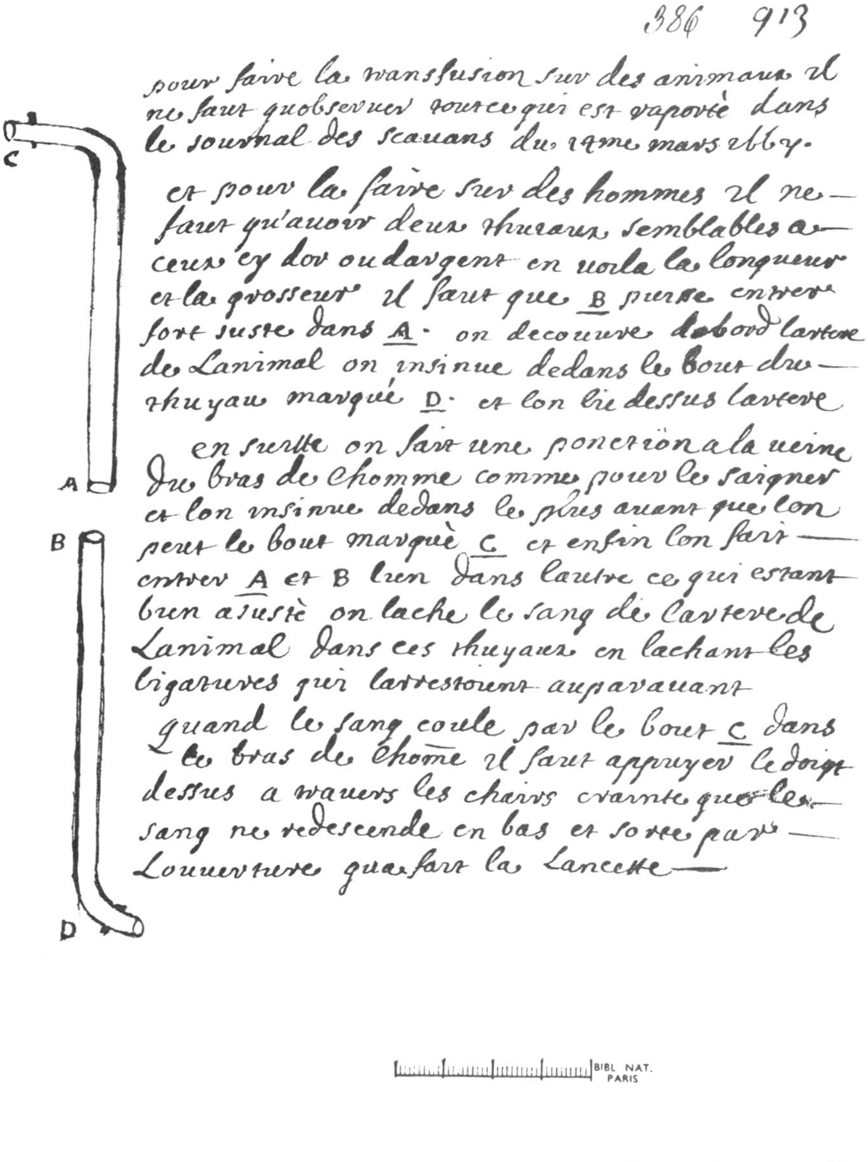

pour faire la transfusion sur des animaux il
ne faut qu'observer tout ce qui est rapporté dans
le journal des scavans du 14me mars 1667.

et pour la faire sur des hommes il ne
faut qu'avoir deux thuyaux semblables a
ceux cy d'or ou d'argent en voila la longueur
et la grosseur il faut que B puisse entrer
fort juste dans A. on decouvre d'abord l'artere
de l'animal on insinue dedans le bout du
thuyau marqué D. et l'on lie dessus l'artere

en suitte on fait une poncrion a la veine
du bras de l'homme comme pour le saigner
et l'on insinue dedans le plus avant que l'on
peut le bout marqué C et enfin l'on fait
entrer A et B bien dans l'autre ce qui estant
bien ajusté on lache le sang de l'artere de
l'animal dans ces thuyaux en lachant les
ligatures qui l'arrestoient auparavant

quand le sang coule par le bout C dans
le bras de l'homme il faut appuyer le doigt
dessus a travers les chairs crainte que le
sang ne redescende en bas et sorte par
l'ouuerture qu'a fait la lancette

FIGURE 4 After watching Denis and Emerez carry out transfusions, the Montpellier doctor Noël Vallant preserved a description and sketch of the equipment among his papers, now in the Bibliothèque nationale (fonds français 17057, folio 386) (photo Bibl. nat., Paris).

results, since the facts will speak for themselves. He now has definite ideas about the preparation of patients for transfusion as well as for post-operative care, and he adds that he knows of many other sick persons who may find relief from this experiment.

One should note that the symptoms described by Denis would be profoundly disturbing to a modern physician. The heavy perspiration, extreme warmth in the arm and elsewhere, the violent back-pains, 'une grande évacuation par haut et par bas,' followed by deep sleep for many hours – all these signs add up to a very bad mismatch of blood, and today one would expect a dead patient in the bargain. But the early adventurers in such dangerous territory may perhaps be excused; blood from any source represented vital strength, modified only by the temperament of its animal or human origin. The copious dark urine would now be interpreted as carrying the 'haemoglobin of destroyed blood cells,' according to Sir Geoffrey Keynes, but Denis, without a suitable microscope or other instruments, had no way of making a sound identification of what was there.

At the end of January the insanity of Saint Amant returned, and Paris was full of rumors that the patient had died as the operators were carrying out a third transfusion. Henry Justel wrote to Henry Oldenburg (3 February 1668) that Denis and Emerez had opened the jugular of Saint Amant, and that without the support of Montmor, who, as a *maître des requêtes*, carried considerable weight in the courts, their rashness could have caused them much trouble. Justel notes that this outcome of the experiments will discredit transfusion, and that no one will perform it on men. This came to be a common attitude, raising the question of the prematurity of the investigation as well as of the responsibility of Denis and Emerez in the death of Saint Amant.

Denis claimed that the third transfusion was performed on the urgent appeal of the wife, who had obtained a calf and engaged the services of the surgeon. Although Denis objected that the condition of the patient was unfavorable, he yielded finally, and the operation was begun; he found it was not possible to draw blood from the patient or to complete the transfer of blood from the calf. During the night Saint Amant died; it was said that he had accused his wife of poisoning him, so that the two operators returned to ask permission to make an autopsy, only to find that the widow had arranged for a hasty burial. She had also been approached by three unnamed physicians who had tried to get her to lay charges against Denis; an accusation of malpractice would effectively stop his tests. Much money had been offered her, but she considered that even more could be obtained from Montmor, who sponsored all this activity.

Now Denis thought he should break silence, and he went to the courts to lay charges against the widow and her abettors. Witnesses were found to sustain the charge of poisoning, and although her case against Denis was thrown out, it was decreed that henceforth transfusion could be performed only with the approval of members of the Paris Faculté. In the course of the following year the widow was tried on the murder charge, and Denis and Emerez were found innocent of having contributed to the death of Saint Amant. This was a *cause célèbre*; an unnamed Englishman who attended the trial wrote that Denis was defended by a son of the Président de Lamoignon, chief justice of the Paris courts, who performed admirably, and that four dukes were present, Enghien, Luynes, Mortemar, and Chaulnes, as well as other great persons, men and women.

In the light of all the circumstances, these efforts of 1667-8 probably should not be condemned as unnaturally rash or premature. After the discussions and trials of infusion of fluids into the veins, it was inevitable that someone would try the final test, the transfusion of blood into the human body. Surgeons had undertaken equally drastic tasks, and *materia medica* included many doses stranger than fresh lamb's blood. The history of medicine cannot be written if it is insisted that the surgery of our ancestors should have been carried out with the precautions suggested by Lister and Pasteur. Knowledge sometimes results from mistakes which horrify posterity, and if Denis' innocent mingling of the blood of different species shocks a modern reader, it may usefully be recalled that there was then much in all fields of life that today seems distasteful and dangerous. In view of the limited knowledge of the nature of blood possessed by his contemporaries, Denis appears to have undertaken a useful task, with an interest in his program which falls short of fanaticism. He prepared his work with care, performing some fifty tranfusions on dogs and other animals before trying the new method on man. He wrote in an honest and workmanlike style, expressing himself clearly, factually, unemotionally, and persuasively. The logic of the situation demanded that the treatment be devised and tried and the remaining questions answered as they came up. One might suggest that the situation resembled that of three hundred years later, when the logical next step in organ transplant was the moving of a heart from one body to another to save a life.

The objectivity of Denis is apparent in the way in which his case histories are written up. The violent and distressing reactions observed in his patients are recorded with much detail, sometimes too vividly for the taste of a general reader; there is no tendency to cover up the pain and physical distress which his transfusions caused. Modern surgeons would have regarded the symptoms as clear warnings that the treatment was not working as expected, and would have taken steps to alleviate them. Sensitivity to suffering has increased enormously since anaesthetics were introduced in the mid-nineteenth century; life was carried on in Denis' day with great indifference to what we would consider agonizing pain. Illustrations in early books of surgery show that even simple operations were sheer torture, and torture itself was never far from the consciousness of any who tangled with the law or authority. Medical treatment often led to violent reactions, regarded by doctors with equanimity as quite normal or even desirable. Denis' work was undertaken because he believed with many men of his time that the blood was not merely a fluid that fed the tissues but also in some sense represented the temperament of the individual human being. In this way, it was supposed that a means of treating the mind or spirit of the individual might well be by way of the blood; if that vital fluid could be changed in character, then affections of the mind and will – lethargy, melancholy, fits of insanity and so on – could be controlled accordingly.

Denis was naturally reluctant to attempt to obtain blood from human donors; early trials using dogs had been accompanied with difficulties in keeping the donors alive. Richard Lower had no scruples in bleeding his animals to death; his interest seems to have been in the technical aspects of the operation rather than in the development of a procedure for use with human patients. In choosing donors, once he had perfected the mechanics of the operation, Denis used animals whose blood would possess qualities complementing the deficiencies of the temperament of his patient. Thus a man given to frenzy and uncontrollable speech and actions should be assisted by the infusion of the blood of an equable and even stolid beast, so that the mixture of characteristics would produce the desired moderation of temper and behavior. Similar results are achieved with more sophisticated medications today, and with more success, but the purposes are analogous. Medicines then were described in terms of their effect on function or temperament. Molière's Argan gives us the adjectives we need: *insinuatif, préparatif, remolliant, détersif, hépatique, soporatif, somnifère, purgatif, corroboratif, anodin, astringent, carminatif, cordial, préservatif*. Some of these are still in use, none of them very far from our modern litany of analgesic, antacid, tranquillizing, antiseptic, stimulant, sedative, narcotic, and so on – words which sometimes have an exact meaning, but which often convey a psychological effect.

The lack of positive results led, of course, to a rejection of the technique until new conditions made it possible to revive interest in it in the nineteenth century. The Dutch physicist, Christiaan Huygens, in Paris where he had been invited to become a member of the new Académie royale des sciences, wrote to his brother Lodewijk on 20 April 1668 that his colleagues

n'ayant pas eu grande opinion dès le commencement de l'utilité de la transfusion, ne voient rien dans ces observations qui les fasse changer de sentiment, puisqu'elles font voir seulement qu'après la transfusion les animaux et hommes ne s'en portent pas plus mal qu'auparavant. Car l'importance seroit de faire voir que les malades se peuvent guérir par cette opération, comme l'on a voulu essayer icy.[12]

This judgment reflects that of the professional scientists of the academy; the view of an intelligent prospective member of the medical profession was expressed by Guillaume Lamy in three pamphlets of this same year, addressed to René Moreau, a member of the Paris Faculté and professor at the Collège royal. His first letter was based on consideration of the problems apparent to any doctor before the method had been tried: transfer of blood would be impossible in some cases, the 'corruption' of the patient's blood would 'corrupt' the new blood just as the saliva of a mad dog infects the blood of another healthy animal, and finally, transfusion, instead of curing one disease, would originate others; moreover, a calf's blood in human veins would reduce the patient to the stupidity and brutal inclinations of the animal. Another letter is more to the point: keeping off theoretic grounds, transfusion is possible, but there is no proof that a dog can be nourished by transfusing the blood of another species. Dogs that have been treated in this way have purged themselves of the foreign blood, but any improvement in their condition has been due to the preparatory bleeding they have undergone before new blood was introduced. The massive bleeding that would be needed before proceeding to replace lost blood by transfusions would be so dangerous that the risks should not be undertaken in any circumstances.

This was a sane and moderate conclusion at this stage of technical development. Much was written and published on the topic, and most was predominantly speculative, as seen in the light of modern science. Many doctors still held that old-fashioned bleeding was a panacea; ancient classics and the routine of the Faculté were not to be rejected lightly.

By 1669 the issue had disappeared from public discussion. Condemnation of the procedure by the Faculté and the Parlement had been supported by a prohibition from the Papacy, and the surgeons and the provincial doctors practicing in Paris had suffered some loss of prestige. The surgeons recovered

12 Christiaan Huygens, Œuvres complètes 6: 209

status with the operation on the fistula of Louis XIV in 1686, with the technique for lithotomy developed and used by Frère Jacques, and with the lectures on anatomy which reached a high degree of popularity at the Jardin des plantes towards the end of the century. Although the Montpellier doctors held positions of importance in royal and princely households, their public standing was still unsatisfactory; the efforts of Charles de Saint Germain in 1668 to set up a royal chamber to represent their interests would doubtless have benefited if Jean Denis had achieved positive results, for he, with Noël Vallant, Jean Pecquet, Marin Cureau de la Chambre, and the royal physician Antoine Vallot, had actively tried to establish a counterpoise to the conservative Faculté. Various minor successes were wiped out when the regents opposed ratification of the edict, so that Colbert was forced to have the approval annulled by action of the Council of State. The ambiguous position of these doctors was resolved when they were admitted to equal standing by diploma after payment of a heavy initiation fee.

There was, however, more at stake than the standing of a group of physicians from provincial medical schools and the company of surgeons. Jean Denis' work represented the ideas of a growing body of opinion insisting that maxims and doctrines deemed self-evident be subjected to experimental test and review by objective reason — in short, that science was not a fixed and unchangeable body of knowledge, but a growing thing capable of unlimited increase and change. The failure of Denis' method of transfusion to impress the profession was due rather to inadequate knowledge of the nature and function of blood than to an incorrect view of how certain disabilities could be set right. He achieved a measure of success, in spite of the debatable outcome of the numerous experiments he tried on men and women, horses, calves, dogs, sheep, and even a parrot, in that he asked the public to think in a new way about the physical world and how men should deal with its problems.

The dozens or more pamphlets and articles published by Jean Cusson and others, commented on in the pages of the *Journal des sçavans*, form the record of a turning point in the intellectual life of Paris, a moment in which readers were asked to face the question of truth, where it was to be found, and how it was to be recognized. There was a public to be reached and educated, and three centuries later one can only regret that a certain professional contempt for the layman, for the man whose credentials were not entirely clear, kept the learned members of the Académie royale des sciences from expressing their views and recording publicly the results of their own tests and their thoughts on experimental method in medical questions. Claude Perrault made his attitude very clear in the last paragraph of his report, on the last page of the final volume of his *Essais de physique*, published twenty years after the dust had settled in the transfusion affair:

Et cela fait assez clairement voir qu'il n'y a guère moins de vanité dans les expériences que dans le raisonnement, quand même il s'agit des choses sensibles, et qu'il est aussi facile de broncher sur de fausses expériences que sur de faux raisonnements: Enfin qu'on ne peut être assuré que ces deux excellens instrumens des plus parfaites connoissances soient exempts de fausseté, à moins que de les faire rectifier l'un par l'autre, ce qui demande une exactitude et une application plus grande apparemment que n'est celle qui a été employée par ceux qui ne doutent nullement de l'utilité que peut apporter la transfusion du sang d'un animal dans un autre.

However, Perrault, judicious conservative that he may be, should not be allowed the last word. He could not see, as could Montmor, that there was a sense in which Denis was correct, that the common function of the blood in mammals justified an effort to discover in what sense there might be a kind of compatibility in the blood of different species, an effort that might lead in the long run to a better understanding of the nature of blood, and beyond that to a comprehension of ways in which blood of various species might possibly afford a means of aiding and preserving life. As a doctor and scientist, Perrault might have been expected to see that much could be learned from the massive rejection of foreign fluids by transfused animals and even human beings, when death did not intervene at once. Nor could Perrault grasp the idea that only by radical imaginative effort can the individual scientist advance his skill towards new generalized techniques and the knowledge of new bases for the advancement of science. Denis may have been rash in the view of his day and ours, but he anticipated medical history by about two centuries. His hard work and the enlightened improvisation of Emerez showed more of the working scientist than Perrault's somewhat supercilious and jaundiced condemnation.

It seems clear, three centuries later, that more was on trial than a particular device, a technique mechanically possible, even though destined to remain therapeutically useless for many decades. It served the cause of science in an age of love-philtres and the black mass, belief in magic, horoscopes, and witchcraft, that literate men, trained in the healing arts, should be seen building on ideas suggested by the discoveries of William Harvey and Jean Pecquet, following the experiments of Richard Lower, perfecting his technique, and facing the crucial trial after much testing of skills and instruments on dogs. Men were weary of controversy and rationalizing, as they were of phlebotomy and purgatives, and many were in a mood to welcome innovation. The intellectual slumbers of the University of Paris obviously could not be moved by street fights over cadavers for dissection or the early farces of Molière; the constant reference to authority had destroyed originality and the sense of fact in all but the most vigorous of minds.

The work of innovators in medicine and science contributed largely to the destruction of the self-complacent miasma into which a merely erudite humanism had declined. The men of the new sciences, Pascal, Pecquet, Auzout, and even Jean Denis, brought a vivid appeal to reality to bear on the human condition; their work demonstrates the charm that the experimental sciences had for readers and thinkers tired of dogmatic definitions and scholastic distinctions. The announcement of the rings of Saturn in Montmor's drawing-room in 1658, the discussions over the dissection of animals from the royal zoo in the royal library by anatomists from the royal academy of sciences, the description of the behavior of insects in hives and swarms, or of the circulation of sap in trees, and, along with this, of the reactions of living beings to the introduction of strange blood into their veins and arteries – all these tended to break the intellectual habits of the time and prepare the way for a century in which everything will be questioned and men will be surprised by nothing new.

Les gens de maintenant: Molière and his creations, Béralde, Toinette, and Angélique; François Bernier and Nicolas Boileau, with Guillaume de Lamoignon ('Proctecteur des Gens de Lettres,' as he is described by Moreri,) presiding in the background; Habert de Montmor, the wealthy *maître des requêtes*, sponsor and host of the chief assembly of scientists in Paris before the founding of the Académie royale des sciences, with his protégés Jean Denis and Paul Emerez – these, with many others, shared an outlook and a vision, a sense that all was not well with the established view of man and his mortal nature, that in spite of what La Bruyère would write, all had not been said, and there was much to learn. Their authorities were less Aristotle, Hippocrates, and Galen than William Harvey, the anatomist, Blaise Pascal, the physicist, and Jean Pecquet, the physiologist. For each of them, experiment, *l'expérience*, was the basis of knowledge, and in due course, *les gens de maintenant*, the now generation, found a way to express their rejection of the teachings of established institutions and break the intellectual authority of the faculties of the University of Paris.

CHAPTER SIX

Science and the human comedy: Voltaire

Nous sommes au temps où il faut qu'un Poète soit Philosophe.

(Voltaire, *Épître à Madame du Châtelet*)

INEVITABLY discussion of the eighteenth century returns to Voltaire. For better or for worse, he represents his time more fully than do any of his contemporaries. The opinions he arouses are expressed with vigor and precision.

He was a man of the Age of the Academies, as Fontenelle calls it; a member of eighteen of them, from Britain to Italy, from Scandinavia to Spain. He knew how to use the journals for the circulation of his ideas and the furthering of his ends. He wrote in every vein, in every style known in his age – heroic epic and its burlesque, satire, epigram, short lyric, long epistle, philosophic poem, ode and chanson, tragedy in five acts or three, comedy in prose and verse of every length, and libretti for the *opéra comique*. His prose ranged from extended history to ephemeral propaganda, in pamphlets of every size, *contes philosophiques* of a couple of pages or book-length novels, diatribes, dialogues, ironic hoaxes, long compendia alphabetically arranged – the substance of all this a private mingling of fact or legend with personal hypothesis and theory. His work shows his understanding of the power of the printed word to reach the reader and influence opinion, a power used sometimes with the generous manner of a *grand seigneur*, and as often with the lack of scruple of one who finds no need to exhibit even moderate honesty towards his public or his publishers.

The seventeenth century he knew well, as one born in its declining years, who had heard of it through men who had seen it at its height and appreciated it according to their private tastes. He wrote its history in his *Siècle de Louis XIV*, whose size impresses without overwhelming the reader with unmemorable detail. Working from documents available to him as *historiographe du Roi*, he enriched his book with chapters of anecdotes told by survivors, some of whom he had met in his youth. A modern historian, Émile Bourgeois, has edited the work for students' use, a congenial task, for he could respect the text even while correcting it in minor detail. Voltaire turned back to *le grand siècle* repeatedly in his literary work, from the early idealization of Henri IV in the epic *La Ligue*, revised in 1728 into *La Henriade*, on which contemporaries based his poetic fame, down to his later work as a literary critic. He produced an edition of the theatre of the two Corneilles with rich commentary for the benefit of an impoverished descendant of the poets' family; he wrote the apparatus for an edition of the comedies of Molière, with a short critique of each play, and he turned with sound judgment and exceptional delight at many points in his work to the high poetry and skilful technique of the tragedies of Racine. His controversial comments on the *Pensées* of Pascal, as read and circulated in his day, were published as the twenty-fifth of the *Lettres philosophiques*. The peculiar atmosphere of the seventeenth century recurs occasionally in his fiction, most notably in *L'Ingénu* (1767), whose hero, fresh from the wilds of the New World, meets several notable figures of that era in the course of unhappy adventures in France.

But most important is his preoccupation with the great movements of the period, its institutions, and its political and philosophical trends. He dwells on the Académie française, on Port-Royal and Jansenism, and on the Jesuit ascendancy; on the patronage of the arts, letters, and science under Colbert, and on the political settlement of Europe by the Peace of Westphalia in 1648. He describes the civil war of the Fronde and the reaction it aroused, the rising power of the monarch and the subsequent decline of the prestige of France under the impact of the military policies of *le Roi soleil*. Aware of the dominant role of king and ministries, and the institutions through which the royal will was expressed, Voltaire was equally alert to the importance of individuals – artists and builders, the original scientists and technicians, engineers of canals and waterworks, the architects of palaces and fortifications. He knew and spoke with knowledge of the work of foreign scientists, perhaps particularly of the English and the Scots, and the contribution they had made to the understanding of the natural world. Thus he came to describe the seventeenth century as *le siècle des Anglais*, so important were the productions of William Harvey, Isaac Newton, Edmond Halley, Christopher Wren, John Locke, the great Lord Bacon, and the indefatigable Robert Boyle.

In Voltaire's perspective, the new sciences had become as important as any other field of activity, not excluding theology, war, or politics. Developments in science had not only advanced knowledge of the external world, they had also created social structures in which scientists came together for the advancement of their work. Cooperation showed how much would be gained through discussion of common problems and the exchange of observations. The scientist had won recognition not only for his discoveries and inventions — the reflecting telescope and the micrometer, the exhaustion pump and the barometer, for instance — but also, and perhaps in the long run chiefly, for the development of a theoretic approach to phenomena which could be applied at any level of perception, in scale with any order of magnitude. By the end of the seventeenth century the informal gatherings and casual habits of amateurs had been replaced by a number of foundations with a newly defined purpose. The humanist academy, reinvented in Italy for social ends as much as for literary and rhetorical exercises, now became a pattern for meetings planned to promote the investigation and discussion of natural phenomena. Oratory, poetry, philosophical and philological debate, and aesthetics and criticism yielded place to experiment and observation, usually in the light of recognized classical and modern antecedents, to the compiling of knowledge of the natural world, the collection of specimens and artifacts, as well as of new books and ancient manuscripts of scientific interest.

While the activities of Blaise Pascal and Jean Denis have shown that the scientist does not always need the help of an academy, it is clear that no scientific institution can long exist merely on the random activity of amateurs. The participation of serious and motivated scientists is essential; substantial work, recognized to be of general utility or theoretical significance, alone could justify the support of an organization with intellectual pretentions. Talk, however brilliant, could not take the place of well-directed experiment and consistent observation. Science has always been expensive to support, and tangible results, either in pure knowledge or in advantages to the community in which the scientist worked, produced fruit for the group, in prestige and material resources for all. Able and commited scientists could look forward to several privileges from their association with a good academy: publication of their work for an audience capable of understanding and assisting them, readers who could offer critical and constructive comment, and the satisfactions derived from participation in the collective effort. Membership in the Cimento of Florence or in the Académie royale des sciences was a mark of status, for in these bodies selection was a recognition of merit. Moreover, especially in Paris, election to the academy gave a man a place to work, instruments and resources for research, the assistance of younger associates, publication in the distinguished *Mémoires*, access to the famous Bibliothèque du Roi, and, not least, a substantial stipend which did not impose regular hours of work. The sense of being a professional in the sciences was growing. Now a man could be set apart from the amateur virtuosi whose standards were not always rigorous, whose work depended on individual whim and private fortune.

At the same time, the publication of scientific works had become a profitable branch of the book trade, with wide international connections. Initiative in this came as much from the booksellers as from the scientists; the academies, with their collective support for significant books, found little difficulty in getting their work into circulation. By Voltaire's time, numerous scientific productions had become classics, reprinted and translated for a cosmopolitan public. Such were the *Saggi di naturali esperienze* of the Accademia del Cimento of Florence, edited by Lorenzo Magalotti in 1668, Thomas Sprat's *History of the Royal Society of London* (1667), the *Principia* of Isaac Newton, and many other works, by such as Descartes and Galileo, Edmond Halley, John Ray, and Robert Boyle. Even periodical literature found itself reprinted: the *Journal des savants*, the *Philosophical Transactions* of the Royal Society, Pierre Bayle's *Nouvelles de la république des lettres*, as well as less well-known serials, may be found in reprints and translations appearing sometimes long after their date of first issue. Most of these were the ventures of enterprising publishers who capitalized on the trends visible in the changing reading public and who sought the cooperation of more or less competent editors to produce the kind of book that would sell in the growing international market. These periodicals for the learned public usually appeared four times a year; the quarterly journal of today represents an old habit, a cultural pattern deeply ingrained.

As time passed, the trend towards specialization in the professions made itself apparent in new periodicals which sought the support of a limited public by catering to specific needs or tastes. Of all these, as Eugène Hatin's *Bibliographie de la presse périodique française* shows clearly, many were ephemeral, and their contents trivial. They had, however, introduced a new era in the literate culture of Europe, and by Voltaire's day they exerted a critical influence on writers and writing in every genre. The journalist opened the way for Marshall McLuhan's role in the multi-media. Voltaire himself was the first and in some ways the most talented exponent of the craft, using theatre, poetry and prose, journals and pamphlets, and hoax and parody, with profligate expenditure of his own energy and the goodwill of his printers. Apart from their value as an outlet for the polygraph, the journals had much serious content; they were the work in large part of educated men, scholars occasionally, who had suffered from intolerance and sought refuge in cities where their skills could be used for the circulation of ideas. News of the sciences and of scientists appeared frequently, and this offered the savant a means of establishing contact with colleagues whom he would otherwise never meet. Discoveries were announced and priorities confirmed – important for everyone who valued personal recognition for his work. And the pages filled with reviews of recent books permitted the general public who bought these periodicals to keep in touch with new ideas and changing taste.

The sense of novelty, implied in the words *news* and *nouvelles*, and the sense of the passing day, suggested by the words *journal, giornale,* and *Zeitung*, indicate an essential element in the attitude of the reading public. Eager for information concerning the latest discovery or the newest theory, the reader of 1700-25 had gained an outlook on the world of ideas very different from that of even a hundred years before. He had become increasingly aware, as discovery succeeded discovery, and as new techniques and theories displaced others, of changes in outlook and principles of thought that could no longer be neglected. The acceleration was perceptible even in the most conservative circles; men were saying, as the Jesuit René Rapin had said about 1675 in the house of the Premier Président of the Parlement de Paris, 'que depuis près de soixante ans, on a plus fait de nouvelles découvertes dans la Physique, par les expériences, par les observations, & par l'invention des nouveaux instrumens d'Astronomie, qu'on n'en avoit fait depuis plus de mille ans.'[1] As time passed, the rate of change increased; the time span fell to fifty years, then to two decades, as Robert Oppenheimer much later observed in a public meeting. That was in 1956; what he might have said today it is rash to guess. Derek Price, however, has been more specific: in 1959 he wrote that over the last three centuries the reach of science has been doubling in each successive generation, with the result that science itself grows as the cube of its reach, increasing two-fold in every dozen years. The statistics on which he based this estimate he found in the size of scientific libraries, in personnel, in expenditures, in the mass of publications, and in such intangibles as the intensity of specialization.

And yet, although libraries and bookstores in 1700 were full of titles in the sciences, many of them popularizations of recent work, along with accumulating numbers of current periodicals, syntheses to replace old philosophies were more and more difficult to achieve. The scientific mode had spread to such titles as William Petty's *Political Arithmetic* (1691) and to the adoption of his term 'political science.' The Abbé de Saint-Pierre, author of numerous 'projects,' the most famous being his *Projet pour rendre la paix perpétuelle en*

1 René Rapin, *Réflexions sur la philosophie ancienne et modern* (Paris 1676) pp. 202-3

Europe (Utrecht 1713), owed his empirical approach and his logic to close association with Fontenelle, the mathematician Varignon, and others in Paris in the 1680s.[2] Giambattista Vico was not sympathetic to the physical sciences, yet the title *La Scienza nuova* (1725, 1730) reflects a mode in his effort to renew historical studies through closer attention to facts. The frivolous appearance of the *Lettres persanes* (1721) does not hide Montesquieu's curious interest in the comparison of cultures and moral codes, developed in the belief that objective analysis of observed instances of human behavior would lead to valid and useful conclusions. The tendency to mathematicize the analysis of human impulses and reactions occurs in many forms; perhaps a kind of climax was reached in Maupertuis' *Essai de philosophie morale* (1749, 1750) in which a calculus of pleasure and pain is developed as a basis for understanding decisions which lead to action. The method is seen in the following axiom, presented early in the little book, setting the terms on which the argument is worked out: 'En général, *l'Estimation des Momens heureux ou malheureux, est le Produit de l'Intensité du Plaisir ou de la Peine, par la Durée.*' The italics are those of Maupertuis; one should add that he makes a fundamental distinction between *les plaisirs du corps and les plaisirs de l'âme*, and concludes that '*Tout ce qu'il faut faire dans cette Vie pour y trouver le plus grand Bonheur dont notre Nature soit capable, est sans doute cela même qui doit nous conduire au Bonheur éternel.*' These lines sum up the effort of a mathematician-*philosophe* to justify the deliberate choice of a Christian life on the grounds of a calculus of pain and pleasure, of physical satisfactions in contrast with pleasures of the soul, which latter may be reduced, he says, 'à deux Genres de Perception: l'un qu'on éprouve par la Pratique de la *Justice*, l'autre par la Vüe de la *Vérité*. Les Peines de l'Ame se réduisent à manquer ces deux Objets.'[3] This argument parallels the earlier paradox of Pascal, who treated the same problem of persuasion in the form of a Wager.

2 Merle L. Perkins, 'The Abbé de Saint-Pierre and the seventeenth-century intellectual background,' *Proceedings of the American Philosophical Society* 97 (1953): 69-76; and 'Late seventeenth-century scientific circles and the Abbé de Saint-Pierre,' ibid 102 (1958): 404-12. These articles open a wide vista on the activity of amateur and professional scientists in the late 1600s, and suggest the prolonged effects of such lines of investigation and speculation on the Enlightenment in general.

3 Pierre Louis Moreau de Maupertuis, *Essai de philosophie morale* (1750) pp. 5, 125,40. The correspondence of Maupertuis with Jean Bernoulli 11 in 1749 and 1750 indicates that this book, as well as the *Essai de cosmologie* and the *Réflexions philosophiques sur l'origine des langues*, was published originally in Basel, most probably by the Deckers, and not in either Paris or Berlin, as suggested by Brunet. See chapter 8 below.

Yet the dominant mathematical and physical modes of interpretation offered no clue to the contemporary scene. Europe in the first decades of the eighteenth century was no simple structure. An overwhelming diversity of governmental systems, republics of many forms, monarchies hereditary or elective, limited and unlimited in every degree, principalities and federations, free cities and theocratic states, lay everywhere to confound the political theorist. The patchwork of governmental systems was matched by an equally complicated medley of cultures. There was no single pattern of taste and tradition; the sophistication of the larger cities, Paris, London, Amsterdam, or Venice, offered no indication of the level of comfort or intelligence of market towns twenty miles away. The commercial usages of different centres, even of major international exchanges, were not affected by rationalizing tendencies: weights and measures, banking and trading practices, even modes of keeping accounts, remained as they had always been, the product of long centuries of slowly developed communal or tribal custom. Reform in this area, as in many others, would await a revolution on a continental scale before ways of doing business could be reduced, not to uniformity, but to reasonable consistency.

If synthesis was to be found, it had to be in the mind of the shrewd observer; little could be expected of practical men. Towards the end of his life, Voltaire wrote a tale, *La Princesse de Babylone* (1768), in which he uses once more his favorite pattern of the intelligent and curious traveler to record the chaos and diversity of the contemporary world. This time a pair of lovers, Amazan the Gangaride from further India and Formosante the princess, pursue one another in a vast *chassé-croisé* across Asia and Europe, from China and Siberia to Spain. As they go, a chapter, or at least a paragraph, is devoted to each country they visit, and the impression is finally conveyed that in all this spectrum of cultures there is no unity or uniformity, no coherence or consistency, that the only order that can be derived from the most extensive travel, the richest possible experience of the manners and customs of mankind, must be found in the tolerance, the liberal intelligence of the enlightened skeptic.

The discovery that liberty lies in the mind and cannot be found in the mechanisms of the natural order or in the laws of institutions is perhaps the chief legacy of seventeenth-century science beyond its own proper area of method and discovery. Voltaire's heroes, from the Sirian giant Micromégas, sired by Jonathan Swift on Maupertuis' version of Newtonian cosmology, through Zadig and Babouc, Candide and the Huron of *L'Ingénu*, to Amazan and his Formosante, all illustrate the same traits: an alert mind, free from prejudice and the limitations imposed by systematic doctrine, quick in sensibility, endowed with common sense and modern mathematics, seeking constantly to organize its knowledge and to understand its world. These heroes of the *contes philosophiques* seem to be the particular invention of Voltaire. They are as remote in their way from the polite gentlemen and comic maniacs of Molière as they are from the heroes of old romance or the Byronic rebels of another century. Their life may be a sequence of wild adventures, full of coincidences and characters in disguise, but it is in essence the life of intellectual comprehension, not the pursuit of an unattainable female, nor yet the search for an impossibly consistent morality desired by an Alceste, nor even for power to change a sorry scheme of things. After seeking knowledge of the world in the hope of finding a balance of good and evil, in the mission assigned to Babouc, or a place where a man can live with his own reason and be content, as does Candide, these heroes settle for a quiet opportunity for useful existence and the increase of knowledge, in company with a compatible female, if such can be found. They are projections of the life Voltaire was to lead at Ferney. The final pages of *Candide* show us the sublimed and rarefied ideal – the life of reason on a fertile and cultivated farm, with companions to share the labor and the satisfactions.

Such tales cannot be explained in terms of sensibility or literary form alone. Their heroes are not, like other figments, a product of the tradition of the novel or a response to social conditions and public taste. They recall Gordon Craig's preference for marionettes over actors, because marionettes do not corrupt ideas with personality. In the term *conte philosophique*, which describes Voltaire's stories and his alone, the operational word is the adjective, which from the mid-seventeenth century on refers more often to the natural sciences than to metaphysics. The word *philosophique* offers a clue to what Voltaire intended in the French edition of his letters about England, as well as in these narratives, long and short, each with a special kind of moral.

His first contact with Newtonian science is described briefly, if not very satisfactorily, in an essay of about 1745, a 'Courte Réponse aux longs discours d'un Docteur Allemand':

Lorsque j'étois en Angleterre, je ne pus avoir la consolation de voir le grand Newton, qui touchoit à sa fin. Le fameux Curé de Saint James, Samuel Clarke, l'ami, le disciple & le commentateur de Newton daigna me donner quelques instructions sur cette partie de la Philosophie qui veut s'élever au-dessus du calcul & des sens. Je ne trouvai pas à la vérité cette anatomie circonspecte de l'entendement humain, ce bâton d'aveugle, avec lequel marchoit le modeste Locke, cherchant son chemin & le trouvant: enfin cette timidité savante, qui arrêtoit Locke sur le bord des abîmes. Clarke sautoit dans l'abîme, & j'osai l'y suivre un jour, plein de ces grandes recherches, qui charment l'esprit par leur immensité. Je dis à un membre très éclairé de la

Société Roïale: Monsieur Clarke est un bien plus grand Métaphysicien que M. Newton; cela peut être, me répondit-il froidement; c'est comme si vous disiés que l'un joue mieux au ballon que l'autre: cette réponse me fit rentrer en moi-même.[4]

And Voltaire adds that he went on to puncture 'quelques-uns de ces ballons de la métaphysique,' and found that they gave off nothing but wind.

The rest of the 'Courte Réponse' is devoted to a defense of the sciences against the old-school philosophers, including even Leibniz and Malebranche, whom he finally compares with the group of fallen angels in *Paradise Lost* 11, who

> reasoned high
> Of Providence, foreknowledge, will, and fate,
> Fixt fate, free will, foreknowledge absolute,
> And found no end.

One wonders why Voltaire did not quote the rest of the last line: 'In wandering mazes lost.'

The first detailed and explicit evidence of Voltaire's Newtonian outlook occurs, of course, in the fifteenth, sixteenth, and seventeenth *Letters concerning the English Nation* (1733), in the composition of which he had had the assistance of Maupertuis, at this time the leading French critic of the Cartesian cosmology. In the preceding year, Maupertuis had published not only his Latin treatise on the shapes of stars, but also a little book on the theory of gravitation, under an innocuous title, *Discours sur les différentes figures des astres*. These scientific publications made it necessary for Voltaire to produce something much more advanced than his superficial knowledge would permit, particularly because the first printing of the *Letters* was to appear in English, for a British public sophisticated in Newtonian ideas.[5]

However, as early as 1730, the new cosmos had had its effect on Voltaire.

---

4 The 'Courte Réponse' is quoted here from the earliest edition available, *La Henriade et autres ouvrages du même auteur, nouvelle édition* ('A Londres' [Rouen] 1750) 2: 312. Alterations of this text in later printings modify the sense somewhat: in the 1757 Cramer *Œuvres complettes* 3: xiv-xv we read 'Clarke sautait dans l'abîme, et j'osais croire l'y suivre. Un jour, plein de ces grandes recherches, je dis à un Membre très-éclairé de la Société Royale: Monsieur Clarke est un bien plus grand Métaphysicien que Mr Newton ... ' This reading is accepted by the 1768 quarto, also from the Cramer presses, except that 'Royale' is omitted after 'Société.'

5 Some of the circumstances under which the *Letters concerning the English Nation* were written are discussed in my article in *The Age of the Enlightenment* referred to above, chapter 2, note 1.

In that year, a new printing of the *Henriade* was published in Paris, imprinted 'A Londres, chez Hierome Boldtruth, à la Vérité,' in which Voltaire's participation is visible in the preface and variants.[6] In a passage in the seventh canto, the new cosmology replaces not only the vortices of Descartes but also remnants of the Ptolemaic heavens as they had been adapted to conventional religious art. In the *editio princeps* of the epic, *La Ligue* (1723), Henri IV, hero of the epic, is visited in a dream by his most famous ancestor, Saint Louis, and is swept into a vision of the celestial universe:

> Henry crut à ces mots, dans un char de lumière,
> Des Cieux en un moment pénétrer la carrière;
> Comme on voit dans la nuit la foudre et les éclairs,
> Courir d'un Pôle à l'autre & diviser les airs.
>
>   Parmi ces tourbillons que d'une main féconde,
> Disposa l'Éternel aux premiers jours du monde,
> Est un globe élevé dans le faîte des Cieux,
> Dont l'éclat se dérobe à nos profanes yeux;
> C'est là que le Très-haut forme à sa ressemblance
> Ces esprits immortels, enfans de son essence,
> Qui soudain répandus dans les Mondes divers,
> Vont animer les corps et peupler l'Univers.
> Là sont après la mort nos âmes replongées,
> De leur prison grossière à jamais dégagées,
> Quand le Dieu qui les fit les rappelle en son sein,
> D'une course rapide elles volent soudain
> Comme au fond des forêts, les feuilles incertaines,
> Avec un bruit confus tombent du haut des chênes,
> Lorsque les Aquilons messagers des Hivers,
> Ramènent la froidure & soufflent dans les airs.
> Ainsi la mort entraîne en ces lieux redoutables,
> Des mortels passagers, les troupes inombrables.

Comment on this mish-mash of conventional imagery is hardly necessary; it is typical of much of the second-rate poetry of the preceding age of classical

---

6 *La Henriade, édition critique*, O.R. Taylor ed., in the *Complete Works of Voltaire* (Geneva, Institut et Musée Voltaire 1970) 2. The edition of 1730 is described on p. 238; the passages cited in the text of this chapter are found on pp. 511-13. I am indebted to Owen Taylor for verifying this variant reading, which confirms his view that Voltaire took an active part in the preparation of this curious clandestine edition.

imitation and popular theology. In any case, Voltaire now replaces it with something much more concrete and acceptable to his *philosophe* public. Saint Louis and Henry together

> dans un char de lumière
> Des Cieux en un moment traversent la carrière.
> Tels on voit dans la nuit la foudre et les éclairs,
> Courir d'un pôle à l'autre, et diviser les airs;
> Et telle s'éleva cette nue embrasée
> Qui dérobant aux yeux le Maître d'Élisée,
> Dans un céleste Char de flamme environné
> L'emporta loin des bords de ce Globe étonné.
>   Dans le centre éclatant de ces orbes immenses
> Qui n'ont pu nous cacher leur marche et leurs distances,
> Luit cet Astre du jour par Dieu même allumé
> Qui tourne autour de soi sur son axe enflammé.
> De lui partent sans fin des torrens de lumière.
> Il donne en se montrant la vie à la matière.
> Et dispense les jours, les Saisons, et les ans
> A des Mondes divers autour de lui flottans.
> Ces Astres, asservis à la loi qui les presse,
> S'attirent dans leur course, et s'évitent sans cesse,
> Et servant l'un à l'autre et de règle et d'appui
> Se prêtent les clartés qu'ils reçoivent de lui.
> Au delà de leur cours, et loin dans cet espace
> Où la matière nage, et que Dieu seul embrasse,
> Sont des Soleils sans nombre, et des Mondes sans fin.
> Dans cet abîme immense il leur ouvre un chemin.
> Par delà tous ces Cieux le Dieu des Cieux réside.
>   C'est là que le Héros suit son céleste guide,
> C'est là que sont formés tous ces esprits divers
> Qui remplissent les corps et peuplent l'Univers.
> Là sont après la mort nos âmes replongées,
> De leur prison grossière à jamais dégagées.
>   Un Juge incorruptible y rassemble à ses pieds
> Ces immortels Esprits que son souffle a créés.
> Sous cent noms différents le Monde entier l'adore.[7]

7 These lines are quoted from the *Œuvres de M. de Voltaire* (Amsterdam 1732) I: 123-4.

FIGURE 5 This ornamental vignette by Jacob Folkema was used to adorn Voltaire's *Elemens de la philosophie de Neuton* (Amsterdam, Ledet 1738). While suggesting the scientific and artistic avocations of the day, none of the instruments shown are Newtonian, nor do any of the sixteen cherubs appear to be engaged in post-Newtonian scientific exercises.

The conventional imagery persists, but in a footnote Voltaire warns the reader of the presence of Newton.[8] The new astronomy has made its appearance in a modern epic. The rotating sun is at the centre of the planetary system; the orbits, the movements, and the mass of its members have been calculated. Solar light is the basic energy, giving life to matter, and establishing units of time – days, seasons, and years. Gravitational force determines the orbits of the planets, even though to an observer these stars seem to approach and separate. And far beyond this realm are countless universes of suns and planets, unveiled by means of telescopes developed since Henri's time, but whose presence here lends a prophetic touch to the whole passage, appropriate in the epic vision. The cosmos of Copernicus and Kepler, Newton and Flamsteed, has found its way into one of the most widely read poems of the century. More and more the traditional bric-à-brac of the seventeenth-century poet yields to the intellectual realities and the perceptions of a new age.

From about this time, Voltaire devoted much attention to the physical sciences and mathematics, in the company of the Marquise du Châtelet and the various scientists who found their way to Cirey – Maupertuis, the young Alexis Claude Clairaut, Samuel König, and others. On 30 October 1732, in a letter to Maupertuis from Fontainebleau, Voltaire asks whether he is to believe in 'le grand principe de l'attraction de mr Newton ... Ma foy dépendra de vous, et si je suis persuadé de la vérité de ce sistème comme je le suis de votre mérite je serai assurément le plus ferme neutonien du monde.' The reader derives little sense of an authentic scientist from these lines, nor yet from a letter of November 3 in which he thanks Maupertuis for two demonstrations which clarify his problems.[9] Now he writes, 'Me voicy neutonien de votre façon. Je suis votre prosélite et fais ma profession de foy entre vos mains.' Voltaire's excitement over the new philosophy breaks out in this second letter; his enthusiasm is not that of a scientist evaluating a fruitful hypothesis, but that of a convert to a new religion. Maupertuis' new book, which Voltaire has not yet seen, the *Discours sur les différentes figures des astres* is awaited eagerly:

Je ne doute pas que votre livre ne vous fasse bien des disciples ... Vous serez l'apôtre du dieu dont je vous parle. Plus j'entrevois cette philosophie et plus je l'admire. On trouve

8 The note is to the line 'S'attirent dans leur course, & s'évitent sans cesse,' and reads 'Que l'on admette ou non l'attraction de l'illustre M. Newton, toujours demeure-t-il certain que les globes celestes, s'approchant et s'éloignant tour a tour, paroissent s'attirer et s'éviter' (edition of 1732, 1: 124).
9 The letters of 30 October and 3 November 1732 are numbered D533 and D534 in *The Complete Works of Voltaire* 86: 243-7.

à chaque pas que l'on fait, que tout cet univers est arrangé par des lois mathématiques qui sont éternelles et nécessaires.

Isaac Newton 'est notre Colomb. Il nous a menez dans un nouvau monde, et je voudrois bien y voiager à sa suitte.' Voltaire's letter is almost incoherent in its excited ejaculatory style. Perhaps he thought this was the best way to impress Maupertuis with his newly found enthusiasm, or it may be that it was a completely spontaneous outburst. In either case, the receipt of such a letter would be unique in the experience of the mathematician; as a working scientist he would scarcely regard its writer as a serious colleague, but rather as a lively young man, potentially useful on some occasions, but necessarily to be watched with care. The amenities of eighteenth-century correspondence can lead the modern reader into interpretational traps. The *serviteur* with which the usual letter ends is rarely *obéissant* and almost never *très humble*, and when the compliments accumulate in the last paragraph, let the reader beware!

The revision of the *Letters concerning the English Nation*, and the preparation of the French version, aptly called the *Lettres philosophiques*, to appear in 1734, had emphasized in Voltaire's mind the differences between the English outlook on natural science and the views generally held in France. This antithesis, extending to other subjects — religion, politics, literature, as well as food and drink — remained part of his mental baggage, elaborated frequently in later writings, the balance of preference wavering according to particular circumstance. Voltaire was not by any means the first to notice the peculiar quality of British science; various French travelers had visited the Royal Society in its earliest days, and some of them, Samuel de Sorbière and Balthasar de Monconys in particular, had written about the meetings in Gresham College. And about 1683, the fabulist Jean de La Fontaine had written, in 'Le Renard anglais' dedicated to Lady Harvey:

> Les Anglais pensent profondément;
> Leur esprit en cela suit leur tempérament;
> Creusant dans les sujets, et forts d'expériences
> Ils étendent partout l'empire des sciences.
> Je ne dis point ceci pour vous faire ma cour;
> Vos gens à pénétrer l'emportent sur les autres;
> Même les chiens de leur séjour
> Ont meilleur nez que n'ont les nôtres.
> Vos renards sont plus fins.[10]

10 This passage was called to my attention long ago by Louis Cons.

The poet was echoing the views of many Frenchmen; the freedom of discussion, the ingenious devices, the new outlook of many British scientists, all were remarked by his contemporaries. In Voltaire's day, however, much had happened; the atmosphere had changed, and in several quarters it was felt that there was disloyalty in writing with favor of foreign science and learning, perhaps especially when the British were involved. The *Anglomanie* so commonly regarded as typical of the French eighteenth century was balanced by a degree of xenophobia in some high circles.

During the years spent with Madame du Châtelet at Cirey and elsewhere, Voltaire read widely in Newton and his commentators, Clarke and Pemberton and others. He was acquainted with Francesco Algarotti, author of *Il Neutonianismo per le dame*, as well as with Charles-Marie de La Condamine of the Académie des sciences; both of these accepted Newton's theory. With them and others, he was following the debate over the shape of the earth, already noticed in the *Letters concerning the English Nation*. The conflicting views were soon to be tested by observation and experiment; the Académie des sciences was organizing expeditions, whose findings were expected to settle the question, the first to the Presidency of Quito, on the Equator, in the Vice-Royalty of Peru, and another, under the direction of Maupertuis, to Lapland. This Baltic adventure will be discussed in Chapter 8; here we may note that the most fanciful product of this prolonged controversy was Voltaire's *Micromégas*, the tale of a giant from Sirius who visits the earth, landing in a little pond, where he finds a company of minute astronomers returning from the Arctic Circle. Their minds are marvelously developed in mathematical matters, but lamentably ignorant of fundamental problems of metaphysics and epistemology.

The agnostically inconclusive ending of *Micromégas* represents as well as any text the general outlook of Voltaire in middle life. His view of the sciences committed him to a neutral position in religion and philosophy; rejecting final causes, he could hope to devise a method deriving from physics useful in analyzing the behavior of human beings in the historical process as well as in the creation of narrative, whether in fiction or in the theatre. He was well aware, as were most men of his time, of the role of chance in the lives of men and nations, but this facile interpretation satisfied neither novelist nor historian. Some means must be found to make sense of the actions and reactions of men as they wrestled with destiny. It was unscientific to assume a providential inspiration for actions that could be explained by traits of character or native genius, by the pressures of politics or social or economic conditions, by impulses deriving from religious emotions or even from philosophic speculations. It was equally unscientific to refuse to seek and evaluate causes, to credit everything to the hazards of daily life. A criterion was needed, a means of classification of the phenomena of history.

The analysis which he finally reached may be seen in the epigrammatic antithesis of *esprit* and *mœurs*, most familiar in the title given to his most comprehensive work of history. *Mœurs*, of course, is the Latin *mores*, the traditional, conservative, stabilizing element in society, while *esprit*, *spiritus*, is the intelligence, the creative, critical, inventive energy, in constant conflict with *mœurs*. Together the words compose the title and describe the substance of the *Essai sur les mœurs et l'esprit des nations*, a general account of some two thousand years of history, not limited, like other 'universal' histories, to the civilization of the west. It should be added that the title was not found all at once; the 'Avis des éditeurs,' signed by les Frères Cramer in the edition of 1756, describes the book as 'cette *Histoire philosophique du Monde*,' and in the next paragraph '*l'Histoire des usages & des mœurs des Nations depuis Charlemagne*.' The title-pages of this edition and of the edition of 1757 read 'Essay sur l'Histoire générale, et sur les Mœurs et l'Esprit des Nations depuis Charlemagne jusqu'à nos jours'; by 1768, the shortened title by which the work is commonly known appears in the quarto edition, also by the Cramers of Geneva.

This gradual evolution of a title suggests that Voltaire was not writing a history based on a model, but rather that after he had laid out his massive work he found that one phrase described its substance better than another, and that all along he had been making the contrast of tradition and original genius, manners and mind – in short, analyzing the facts recorded for their contribution to the processes of the history of mankind. The antithesis of *esprit* and *mœurs* permits the description of events as the product of two forces, custom and inventive deviation, related much as momentum and gravitational pull combine to produce a trajectory or orbit, so that the course of events may be traced in terms of a parallelogram kin to that used in ballistics. This kind of diagram was quite familiar to Voltaire; in fact his letters to Maupertuis of 1732 contain rough sketches of lunar orbits in which the diagram is clearly seen. As one reads the historical works, as well as the fiction, one finds that what is customary and traditional combines with what is novel, even revolutionary, to produce events and dénouements. This analysis permits insight into movements and trends; it introduces a measure of causal explanation where nothing very satisfactory had been possible before. The two concepts, *esprit* and *mœurs*, have the advantage of being precise enough for most of Voltaire's readers. The categories are capacious, and justified by common usage.

In this way, history, the most complex of the humanist disciplines, including as it does an account of politics and war, and, particularly for Voltaire, the development of the arts and sciences, of manners and customs, becomes intelligible only as recognizable and measurable patterns may be found in it.

The philosophical tales illustrate Voltaire's analytic method as well as his histories; they are indeed a commentary on his own time, in which even the oriental fiction of *Zadig* allows the critic of society his moments of pointed satire. The sequence of events, the chain of action and reaction, cause and result, presented in backgrounds easily recognized by readers, interests Voltaire much more than the development of character, the analysis of motive and sentiment, or the creation of emotional catharsis. Intellectual attitudes and instinctive impulses of personages are never in doubt, even in moments of lively comedy. Each tale presents its little problem in dynamics: a group of persons, objects in unstable equilibrium, is given a push, the resulting oscillations and repercussions are recorded, and the tensions revealed produce the final pattern as their energies are absorbed. *Candide* offers a typical example of a chain of events moving by interacting causes to an unforeseen conclusion, which is the only possible dénouement once the various impulses are resolved.

There is, of course, a major difference between the play of natural forces in the physical universe and the operation of human energies in history, the evolution of institutions in society. While what may happen in the mechanics of the cosmos is not subject to moral judgment, being neither good nor bad so far as human responsibility is concerned, the deeds of mankind in history must be viewed and valued according to their capacity to produce happiness or one or more of its innumerable opposites. Voltaire's lively indignation at man's capacity for inhumanity, even in the throes of an entirely impersonal earthquake, is evident in numerous chapters of the *Précis du Siècle de Louis XV*, which narrate in sober prose events that only too dismally anticipate most of the anecdotes so vividly combined in the most famous of the *contes*. Here also, Voltaire's respect for ingenuity, for the trades and skills that are the mark of man's dignity as well as the source of most of his science, is made as clear as is his dislike of the cruelty and brutality of the ignorant and the intolerance and arrogance of the powerful. The ultimate ideal is the garden to be cultivated, physical reality to be understood and managed with intelligence and taste, in fuller comprehension of natural process and natural law. Finally, conflicting motions come to rest, the momentum of life itself dominates the present and its sequel.

In this way, among the contributions of the science of the seventeenth century in France to the culture of the era of Voltaire, nothing is more evident than the emphasis on the role of experience, the importance of the raw material of life, recorded and analyzed by the use of carefully tested methods. With the rest of his contemporaries, Voltaire took an outlook as well as material from those who had something new to say. To subject matter of current significance he brought a spirit usually empirical, and sometimes disillusioned to the point of pessimism. He did not entirely forsake the aristocratic, historically humanist poetic tradition; in the last year of his life he wrote a tragedy, *Irène*, on a Byzantine theme in alexandrine couplets. At the very end of the *ancien régime*, the best French poet of the age, André Chénier, wrote, in his *Invention*,

Sur des pensers nouveaux, faisons des vers antiques!

The scientific revolution of the seventeenth century produced an intellectual attitude – *des pensers nouveaux* – rather than anything so comprehensive as a culture. The verses were still *antiques*. It did not reach any very large proportion of the educated public; the noise scientists have made in modern history is often a little out of proportion to their numbers. It affected some non-scientists very deeply, among them Voltaire, Montesquieu, and Diderot. Others – poets, dramatists, novelists – were mostly untouched by it. The effect on morals, on social relations, on the law, was delayed by the inertia perceptible in those areas except in revolutionary times. Thus Voltaire, among a few others, marked a stage in the separation of the loyalty of the man of letters from the humanist culture in which he grew up. The issues posed by science led him to add new dimensions to the skeptical tradition to which he naturally belonged as a French moralist, and so we have, finally, a tendency to bring the creative writer to fruitful acceptance of new lines of investigation and analysis.

As we have seen, this is late, a century late, and one wonders why. Any answer must be tentative, but it might be suggested that there had been no persuasive synthesis of the new knowledge before that of Isaac Newton, that the Cartesian and Gassendist systems had made little appeal to the imagination or the common sense of writers and readers. In *Les Femmes savantes* (1672) Molière had mocked the pedantic women who simultaneously admired the atoms of Epicurus and the subtle matter of Descartes, quite unaware of the inconsistency of their views. For Molière, these phrases were in the vogue, and the scientific movement of the age of the academies was ironically reflected in the sophisticated ambition of the blue-stockings. Voltaire's distrust of systems was evident in others long before he was born: the shrewd observer Molière knew there was no virtue in phrases without objective reference, just as the nascent Académie des sciences rejected doctrine without substance in perceptible fact. Molière was not here, nor even in *Le Malade imaginaire*, attacking science and its true directions, nor its view of truth as an hypothesis to be tested. On the contrary, he accepted the radical skepticism that science involves, its suspension of judgment until the truth is made clear by experiment. The brief reference in the mouths of his learned ladies, almost unique in his major comedies, is sufficient indication that he shared the outlook of the scientists of his day, that he knew there was but slight understanding of such matters in his audience, and that he could put in a word, almost unnoticeable in its context, for *la saine philosophie*, as Voltaire would call it.

On the basis of this and other references it could reasonably be suggested that men of ordinary common sense rejected both the corpuscular theory, with its round or hooked particles as the invisible basis of all matter, and the fantastic vortices of Descartes, operating in a plenum which still permitted comets and satellites to wander apparently at random through a universe which, though full, yet allowed free movement to all astronomical objects. Lying beyond perception, these concepts were in no wise demonstrable by experiment. As cosmic metaphors they had no possible use in a scheme of things of which a man could make a working model, a system of parts in which real movement could be envisaged.

On the other hand, by the use of Newton's laws, astronomical observations could be related with daily phenomena. The flight of a stone from a sling and the motion of planets and comets could be calculated with equal precision. The force that brought the apple from the tree at Woolsthorpe was the force that held the moon in orbit and determined the shape of the earth as well as that of Saturn's rings, and the light that criss-crossed infinite space was the light dispersed by a prism on the wall of a darkened room.

That all these stimulants for a dormant imagination were based on simple mathematical laws was of the utmost importance to the minds of those ready for a fresh outlook. From this revolution came in the long run a new analysis of history on a world-wide scale, extending over a period vastly longer than the six thousand years calculated from the Old Testament by Archbishop Ussher. This opened an immense range of new ideas on the history of the earth and the origins of the solar system, and destroyed the barrier that had held man earthbound in spirit as well as in body. So many old explanations long taken for fact were now destroyed; so many ancient symbols of permanence now became fugitive appearances. But it must be repeated: all this did not come at once, nor for everyone; for many men of the eighteenth century, it was as if Newton had not lived.

No doubt it should be added that the worth of a novel, by Voltaire or by anyone else, does not spring from the fact that it is coherent with the Newtonian world scheme, or that it embodies a scientific outlook or analyzes events by a method parallel with one of those used by scientists. Its value depends on organic aesthetic qualities independent of philosophic assumptions. One does not have to have a conscious world view in order to create characters; the interplay of personalities and the discovery of comedy and tragedy in daily life are recorded from intuitive and unscientific observation. The eighteenth century managed to produce literature of permanent value without a basis in scientific psychology; it learned how to go beyond the type patterns of traditional comedy by seeking out features of class and status, by studying the influence of trades and professions on the minds and behavior of human beings.

But even in all this there was still something lacking, something an expanding science could contribute. Voltaire's view of man, in history, in fiction, or in the theatre, hardly succeeded in organizing the life of the individual on the basis of drives and impulses analytically conceived. The pathmaking work of the introspective Rousseau was not yet woven into the fabric of the time. The creation of characters whose lives were so many evolving sequences of states and outlooks, each depending on the complex of preceding experience, merging imperceptibly into its successor, had to wait for the development of a new range of perception in a form available to author, publisher, reader and critic alike. There is a history to be written of the debt of the Romantic novelists and historians, poets and dramatists as well, contemporaries of Balzac, Stendhal, Sainte-Beuve and Guizot, as well as of Hippolyte Taine, to the various branches of biology explored in the Jardin des plantes and elsewhere, to the associationist and other schools of psychology, and to the great teachers in the medical schools.

In the age of Voltaire, the physical world was not a habitat for natural man viewed biologically; it was a stage on which rudimentary organisms played out a human comedy. Nature was a *décor* with small value beyond that of pointing up the drama. The development of a literature in which there would be really interesting relationships between men and their world had to wait for sciences other than physics and astronomy — for geology, for a more complete geography, for the understanding of climate and the biosphere that Alexander von Humboldt would bring, for a synthesis of man in nature. The science of the early eighteenth century could not contribute in these respects, because it had not faced problems on this scale. It could not offer the creative writer, the historian, the dramatist, the novelist, and the poet the method and criteria he would need. Valid and useful as it may have been, the synthesis which that century reached in what it called 'natural philosophy' was in many ways far from complete.[11]

Much of this chapter has been revised from a contribution to a symposium held at Harvard University on the occasion of the retirement of Percy Bridgman and Philipp Frank in 1956. In its original form this article was published in *Daedalus* 87 (1958): 25-34, and again in Gerald Holton, ed., *Science and the Modern Mind* (Boston, Beacon Press 1958) pp. 19-29. Permission of the American Academy of Arts and Sciences to use the text of this article and its title for this book is gratefully acknowledged.

Quotations from Voltaire in this chapter are taken from editions as nearly as possible contemporary with their composition, and have been left with spelling and punctuation untouched. There is no specific source for the ideas presented here; Voltaire has been a topic for discussion and reflection since about 1720, and the vast literature about him forms an indigestible and sometimes unappetizing mass. As his own work is much more agreeable to quote than that of most of his critics, it has seemed invidious to single out any for special notice. R.I.P.

11 See Harcourt Brown, ed., *Science and the Creative Spirit* (see bibliographic note to chapter 1) pp. 110-20, where some of the topics suggested here receive further development.

CHAPTER SEVEN

Voltaire and
British science

IN THE twenty-fourth and last of the *Letters concerning the English Nation*, 'On the Royal Society and other Academies,' Voltaire turns from the theatre and 'The Regard that ought to be shown to Men of Letters' to the topic of academics. Here he makes special reference to the Royal Society of London and, in the latter part of the letter, to the functions performed by the three most important French bodies, the Académie française, the Académie royale des sciences, and the Académie des inscriptions et belles lettres. The reader of the mercurial Voltaire has learned not to expect a formal conclusion in his books; there is no reflection on preceding chapters, no résumé of their content. The tempting possibilities of a witty analysis of English character or of a sage prediction of the results of the interaction and mutual influence visible in the ranks of the leisured classes of France and England do not lead him to skate on the thin ice of generalizations over the uncertain waters of national differences (figure 6). Typically, he shoots his bolt on each topic in its respective chapter, and shows no desire to coordinate his findings into a larger and perhaps more revealing synthesis. Voltaire's world is a place where countless independent processes go on together, offering small hold for the mind that must seek a unity to relate parts to one another or to a hidden purpose.

This is his way in the histories: *Le Siècle de Louis XIV* and the *Histoire du Parlement de Paris*, for example, each end with a chapter seemingly chosen at random, leaving the reader to come to his own conclusions, to think about the problem as may please his fancy. One can forgive the witty endings of *Micromégas*, *Zadig*, and *Candide*, which tie the knot without ending the train

232 LETTERS *concerning*

LETTER XXIV.

ON THE

ROYAL SOCIETY

AND OTHER

ACADEMIES.

THE *Engliſh* had an Academy of Sciences many Years before us, but then it is not under ſuch prudent Regulations as ours, the only Reaſon of which very poſſibly is, becauſe it was founded before the Academy of *Paris*; for had it been founded after, it would very probably have adopted ſome

of

FIGURE 6 A product of exile in England, Voltaire's *Letters concerning the English Nation* were in large part composed for publication in London before being rewritten in French as the *Lettres philosophiques*. Most of the twenty-fourth chapter appears to represent the author's command of the language; this page is taken from the first edition (London 1733).

of thought. However, in the last of these brilliant and often profound letters, with its curious reversal of the general trend of Voltaire's judgment on English institutions and its avoidance of any examination of the historical reasons which might explain the different forms taken by scientific and literary organizations in Paris and London, the reader feels with some justification that more might and should have been said. One is therefore willing to admit that when Voltaire settled down at Cirey seriously to rework his early writings, he could reasonably accept the censorship of the *Lettres philosophiques*, particularly as the ban extended only to the title of the book, without reference to the text of the various letters. The identity of the book was destroyed with its structure, while the content could be reprinted, revised, augmented, under the non-committal title of *Mélanges d'histoire et de littérature* and issued separately or as part of an edition of his collected works. A writer who already had a sound piece of work, the *Histoire de Charles XII*, published in several editions in two languages, who had announced a history of the age of Louis XIV on revolutionary lines, and who was planning a universal history as well as numerous contributions in other genres, could well spare what added reputation these uneven and ill-assorted letters could bring.

It is not original to remark that events in the life of Voltaire had much influence on the composition and timing of his books, and that his social and public relationships created changing points of view even in the most objective of his writings. Reversals of outlook in him do not always exhibit weakness; very often the converse is true, and a revision of an attitude demonstrates courage in supporting an unpopular cause and insisting on the need for an appeal against an accepted verdict. In the revisions of this chapter another aspect of the growth of Voltaire may be traced, development in an area in which the counsel of friends, the increase of information, and the maturing of judgment, working with changes in the structure of his subject-matter, simultaneously with the variables in the poet's own irritability, bring him ultimately to adopt a friendly view where once he had been inclined to scoff. The *Letters concerning the English Nation* were Voltaire's first venture into prose on other than conventional historical and literary topics, and the book's success, commercial as well as polemical, was sufficient to turn him quickly into what may loosely be called a publicist, although it did not lead him to abandon his role as dramatist and poet. In spite of prohibitions the book circulated widely, as such books will. Its place in the English trade was maintained long after its identity in French was lost; editions in its original form have been produced at intervals down to the present day, in spite of a version closer to Voltaire's changing taste in the translation attributed to Smollett late in the eighteenth century.[1]

To Voltaire in 1733 the Royal Society of London appeared less effective than the Académie des sciences because the latter was 'bien réglée' as well as endowed with stipends for its members, two qualifications which Voltaire regarded as 'les plus nécessaires aux hommes.' Older than the French foundation, the English organization had not been able to benefit by the experience of others, 'for had it been founded after, it would very probably have adopted some of the sage laws of the former, and improv'd upon others.' Another advantage of the French body lay in its rigid requirements for admission:

In France, 'tis not enough that a Man who aspires to the Honour of being a Member of the Academy and of receiving the Royal Stipend, has a love for the Sciences; he must at the same Time be deeply skill'd in them; and is oblig'd to dispute the Seat with Competitors who are so much the more formidable as they are fir'd by a Principle of Glory, by interest, by the Difficulty itself, and by that Inflexibility of Mind, which is generally found in those who devote themselves to that pertinacious Study, the Mathematicks.

The encouragement given to men of science and the defined scope of the French society were two reasons why its publications were better. The fact that Sir Isaac Newton was a Fellow of the Royal Society was not enough to give it a superior position in the esteem of the unprejudiced, for such a genius as his belonged 'to all the Academies in the World, because all had a thousand Things to learn of him.'

This letter gives the impression that in 1729 or 1730 Voltaire had had slight acquaintance with scientists and science. It is not easy to account for the general tone of his comments on the Royal Society. Gustave Lanson's elaborate investigations into the sources used offer no plausible explanation, and one can but surmise that Voltaire was repeating with slight variation comments heard in circles he had frequented in London or absorbed from various books which satirized that obvious butt, the virtuoso, and his preoccupation with material things. Very few of those under whose influence Voltaire came in England were associated with the scientific movement; there is no indication that in his three years in England he exchanged letters with any known scientist. On the other hand, Jonathan Swift was the author of the satire on the scientific academy in Laputa, and Alexander Pope was to publish his *Essay on Man*, with its passage on the limitations of science, in the same year

1 The variants of the numerous French printings of the *Lettres philosophiques* may be studied in the edition by Gustave Lanson, Société des textes français modernes (Paris, Marcel Didier 1909) revised by A.M. Rousseau, 1964. Citations from the *Letters concerning the English Nation* are taken from the London *princeps*, 1733.

as Voltaire's *Letters*. His correspondence during his exile was largely concerned with his private affairs – money, his movements in and out of England, and the publication of *La Henriade* and the short writings connected with the epic – not at all with philosophical questions, including science.

On the other hand, the Royal Society itself, with its relatively large membership, including many dilettanti, its flexible requirements for admission, and its laxness in collecting dues, was open to criticism as a typical product of the empirical British, another product of the confusion and compromise so often found when a committee of Anglo-Saxon amateurs undertakes a project demanding precise thinking and coordinated effort. In comparison, in Voltaire's mind, as no doubt in that of many Englishmen of the day, the professional qualifications of the membership of the Académie royale des sciences, its regulated program for the advancement of the various sciences in balanced order, and its permanence assured by the royal purse, must have justified a degree of contempt for the badly organized amateurs of London.

These considerations may explain a little more clearly why Voltaire can praise the academies of Paris in so far as their work is useful and planned for the prestige and advantage of the nation, even though he may be critical of the futile compliments and formal discourses of the Académie française. This latter body, he says, could justify its existence by producing the useful books planned at its inception, the grammar and dictionary, as well as modernized editions of the classic authors of France, so that there might be a perpetually renewed stock of texts suitable for the moral, aesthetic, and linguistic instruction of the young. The emphasis placed on the French academies and their functions makes it plain that Voltaire at this moment had only the slightest interest in describing the Royal Society, and no great desire to praise it. His purpose was to speak of intellectual affairs in France, utilizing the scheme projected by Jonathan Swift in order to suggest how the bodies already existing in France could be made of greater use to the nation. The point of reference central to the whole discussion is Swift's project for a British academy; it is with this that French institutions are compared, and only secondarily with the Royal Society.[2]

Subsequent French printings of this letter show many revisions of the paragraphs concerning the scientific organizations, while the rest of the text remains largely unchanged. By 1748, Voltaire will have reversed his position

2 The project of Jonathan Swift was set forth in a pamphlet, *A Proposal for Correcting, Improving & Ascertaining the English Tongue in a Letter to the Most Honourable Robert Earl of Oxford & Mortimer* ... (London 1712); *Prose Works of Jonathan Swift*, Herbert Davis, ed. (Oxford, Oxford University Press 1957) 4: 5-21. See Davis' discussion in the introduction, pp. xi-xvi.

on the value and functions of the Royal Society. While his knowledge of British science grew and deepened in the years at Cirey, particularly from 1732 to 1739, at the same time he was developing from a clever and somewhat superficial literary man into one of the most alert and subtle interpreters of human affairs that the eighteenth century would produce.

The transformations of this letter do not, however, solely represent changing perspectives and purposes on the part of Voltaire; there were numerous developments in the customs and usages of the Royal Society itself. That body had been open to legitimate criticism in the last years of the presidency of Isaac Newton, up to his death in 1727. Publication of the *Philosophical Transactions*, never very prompt, had fallen seriously behind; the fees of many Fellows were in arrears; the practice of election on the nomination of a single member had been abused. The meetings themselves seem to have lacked interest; the account of a French visitor in 1725, a year or so before Voltaire's arrival in London, suggests that a lack of order characterized the assemblies. This visitor, the Abbé Joseph Alary, a moving spirit of the Club de l'Entresol which was to annoy the police of Paris a few years later, attended the session of 1 July 1725 in the company of the president, Newton himself, who placed his guest beside him, opened the meeting, and promptly fell asleep. At the end of the session, everyone, including the Abbé, signed the register; then Newton took Alary home to supper, where the talk that had begun early in the morning began again and continued until nine o'clock at night.[3] In passing, one notes that Voltaire does not appear to have been present at a session of the society; a member a few years later of eighteen of the academies of Europe, he took more pleasure in the prestige of belonging than in the occasion for academic activities. His description of the Royal Society always lacks the sense of reality that such travelers as Monconys and Sorbière were able to offer after visiting England in 1663.

The death of Newton marked the end of an era in the history of the society, and with the election of Sir Hans Sloane, and a consequent change of focus, a period of activity and reorganization began. A strong effort was made to bring the *Philosophical Transactions* up to date; new statutes for the election of members were proposed in 1728 and revised in constitutional form in 1730. Attempts were made to collect fees from delinquent Fellows and to clear the lists by limiting membership to those who had a genuine interest in natural philosophy. Leaders in European science were now invited to membership in the society. While under Newton there was no consistent policy in

---

3 Joseph Alary's visit to the Royal Society is described in Grimond's 'Essai historique sur Bolingbroke' in his *Lettres historiques de Bolingbroke* (Paris 1808) 1: 155.

this respect, during Sloane's presidency hardly a year passed without the addition of a notable figure from the ranks of French science. In 1727 Bernard de Jussieu was enrolled, followed in 1728-9 by Maupertuis and three less well-known men, and in 1730 by Montesquieu and the Jesuit Louis-Bertrand Castel of color-organ fame. Fontenelle, secretary of the Académie des sciences, was elected in 1733; next year he was followed by Dortous de Mairan, Duhamel du Monceau and J.-A. Nollet, and in the four years from 1737 to 1740 Clairaut, Réaumur, Le Monnier, and the famous Buffon were admitted. In this way a large proportion of the members of the Académie des sciences came to be Fellows of the Royal Society. The new statutes permitted foreigners to become members without the payment of dues or immediate formal registration at a regular meeting, and so the foreign list grew continuously until another change of circumstance led to further reorganization. Not all the later elections brought in men as high in scientific esteem as those listed here.

In these years, roughly 1733 to 1748, the revisions of the paragraphs on learned societies reflect changes in the Royal Society itself as well as in Voltaire's own circumstances and thinking. He had begun to understand more clearly the function of such an organization, and could recognize its potential value to French and other scientists. Yet in spite of a personal conviction that the quaint English had certain advantages over the more civilized French, the *Letters concerning the English Nation* are not free of a sense that matters concerning the higher faculties would be handled better in France if only official circles could accept the implications of the new sciences, *la saine philosophie*, as they had come to be called. It is not always clear just what impulse may have determined the tone of any specific comment; Voltaire could react quickly to the obvious and striking, and come more slowly to a balanced view, a more mature judgment. He had been impressed by the elegant and massive format of the *Histoire* and the *Mémoires* put out each year by the Académie, as well as by the elaborately equipped missions sent out from time to time to observe and experiment in distant lands; he was not yet ready to undertake the critical reading of scientific work. The passage of years, especially those spent at Cirey with Madame du Châtelet and her learned guests, brought him to a judgment based on fuller knowledge of the facts as well as to a better understanding of the strange processes responsible for the institutions that man builds to free his spirit for the work that he must do.

The revisions of this letter in subsequent years represent successive stages in Voltaire's opinions at the same time that they reflect developments in the historical context. Almost all of the *Lettres philosophiques* reappeared in the

Œuvres of 1739, published by Ledet of Amsterdam, rearranged, and augmented by new writings in prose and verse under the non-committal title of *Mélanges*, which circumvented the prohibition that had fallen on the original book. In the passage that concerns us, the first three paragraphs and one sentence of the fourth are retained without major alteration; at that point the vague reference to Newton 'who belonged to all the Academies of Europe' is replaced by a passage in which it is pointed out:

C'est de l'Académie de Londres que nous tenons les expériences sur l'Electricité, la téorie du feu, celle des fluides, les Loix de la gravitation, les Expériences sur la lumière, celles sur la pesanteur, la réfraction dans le vuide, les phosphores, l'aberration de la lumière, les Telescopes de réflexion, le plomb laminé, la machine qui tourne par le moyen du feu, les sphères qu'on nomme oreri, etc., que de sujets d'Emulation!

This is the first reference to the diversity of fields in which British scientists had reached significant results, and the first hint that there was much in the moral and social atmosphere of London that was advantageous to the life of the intellect. These words result from days and nights at Cirey, divided between extensive reading, experiments, and discussions of questions of natural philosophy.

This first hint of the reversal of Voltaire's position leads to a complete rewriting of the opening paragraphs of the chapter. In 1742, in another edition of the *Œuvres*, under the imprint of Bousquet of Geneva, Voltaire has rewritten the fourth paragraph, omitting the comparison of the publications of the two academies; he now sees that, impressive as the French *Mémoires* and *Histoire* may be, they are not essentially superior to the *Philosophical Transactions*. Revising the text of 1739, he writes with more emphasis,

Quoique la Société royale de Londres manque de l'encouragement, c'est elle cependant qui nous a fait connaître la nature de la lumière, les loix de la pesanteur, la réfraction dans le vuide, l'étendue de l'électricité, l'aberration de la lumière, le secret du Phosfore, la machine Hidraulique à feu, le calcul de l'infini, etc. Cette Compagnie auroit-elle mieux fait, si elle eut été bien payée?

The new sentences are brief, but they suggest that Voltaire had been profiting from a reading of the *Transactions*, and reflecting to good purpose on the comparative values of different kinds of scientific work. They are not unworthy of a man who has brought out one of the earliest books on Newtonian philosophy for the French public, and presented a memoir on 'Fire' to the Académie des sciences. It is not surprising to find that he has been in touch with British scientists and amateurs, and that his contacts are not solely through books.

Among several who had been active in bringing French and English scientists into closer contact was the wealthy Martin ffolkes, at this time (1739) vice-president of the Royal Society, who would be elected president to succeed Hans Sloane in 1741.[4] He was no scientist, as were his immediate predecessors, but it should be said that this amateur of books, antiquities, scientific instruments, and the arts did as much by means of his genial personality and his assiduous attention to the social graces as another might have done by eminence in strictly scientific circles. Anxious to continue Sloane's work of renewal in the society, ffolkes had travelled widely, and established contacts in many places. His interest in books was not merely that of a collector, and he was interested in seeing good books published appropriately. A visit to France in 1739 strengthened his position in the community of virtuosi, and on his return his contacts with French and other scientists were maintained by correspondence.

The two known letters which passed between Voltaire and ffolkes in 1739 and 1743 may not be all that were exchanged at this time, but they offer some details of the relationship between two amateurs of the sciences.[5] The first is a brief note dated from Paris 'the 10th october n.s. 1739' and reads:

I do myself the honour to send you this little answer i was oblig'd to write against our antineutonian cavillers.

I am but a man blind of one eye expostulating with stark blind people who deny, there is such Thing as a sun.

I'll be very happy if this conflict with ignorant philosophers may ingratiate my self with such a true philosopher as you are. I am
    Sr

        yr most humble obedient servant

                                      Voltaire

The 'little answer' was a copy of Voltaire's *Réponse aux objections principales qu'on a faites contre la philosophie de Newton*, a tract written in

4 Martin ffolkes is discussed in the introduction to my article 'Mme Geoffrin and Martin ffolkes: six new letters' in *Modern Language Quarterly* 1 (1940): 215-41.

5 The letters to Martin ffolkes of 10 October 1739 and 25 November 1743 are taken from the edition of the correspondence of Voltaire by Theodore Besterman in the *Complete Works* (see chapter 6, note 6) volumes 91 and 93; the letters are numbered D2088 and D2890 respectively. Sir Gavin de Beer reviews some of the subject matter of the present chapter in an article 'Voltaire et les sciences naturelles' in *The Age of the Enlightenment* (see chapter 2, note 2) pp. 35-50; the letters to ffolkes are also indispensable to his account.

support of his *Éléments de la philosophie de Newton*, published in Amsterdam in 1738, and already in circulation in Paris. Another copy of the *Réponse*, with a similar brief note was sent to Robert Smith, professor of astronomy at Cambridge.

At the time of these letters Voltaire was well known to English readers. Several of his works had been published in London: the quarto *princeps* of *La Henriade* (1728) had been followed by three or four editions, in one of which we have seen a solidly Newtonian variant reading. The most popular of Voltaire's works was the *Histoire de Charles XII*, circulating in English editions from 1732, and reprinted at once in Dublin; at least ten printings were made before 1740, not counting the editions in French, some of them under a 'Basle' imprint, which were obviously of London origin. The *Letters concerning the English Nation* date from 1733 in London and Dublin printings; the Irish publishers worked from proof sheets sent from London by fast mail before final revision and date of issue. Most of the early tragedies appeared in England: *Œdipe*, with a dedication to George I, has become a rarity, but *Zaïre* and *Alzire* were well known, particularly in the translations by Aaron Hill (1736); both plays had been presented successfully in the London theatres. *Brutus* and *La Mort de César* had not been so well received. John Hanna's book *The Elements of Sir Isaac Newton's Philosophy... Translated from the French* had been published in 1738, and Voltaire's name was already associated with current science.

It may be, therefore, that the sending of the *Réponse aux objections* to Martin ffolkes and Robert Smith can be interpreted as an attempt to indicate that the French poet and dramatist, the author of a popular history, had some claim to serious recognition in English intellectual circles. The letter quoted above does not read like an overture to a new acquaintance; its wording and manner indicate that the two men had met, and that Voltaire felt sure enough of ffolkes' attitude to justify this invasion of privacy. It is perhaps not unfair to associate these two letters with a rather devious attempt to promote his candidacy for the forthcoming vacancy of the secretaryship of the Académie des sciences. Martin ffolkes was worth cultivating; as a prospective president of the Royal Society and a correspondent of Réaumur, Maupertuis, and the witty hostess of *philosophes*, Madame Geoffrin, his approval could not fail to aid the repute of Voltaire in Paris.

The life of Voltaire is full of periods in which one feels the need of even more documents than we have or are likely to possess. In these years, 1739-43, Byron's phrase, 'historian, bard, philosopher combined' is singularly apt. Voltaire turns with meteoric speed from verse to prose, from theology to the theatre, from new publications to hasty revision of the old.

The scientific period of his life is not entirely over, but the historian has begun his work in earnest, and Voltaire is busy with criticism of Biblical fundamentalism. On a mundane level, he is entangled in the interminable lawsuits of the Châtelet household; he spends much time in Brussels; he meets Frederick of Prussia at Cleves and Rheinsberg; he is confined to Paris with illness; he struggles to get *Mahomet ou le Fanatisme* adequately staged and published; and he is busy with the publication, suppression, and finally the revision of the *Anti-Machiavel* of a new and squeamish king of Prussia. Voltaire can live through these things and much more, keeping his head and a sense of direction; the student of his life plods after him, trying to play Boswell to a Catherine-wheel, and finding the flying sparks a little hard to follow.

The occasional biographer who mentions it regards Voltaire's election to the Royal Society of London as a kind of miraculous honor conferred on him without sufficient reason or justification by works. Churton Collins, Archibald Ballantyne, and S.G. Tallentyre, not to mention more recent writers, barely mention the fact; further elections to academies in Bologna, Edinburgh, Berlin, and other cities arouse little interest. The deliberate quest for academic recognition is often not understood, or is perhaps disapproved of, by the modern biographer or historian. It seems clear that Voltaire was seeking status as a man of European letters, that he wished to claim kinship with forward-looking men in every nation, without antagonizing any establishment. Many interests had come to complicate his originally rather simple concern with England and British affairs. He had had to publish abroad; now he would benefit from necessity, and through the booksellers and publishers he would seek out a wider reading public, the intellectual elite, men of science and philosophy, with new books, revisions of his older works, translations, and perhaps even an edition of *Complete Works*, modeled on the *Œuvres complètes* pouring from presses in the Netherlands and Switzerland.

Another goal, and one less nebulous, was that of the post of secretary to the Académie des sciences. Fontenelle had been *secrétaire perpétuel* since 1699, and now, at well over eighty, was being permitted to retire. Voltaire thought his own qualifications as a writer would make him a competent candidate; he had read and written on science, which in the usage of the day entitled him to think of himself as a *philosophe*. As a disciple of Isaac Newton, author of a notable popularization of the new theories now becoming the vogue in France, he felt sure that his position among the younger academicians was secure enough to allow himself to count on their support. What he had not considered was that he had very little of the temperament of a *secrétaire perpétuel*; no person who knew him would expect that he could confine himself to academic business for more than a few weeks or days, or that he could, as he had said of Fontenelle, 'rendre fort bon compte des idées des autres.'[6] Impersonality was the last trait that one could expect to find in Voltaire. Behind closed doors, the post was offered to Dortous de Mairan, whose qualifications were impeccable: he was a physicist and mathematician, and a professional on whom all could count for loyal service. He accepted for three years only, and Voltaire began to think that he might have a second chance when de Mairan retired. The post of secretary would lend prestige to the deistic, philosophic, and humanitarian ideas he held dear.

But in 1743 Dortous de Mairan was replaced by the relatively unknown Grandjean de Fouchy, and Voltaire's path to this particular position of influence was indefinitely closed. He turned instead to seek a chair in the older Académie française, less significant in terms of ideas, but ranking higher in social eminence. There had been many occasions on which he could have been a candidate for one of the forty *fauteuils*, for the turnover in this body is fairly constant; now it was the turn of the elderly Cardinal de Fleury to vacate his seat, and with the death of one of his chief opponents, Voltaire thought that election in his place would be a sweet revenge. Once more he failed, losing to the obscure Bishop of Bayeux, and his letters tell of his exasperation. Repeated efforts to gain academic recognition were typical of his time and culture, common in Paris of the *ancien régime*, and even much later.

The grapes were sour, and he turned to the pursuit of still another objective, in which success brought an emotional satisfaction that shines clearly through many pages of his writing of these and later days. He presented himself according to the statutes for election to the Royal Society of London, and to assure himself of success, he obtained, in ways that the documents do not make clear, the support of a number of distinguished Fellows. Highest in rank was the Duke of Richmond, Lennox and Aubigny, grandson of Charles II and Louise de Kéroualle; with him was the Earl of Macclesfield, who became president of the society in 1751, succeeding ffolkes. James Bradley, astronomer royal, whose brilliant work on the aberration of light had been mentioned in the latest revision of the 'Letter on the Royal Society and other academies,' also signed, along with ffolkes himself. A former secretary of the society, James Jurin; Shallett Turner, regius professor of modern history at Cambridge, and William Jones, mathematician and a member of the house-

---

6 Gustave Desnoiresterres came to a different conclusion, largely on the basis of a somewhat satiric comment by La Beaumelle: 'Cet emploi convenait singulièrement à M. de Voltaire qui est le premier homme du monde pour écrire ce que les autres ont pensé.' It is not clear that the author of *Voltaire et la société au XVIIIe siècle: Voltaire à Cirey* (Paris 1871), p. 356, was entirely aware of what traits of character could be expected of a *secrétaire perpétuel* by his professional colleagues.

hold of the Earl of Macclesfield, completed the list of sponsors. Perhaps ffolkes mobilized this impressive group on Voltaire's behalf; in any case it would be difficult to select from the roll of Fellows of 1743 seven men of equal eminence in as many fields, representing the various classes that offered support and dignity to the rank of Fellow.

The sponsorship of Voltaire's application was an unanswerable argument for his election once the set course of ten successive postings in meeting had been run, and on 3 November 1743 the vote to admit him was favorable. The certificate, number 271 in the first volume (1731-50) in the archives of the Royal Society, dated 14 April 1743, was posted at weekly intervals from April 21 to June 23, with the exception of 26 May, presumably for a holiday, and finally on 27 October. In the text of the certificate, Voltaire is described as 'A Gentleman well known by several curious and valuable Works,' recommended 'as well skill'd in Philosophical Learning, likely to be a useful member, and in every way well qualified and deserving of the Honour he desires.'

Voltaire expressed his thanks for this election in a letter to Martin ffolkes written from Paris on 25 November 1743; as its language characterizes its writer better than any words of a commentator, it is given here verbatim:

Sr,

One of my strongest desires was to be naturaliz'd in England; the royal society, prompted be you vouschafes to honour me with the best letters of naturalisation. My first masters in yr frée and learned country, were Shakespear, Adisson, Dryden, Pope; j made some steps afterwards in the temple of philosophy towards the altar of Newton. J was even so bold as to introduce into France some of his discoveries; but j was not only a confessor to his faith, j became a martir. J could never obtain the privilege of saying in print, that light comes from the sun and stars, and is not waiting in the air for the sun's impulsion; that vortices cannot be intirely reconcil'd with mathematics; that there is an evident attraction between the heavenly bodies, and such trash.

But the liberty of the press was fully granted to all the witty gentlemen who teach'd us that attraction is a chimera, and vortices are demonstrated, vho printed that a mobile lanch'd out from on high describes a parabola because of the resistance from the air below, that t'is false and impious to sai, light comes from the sun. Even some of them printed, *colla licenza dei superiori*, that Newton ridiculously mistook, when he learn'd from experience the smaller are the pores of transparent bodies, the more pellucid they are; they alleg'd very wisely that the widest windows give the greatest admittance to light in a bed chamber. These things j have seen in our booksellers shops, and at their shops only.

You reward me sir for my sufferings. The tittle of brother you honour me with is the dearest to me of all titles. J want now to cross the sea to return you my hearthy thanks, and to show my gratitude and my veneration for the illustrious society of which you are the chief member.

Be pleas'd sir to be so Kind as to present yr worthy bretheren with my most humble respects. J hope you will sai to mylord duke of Richemont, to mr Jurin, mr Turner etc. how deeply j am sensible of their favours.

J am with the greatest esteem, and the most sincere respect
    Sr
        yr most humble and faithfull servant, j dare not say brother

                                                Voltaire[7]

This letter, now in the collections of the Royal Society, justifies the view that Voltaire did not come seriously under the influence of British science during his exile and that his early contacts had been literary and political. He seems to regret that he had not sought to meet scientists; at times in other letters of this period, to César de Missy for example, he talks of making a leisurely way over the white roads of Picardy and the uncertain waters of the Straits of Dover to the home of liberty in politics and science, where a poet is not condemned to lies and flattery. There is a bitterness in the letter, too; now close to fifty years old, with a record of publication more diversified and more solid in worth than any Frenchman of the time, Voltaire is justifiably harsh with his compatriots who are firmly entrenched in the senior academies and reject his claim to recognition. And there is a clear sense that there are qualities in the British outlook, in the open atmosphere of the Royal Society, that will have much to contribute to the academies of Europe. Voltaire could not have torn himself from the society of his Lady Newton, but at least he was now able to come closer to understanding a great English institution than he had as an exile fifteen years before.

By 1748, then, he was ready to give this much altered chapter on academies its final form, and he seized the opportunity offered by the new edition in preparation in the shop of George Conrad Walther in Dresden to bring out a thoroughly revised text. Suppressing entirely the outdated comparison between the Académie des sciences and the Royal Society, he begins with an assertion that great men, Homer and Phidias, Sophocles and Apelles, Vergil and Vitruvius, Ariosto and Michelangelo, were all formed independently of academies; Tasso had nothing but criticism from the Accademia della Crusca, and Newton did not owe his discoveries on optics, on gravitation, on the integral calculus, or on chronology to the Royal Society. 'A quoi peuvent

7 See note 5 above.

donc servir les Académies? à entretenir le feu, que les grands génies ont allumé.'

Then a brief paragraph descibes the form and functions of the British organization. Formed in 1660, it is older by five years than the Académie des sciences:

Elle n'a point de récompenses comme la nôtre. Mais aussi elle est libre. Point de ces distinctions désagréables, inventées par l'abbé Bignon, qui distribua l'Académie des sciences en savans qu'on payait, & en honoraires, qui n'étaient pas savans. La Société de Londres, indépendante, & n'étant encouragée que par elle-même, a été composée de sujets qui ont trouvé, comme je l'ai dit, le calcul de l'Infini, les lois de la lumière, celles de la pesanteur, l'aberration des étoiles, le Télescope de réflexion, la pompe à feu, le microscope solaire, et beaucoup d'autres inventions aussi utiles qu'admirables. Qu'auroient fait de plus ces grands hommes, s'ils avoient été pensionaires ou honoraires?

The rest of the chapter remains without notable change. The description of Swift's proposed academy, the weakness of the oratory of the Académie française, the wise utility of the publications of the Académie des belles lettres, marred in places by triviality, the purposes of the Académie des sciences – all are set forth with only minute verbal changes. Finally the chapter expresses Voltaire's desire to see men of science undertake to unite theory and practice for the utility of all, while men of letters undertake the preparation of a set of revised classics for the education of youth.

These last comments on the Royal Society mark a point beyond which the present letter does not go. Voltaire has gained access to documents which permit him to be more precise about the dates of foundation of the two scientific academies, and one may surmise that it was at this time that he wrote various passages about scientific matters in the *Siècle de Louis XIV*. The book is in general eulogistic of Louis and his government, which lends a little significance to a passage in a chapter 'Des Sciences':

Quelques philosophes en Angleterre, sous la sombre administration de Cromwel, s'assemblèrent pour chercher en paix des vérités, tandis que le fanatisme opprimait toute vérité. Charles second, rappellé sur le trône de ses ancêtres par le repentir & par l'inconstance de sa nation, donna des lettres-patentes à cette académie naissante; mais c'est tout ce que le gouvernement donna. La Société roiale, plustôt la société libre de Londres travailla pour l'honneur de travailler. C'est de son sein que sortirent de nos jours les découvertes sur la lumière, sur le principe de la gravitation, sur l'aberration des étoiles fixes, sur la géométrie transcendante & cent autres inventions qui pourraient à cet égard faire appeller ce siècle, le siècle des Anglais, aussi bien que celui de Louis XIV.[8]

This passage appeared in the twenty-ninth chapter of the first edition of the *Siècle de Louis XIV*, and remained unaltered through subsequent printings. The text of the whole book was included in the *Essay sur l'histoire générale, et sur les mœurs et l'esprit des nations* as published by the Cramers of Geneva in 1756, where it is numbered 203; now a final chapter, 212, 'Des Beaux-arts en Europe du tems de Louis XIV,' a temporary conclusion of this vast panorama of history, attempts to lend perspective to the *Essay*. Voltaire begins by remarking that the great public disasters with which his pages have been filled 'sont à la longue effacés des régistres des tems. Les détails et les ressorts de la Politique tombent dans l'oubli. Les bonnes loix, les instituts, les monumens produits par les Sciences et les Arts, subsistent à jamais.' And he proceeds to point out that Michelangelo, Raphael, Ariosto, Tasso, and Galileo count for more than the most famous popes, that Cromwell may be forgotten but Newton remains, and that in the age of Louis XIV, which he describes as extending from about 1640 to 1730, the greatest progress was made by the English, listing Milton, Dryden, and Pope as poets, Addison in prose, and the scholars and theologians for their vigor and learning. Then he adds:

C'est surtout en Philosophie que les Anglais ont été les Maîtres des autres Nations. Il ne s'agissait plus de systèmes ingénieux. Les Fables des Grecs devaient disparaître depuis longtems, & les Fables des modernes ne devaient jamais paraître. Le Chancelier Bacon avait commencé par dire qu'on devait interroger la Nature d'une manière nouvelle, qu'il fallait faire des expériences: Boyle passa sa vie à en faire. Ce n'est pas ici le lieu d'une Dissertation physique; il suffit de dire qu'après trois mille ans de vaines recherches, Newton est le premier qui ait découvert & démontré la grande loi de la Nature, par laquelle toute partie de la matière pèse vers un centre, & tous les Astres

---

8 *Le Siècle de Louis XIV publié par M. de Francheville, conseiller aulique de sa majesté, et membre de l'académie roiale des sciences et belles lettres de Prusse*, 'A Londres, chez R. Dodsley, à la Tête de Tully en Pallmall. M.DCC.LII' (2: 327). A 'Préface de l'editeur' reprinted here from the Berlin edition of 1751 is of more than passing interest, as its author takes the occasion to praise 'un monarque à qui la vérité n'est pas moins chère que la gloire, & qui, de l'aveu de l'Europe, est aussi capable d'instruire les hommes que de juger de leurs ouvrages.' If, as seems probable, Voltaire himself is the author of these words, it is not impossible to find in them an echo of the discontents which had led him to leave Paris in 1750 and take refuge at Sans Souci. The 'monarch who loves truth no less than glory' is, of course, Frederick II.

sont retenus dans leur cours. Il est le premier qui ait vû en effet la lumière; avant lui on ne la connaissait pas.[9]

After this there are three paragraphs on aspects of Newtonian science and one devoted to Halley's charting of the stars and his observation of the variation of the compass needle. Then Voltaire adds:

Cette indifférence que nous avons pour les grandes choses devenues trop familières, et cette admiration des anciens Grecs pour les petites est encor une preuve de la prodigieuse supériorité de notre siècle sur les anciens ... Cette dispute entre les Anciens et les Modernes est enfin décidée, du moins en Philosophie. Il n'y a pas un ancien Philosophe qui serve aujourd'hui à l'instruction de la jeunesse chez les Nations éclairées.

This leads to his famous comparison of Locke and Plato, after which he passes to the contributions of the north of Europe; the work of Hevelius and Leibniz leads to Italy and the science of Galileo. The chapter hardly lives up to its title; what a modern reader thinks of as *les beaux arts* is not much discussed, but the chapter indicates a serious revision of the outlook of 1750, illustrating the fact, perhaps obvious by now, that Voltaire long continued to broaden the basis for his comments on the learning and science of Europe, embodying results of reading and reflection in the texture of his major works.

The original *Letters concerning the English Nation* were soon outdistanced in the years of omnivorous reading at Cirey; the structure of that book in its French form was destroyed, its components passing into the continually growing series of *Mélanges*. The tone of the letters on religion, literature, and institutions in England was not lost, even though their impact was reduced when other topics were added as Voltaire's range of interests grew broader. Comments on British ways and manners continue, in the historical works, as we have seen, and in some of the latter *contes philosophiques*, in a wisely comic chapter of the *Princesse de Babylone*, in the *Histoire de Jenni* – which Voltaire took to be a boy's nickname – and the *Oreilles du Comte de Chesterfield*. The criteria which Voltaire derived from his experiences in London persist, and have their influence in the *Dictionnaire philosophique* and the *Questions sur l'encyclopédie*.

Through these years, the chief British organization with intellectual pur-

9 Voltaire, *Collection complette des œuvres* (Geneva 1756) volume 17, *Essay sur l'histoire générale* vii, p. 157

poses remained a landmark in Voltaire's thinking, its standing enhanced in his mind in the course of some ten years of scientific writing and reading. He never became a scientist in any valid sense; he remained an amateur who played with words and ideas, interested in little beyond what was immediately in sight. Because he was averse to systematic thinking, he could hardly understand a theory except as something to believe in or reject, never outgrowing the frame of mind in which he had written to Maupertuis at the time of his conversion to Newtonian ideas. To the end he clung to a few firmly held views which prevented him from understanding a scientist whose imagination was not bound by conventional perspectives. He went so far in the interpretation of contemporary thought and institutions, and could go no farther. His writings are useful as a guide to what much of the eighteenth century thought and believed; they hardly point to areas in which science or philosophy could make notable advances.

Voltaire had great gifts: an impeccable style, a sense of comedy, and a skill in satire; he saw mankind with much objectivity, and he understood many of humanity's motives, in so far as a highly personal irritability would permit. He could evaluate human deeds and social structures in terms of the suffering they inflicted or the degree in which they were economically desirable and good. His art with words contributed to his influence; precision of statement and clarity of argument made him the leader of men and women in many lands, as well as the arch-enemy of innumerable others. This facility of expression does not make him easier to comprehend, for personal traits which surface in his work impede the evaluation of his intent. These are particularly evident when he is on the attack, determined to destroy someone deemed his foe. His relationship with Maupertuis is a case in point, in which one can see the immense danger of a little knowledge, and the havoc that an arrogant amateur can produce.

An earlier form of this chapter appeared as an article in the *University of Toronto Quarterly* 13 (October 1943): 25-42.

CHAPTER EIGHT

From London to
Lapland and Berlin

WHEN PIERRE Louis Moreau de Maupertuis left Paris for London late in May of 1728, he carried letters of introduction to Sir Hans Sloane, successor to Isaac Newton in the presidency of the Royal Society, and *associé étranger* of the Académie royale des sciences. In a brief letter of 22 May, the botanist Bernard de Jussieu remarked he would have liked to accompany Maupertuis 'qui porte cette lettre.' Just over three months later, on 4 September, Maupertuis wrote from Paris, thanking Sloane for courtesies and kindnesses, in particular that he had been admitted as a Fellow of the Royal Society. Thus the 'six months' usually assigned to the visit to England is an exaggeration, and Maupertuis' exposure to science and life in London must be limited to about twelve weeks in June, July, and August of 1728.

There seems to be no record of what Maupertuis did during those weeks. The usual educated visitor would see the Tower, St James's Palace, some of the new Wren churches, and most particularly St Paul's, completed in 1710 and still brilliantly white at the time of Maupertuis' visit. Of special interest would be Sloane's house in Bloomsbury and his rich botanical garden in Chelsea, as well as the Royal Observatory where Flamsteed had worked with notable results until his death in 1719. The *Journal Book* of the Royal Society records his presence at two meetings, 23 May and 27 June, both old style; on June 20 he was proposed as Fellow by the mathematician Abraham de Moivre, and a week later he was ballotted and elected. Although the society did not meet during July and August, there would have been other occasions in which he could gather first-hand impressions of Newtonian scientists, a breed of men he had not frequently met before. Pierre Brunet says that one cannot exaggerate the scientific importance of this visit, 'qui apparaît vraiment décisif dans l'orientation ultérieure des travaux de Maupertuis.'[1]

However, the influence exerted on Maupertuis by English culture in general was much less profound than that felt by Voltaire, whose contemporary sojourn *outre-Manche* extended from 1726 to some time in 1729. The mathematician seems to have felt no impulse to learn English. Most of those he met would be more or less fluent in French or Latin; the education and travel of young Englishmen of those days gave them some skill in languages. Sloane, for instance, had been in Paris and Montpellier in 1683-4, and had been given a medical degree by the shadowy university in Orange. Pierre Desmaizeaux, with whom Maupertuis later exchanged letters, and de Moivre were both Huguenot refugees; a letter of 1 September 1729 to William Jones, also a mathematician, was written in Latin.[2] Cromwell Mortimer, one of the secretaries of the society, who was at this time editing the *Philosophical Transactions*, would be using both French and Latin in his daily occupations.

All the evidence indicates that Maupertuis' purpose in visiting England was quite different from that of the exile Voltaire. As a professional scientist of standing among his colleagues, Maupertuis' use of time was subject to the standards expected of an academician as well as to the strictures of his conscience. On the other hand, Voltaire was an amateur in every sense of the word; a product of the Jesuit educational system as well as of the libertine society of the French Regency, he had wide and uncoordinated interests, and followed his whim into almost every corner of English life. The intellectual chaos of his *Letters concerning the English Nation* makes his position as a dilettante quite clear. In contrast, Maupertuis was no amateur of human affairs; he showed no interest in British politics or religious variations, or in literature, the theatre, or history, so far as his subsequent writings indicate. He was a scientist, a mathematician, convivial and a good mixer in social gatherings, but he was not seriously interested at this time in anything beyond his mathematics and his own branch of the physical sciences.

In 1728 the work of Newton was already known in French scientific circles, even if not accepted as sound theory. Newton had been named one of the first eight *associés étrangers* on the reorganization of the Académie in 1699; the *Principia* had been reviewed in the Netherlands soon after publication, and discussed in the *Acta eruditorum* of Leipzig in the 1690s. The

---

1 Pierre Brunet, *Maupertuis* (Paris 1929) is a good general account of the man and his work.
2 The letter to William Jones, dated 'Parisiis, 1ª Sept. 1729' has been published by S.P. Rigaud in *Correspondence of Scientific Men* (Oxford 1841) 1: 281.

second edition of the *Principia* had been sent in 1714 to Fontenelle, secretary of the Académie des sciences, to the Abbé Jean Paul Bignon, in charge of the Bibliothèque du Roi, and to the Académie, to which institution went also six copies of the third edition in 1728. The more accessible *Opticks* had been analyzed in ten sessions of the Académie by Étienne François Geoffroy in 1706, and a copy of the English edition sent to Varignon in 1718. Pierre Coste's translation of this work (Amsterdam 1720 and Paris 1722) was presented to the Académie in 1722.

Meanwhile the resistance of the Cartesians was growing; a widely read book by the Abbé Philippe Villemot, *Nouveau Système ou nouvelle explication du mouvement des planètes* (Lyon 1707) had appeared, offering arguments regarded as trivial by such leading Cartesians as Johann Bernoulli and Leibniz, but still influential among the reading public who found the *tourbillons* easy to understand. It cannot be denied that many Frenchmen and others hesitated to accept the idea that an Englishman who had shown no great respect for the academies and scientists of the continent could possibly develop a theory that would put the vortices to rout. Science was still a matter of belief and unconscious prejudice for the majority, and it would take much education and liberation of spirit to accept the view that truth has no nationality and demands no patriotism.

Maupertuis was a Newtonian before he left France, but he gained confidence in England from the discovery that an entire academy of intelligent men was convinced that the Cartesian cosmos of vortices, nearly unanimously accepted in France, was without foundation in observed fact or confirmation in mathematical or physical theory, and was, in fact, a figment of the imagination, a useless substitute for a sound theory of the universe. For British scientists, Newton's universe, subject to the operation of simple laws capable of mathematical expression, made much more sense, even if it seemed to depend on the acceptance of the possibility of gravitational attraction over immense distances and the denial of a theory of orbital motion by means of impulses in a plenum. This reciprocal attraction exerted by bodies remote from one another, an 'occult quality' as the French were inclined to call it, was the chief obstacle to the understanding of Newtonian physics on the continent, and it took much discussion and a monumental experimental effort to overcome this particular stumbling-block. Returning to France, even more convinced that Newton was right, Maupertuis was determined to produce the evidence that would persuade his colleagues that their views needed revision. To this end, he began a series of theoretical investigations, to be followed by observations, which resulted ultimately in the recognition of the new physical theory as fundamental to the understanding of the shape and motions of the solar systems and its components, as well as to geodetics and navigational science.

Maupertuis' movements in the months that followed his return to Paris are unrecorded. He seems to have paid a short visit to Montpellier, probably for his health, a recurrent problem. Late in 1729 he was in Basel, to study with Johann Bernoulli (1667-1748), an *associé étranger* of the Académie des sciences, and one of the leading mathematicians of Europe. This was an important move on the part of the younger scientist. Among all the thinkers of the day, Bernoulli was the man whose views had to be met with the maximum of precision in argument, for he was an outspoken adversary of Newton, and a leader in the development of the theory of the Cartesian vortices. The record of this challenge to the accepted system of the Académie is preserved in the copious correspondence between the friendly antagonists, which is preserved in the library of the University of Basel and on which much of this chapter is based.[3]

Fortunately for the historian, the massive Bernoulli collection is quite literally a *Briefwechsel*, an exchange of letters, in which those sent by Maupertuis can be read in the light of replies drafted by the Bernoullis, Johann I and II, thus permitting an understanding of their individual interests as well as of their contrasting personalities. Comments on third persons are frequent, the elder Bernoulli's caustic references to some of Maupertuis' associates adding spice to pages of mathematical calculations. In view of the inadequacy of most publications from the correspondence of Maupertuis, and the war-time destruction in 1915-16 of the bulk of his papers left in the hands of La Condamine, the Basel collection offers perhaps the best available unexploited source of information concerning the latter part of Maupertuis' career and the development of his work as scientist and public figure.

Well before Maupertuis' visit, Jakob (1654-1705) and Johann Bernoulli had welcomed foreign students to Basel, and to their house up the hill from the university. In the Engelhof, in recent years a pension much used by students, Jakob Bernoulli had formed, as Fontenelle says in his *éloge*, 'des Assemblées et une espèce d'Académie' in which he performed experiments, 'ou le fondement ou la preuve des calculs géométriques,' thus becoming the

---

3 Letters which passed between Maupertuis and the Bernoullis are preserved in the Öffentliche Bibliothek der Universität Basel (mss L/Ia, 2/218). Passages quoted from this remarkable collection have been taken from a partial transcript made for me by Mlle N. Alexath, secretary of the Bernoullikommission, with the kind permission of the late Dr Otto Spiess. The Kommission projects a comprehensive publication of the Bernoulli papers.

first to establish in Basel 'cette manière de philosopher, la seule raisonnable, et qui cependant a tant tardé à paraître.' Johann continued this hospitable device for promoting the sciences, and Maupertuis would revisit the house several times in the next thirty years, although there is reason to believe that his way of life, developed in the lively society of a brief career in the *mousquetaires gris* and the cafés of Paris, was not entirely to the taste of the older Bernoullis, firmly Protestant and supporters of the Peterskirche round the corner from their house. But in spite of differing tastes, gifts and services were exchanged between Maupertuis and his friends; spectacles were sent from Paris for the older couple, and extra copies of Johann Bernoulli's award-winning dissertation of 1730, *Nouvelles Pensées sur le système de Descartes*, printed at Maupertuis' expense. Bernoulli balanced the account by comments and suggestions for Maupertuis' mathematical productions, his constructive suggestions being of considerable importance to the younger man.

The *Philosophiae naturalis principia mathematica*, commonly called the *Principia*, was published in 1687, and Bernoulli's critical comments appeared soon after in the *Acta Eruditorum* of Leipzig. The substance of them was repeated from time to time in publications and correspondence; their author was clearly piqued that Newton had not deigned to refute the criticism or to act on it in preparing the second edition.[4] Everything that passed between Maupertuis and Bernoulli in later years has to be read in the light of this basic opposition. Each hoped to bring the other to his own point of view, Bernoulli holding that the stellar universe was full of a subtle matter arranged in whirlpools which shared their motion with planets, satellites, and even suns (fundamentally the system of vortices or *tourbillons* invented by Descartes with such elaboration as the refined observations of astronomers and mathematical theory might demand), while Maupertuis worked from the hypothesis that celestial objects moved freely in an essentially empty universe, subject only to their own inertial velocity and the gravitational pull of other similar bodies. In this Newtonian scheme of things Maupertuis saw that one of the most interesting problems would be the determination of the shape of a rotating body in its own field of gravitation, assuming a degree of fluidity in its matter and a speed of rotation sufficient to produce tangential force great enough to affect its shape without causing it to fly apart.

The two systems were mutually incompatible: no compromise was possible between the universe full of vortices and a solar system consisting of

---

4 Newton's failure to discuss or acknowledge the criticisms made by the Bernoullis is placed in another context by A. Rupert Hall in the Wilkins Lecture of 1973, 'Newton and his Editors' in *Notes and Records of the Royal Society of London* 29 (October 1974): 29-52; see especially pp. 45 and 48.

planets and satellites unconnected by a material medium moving freely in orbits determined by their tangential inertia and the gravitational force of the sun. Bernoulli held for the one, Maupertuis for the other; they could understand each other's calculations and respect each other's integrity, if not their basic assumptions. They recognized that the positions to which each clung were sincerely held and would not be abandoned without some final physical demonstration. Argument and mathematical proof could not suffice to break each one's faith in his own interpretation of the phenomena.

During 1729 and 1730 Maupertuis had begun work on the theory of spheroids rotating in their own field of gravity, and had kept Bernoulli in touch with his developing calculations. On 11 June 1731, he wrote that his 'pièce sur les sphéroïdes et sur les anneaux' was nearing completion, the rings in question being suggested by the rings of Saturn first observed by Huygens and announced in 1658, since when they had been a matter of much speculation. Acting on advice from Bernoulli, Maupertuis had put his dissertation in Latin, because he believed 'qu'elle seroit mieux reçue en Angleterre qu'ici; j'ai envie de l'envoyer aux *Transactions philosophiques*'; an argument based on Newtonian theory would be more welcome in London than in Paris. Bernoulli was now asked to examine the article for its geometry and for its Latin as well: 'Corrigez donc, Monsieur, effacez, ajoutez ce que vous jugerez à propos, et ne me refusez pas ce plaisir. Je ne veux point lire cette pièce dans nos assemblées, où il y a des gens que le seul mot d'attraction épouvante.' Bernoulli returned the *pièce* on 26 June, describing it as 'très beau, et très bien écrit en latin'; he had made some corrections, suggesting especially a word to describe Saturn's rings as *fluentum*, defined as 'un amas de matière fluide qui coule doucement et avec une vitesse uniforme,' rather than *effluvium*, which would indicate an outpouring as from a spring or a comet's tail. Accepting the correction, Maupertuis wrote to Bernoulli on 30 June 1731 that he was sending his dissertation to England, 'la doctrine qui y est répandue étant un peu odieuse dans ce pays-ci ... où l'on croit que les tourbillons expliquent tout sans s'embarrasser des couleuvres qu'il faut dévorer pour les concilier avec les phénomènes.'

Maupertuis sent his *pièce* to Sloane on July 9, with a letter in which he repeated his thanks for election to the Royal Society and expressed the hope that his contribution would be accepted for publication in the *Transactions*. Appearing in England, it would need to contain no defense of the theory of gravitation, because that was accepted by everyone, while in France, as he repeated in a letter to Bernoulli, such a development would be badly received, adding:

Quant à faire ma cour à mes compatriotes, je ne crois pas que l'amour de la patrie doive gêner le moins du monde les opinions purement philosophiques. Et quelque respect que j'aie pour l'Académie, je ne voudrois pas qu'elle exigeât de moi aucun sacrifice sur ces sortes de choses, quelque chose qui en pût arriver ... Je ne serois jamais de tel ou tel sentiment par politique, et l'Académie ne l'exige pas non plus.

Publication of such things went a little faster in his day than in ours, but in September he had had no word from Sloane that his article had been received. However, on 27 March 1732 his essay on spheroids had been seen and approved by the mathematician John Machin, one of the secretaries of the Royal Society, and early publication was planned. In a letter to Cromwell Mortimer, Maupertuis expressed his pleasure at the approval of his purely mathematical solution of a problem which in time would affect the observational sciences; not only was he aware of the empirical British spirit, but he knew that his work would have important bearings on the mapping of the earth and so on navigation as well. At this time he submitted a *petit scholion* which made it clear that he did not regard "comme des déterminations vrayes et exactes ce que je dis dans les deux problèmes ... sur la forme des sphéroïdes et des anneaux,' because he feared that some readers might be prejudiced against him for finding other proportions for the two diameters of the earth (polar and equatorial) than those calculated by Newton: 'ce grand homme n'a point d'admirateur si zélé que moi. ' – a statement which perhaps has a modicum of *politique* in it, in spite of a previous protestation to Bernoulli.[5]

In number 422 of the *Philosophical Transactions* 'for the months of January, February, and March' of 1732, Maupertuis' paper was published under the title 'De figuris quas fluida rotata induere possunt problemata duo; cum conjectura de stellis quae aliquando prodeunt vel deficiunt; et de annulo Saturni.' And in spite of his anxieties over French views about Newtonian thought, he published in the same year in Paris his *Discours sur les différentes figures des astres, où l'on essaye d'expliquer les principaux phénomènes du ciel*, a little book which offered, two years before Voltaire's *Lettres philosophiques*, a readable and accurate account of the principles of the theory of gravitation. Some twenty-six years later, justice was done: in his *Histoire des mathématiques* of 1758, J.E. Montucla of the Académie des sciences would credit Maupertuis with a large part in a 'révolution presque subite et générale dans la manière de penser,' created by his 'exposition lumineuse ... de la théorie de l'attraction dans son livre *de la Figure des Astres*.'

Relations between the elder Bernoulli and Maupertuis continued more or

5 The additions and corrections which Maupertuis wished to include in his 'De figuris ... problemata duo' arrived in London too late to be printed in the *Philosophical Transactions*.

less evenly through the next two years. In September 1732 Maupertuis asked permission to communicate two of Bernoulli's papers to the Académie, mentioning the interest taken by François Nicole (1683-1758) and Alexis-Claude Clairaut (1713-65) in Bernoulli's investigations. A little later, expressing his wish to see Bernoulli in Paris occupying the post of astronomer, he adds, 'Nous ne sommes pas dans un temps où l'on puisse espérer que le ministre paye des gens tels que vous et leur donne les pensions qu'il leur faudrait ... Cela étoit bon dans les années magnifiques du règne de Louis XIV.'

But the fundamental difference over Newtonian physics was not forgotten. On 26 April 1733, Bernoulli remarks that he still finds it better to explain phenomena of movement by impulsion than by Newton's obscure concept of attraction; there may even be an element of pique in this attitude, deriving from Newton's indifference to Bernoulli's comments on the *Principia* and the failure to correct errors in that book in its later editions of 1713 and 1726. He recognizes the influence of Newton on the younger generation, both in France and England, when he describes them as 'sectaires ... indiscrets jusqu'à tel point qu'ils prétendent qu'on doive approuver aussi les bévues sur cela seul qu'elles viennent de Mr Newton.'

Meanwhile the search for objective observational support for the opposing views continued. Jacques Cassini had spent the summer of 1733 in measuring a degree of longitude between Paris and Saint Malo, on which Maupertuis remarks that 'de sa mesure résulteroit encore que la Terre seroit allongée; mais je crois qu'il manque à tout cela bien des choses pour pouvoir rien assurer.' A letter of Bernoulli's about this time refers to Cassini's visit to Landau, a town in the Palatinate under French control; this visit was doubtless in connection with the general mapping of France in progress at that time. On 17 February 1734, Maupertuis had spoken of a decision to send an expedition to the west coast of South America to measure a degree along a meridian crossing the equator, but the astronomers Bouguer and La Condamine could not leave so soon, because 'nos escadres ont autre chose à faire que des observations astronomiques.' In a letter of 8 May 1735, Bernoulli expresses surprise that 'Messieurs vos Amériquains' are still in Paris, and continues:

Mais, dites moi, Monsieur, les Observateurs ont-ils quelque prédilection pour l'un et l'autre des deux sentiments? car s'ils sont portés pour la Terre applatie, ils la trouveront sûrement applatie; si au contraire ils sont imbus de l'idée pour la terre allongée, leurs observations ne manqueront pas de confirmer son allongement: le pas du sphéroïde comprimé pour devenir allongé est si insensible, qu'il est aisé de s'y tromper, si on veut être trompé en faveur de l'une ou l'autre opinion. Toutefois supposé que les observations décident contre moi, je me suis déjà muni d'une réponse convenable, qui me mettra à l'abri de toute objection; ainsi j'attendrai de pied ferme le résultat des observations Américaines.

One notices the almost religious fervor with which Bernoulli clings to his point of view and is tempted to recall the early theologian's 'Credo quia absurdum.'

Finally on 12 September 1735, Maupertuis writes from 'Turi' (Thury, where the Cassinis had an estate, whence they took their title) that the Lapland expedition is planned:

Nous allâmes il y a 15 jours à Versailles comme nous faisons tous les ans, présenter le volume de nos Mémoires au Roy, à la Reyne et aux Ministres; on y parla beaucoup d'un voyage vers le pôle dont il avoit été question dans nos assemblées. M. de Maurepas vint quelques jours après à l'Académie et nous annonça que le Roy avoit ordonné ce voyage. On ira dans le Golfe de Bothnie mesurer quelques degrés et faire des observations sur la longueur du pendule, etc. On sçaura peut-être aussy tost par ce voyage que par celuy du Pérou quelle figure a la Terre: car si elle est aussy allongée que m. Cassini le pense, la différence entre un degré de latitude en ce pays-là et un degré vers Paris doit être sensible. Comme je dois faire ce voyage je vous prie, Monsieur, d'avoir la bonté de penser à ce que nous pouvons faire de mieux et de m'envoyer vos Reflexions. Les distances sur le Terrain se mesurent assez seurement avec des quarts de cercle tels que ceux qu'on emporte de 2 et 3 pieds de rayon, mais l'opération délicate c'est celle de la différence en latitude ou la différence de distance d'une mesme étoile au zénit, aux deux extrémités de la distance mesurée sur Terre. On prend comme vous sçavez cette différence avec quelque secteur de 10 ou 12 pieds de rayon; mais malgré l'énormité de l'instrument on a encore bien de la peine à parvenir à l'exactitude qu'il faut pour établir une différence entre les degrés. Comme le voyage du Nord se fera avec le même appareil que celuy du Pérou et que nous sommes les maîtres de porter tant d'instruments que nous voudrons, faites moy la grâce de me dire ce que vous me conseillez là-dessus, et quand mesme il arriveroit que nous trouvassions la Terre applatie, je vous promets de rendre le prix pour vous si on vous le redemande.

C'est asseurément une très belle chose que fait la France au milieu d'une grande guerre, d'envoyer aux deux bouts du Monde mesurer la Terre. J'espère donc Monsieur, que vous me feres part de quelqu'une de vos industries qui s'étendent à tout et que vous me mettres en état de faire sur cela un ouvrage auquel les Anglois ny autres n'auront rien à dire soit qu'il les justifie soit qu'il les condamne. Cleraut sera du voyage et nous allons l'un et l'autre passer les vacances chez M. Cassini pour nous exercer à l'Astronomie.

In a lengthy reply to this letter (13 October 1735) Bernoulli expresses his surprise:

J'ai appris avec étonnement le voyage du nord, auquel vous êtes destiné avec Monsieur Clairaut ... Pour avouer la vérité, je ne vous croyois assez routiné en fait de pratique pour les observations; vous et moi, nous sommes plus faits pour le cabinet à y vaquer aux méditations; cependant votre adresse naturelle et un peu d'exercice que vous allez vous donner chez Mr Cassini vous mettra en peu de temps au fait de la pratique pour devenir observateur adroit et habile. Mais quant à Mr Clairaut je n'ai pas si bonne espérance qu'il puisse bien réussir dans l'art de faire des observations à cause de sa myopie ... qui n'est point du tout propre pour cet exercice.

The letter is long, and it indicates a good deal of thought on the part of Bernoulli. He confesses his lack of experience in observational astronomy, as he has been hampered from childhood with weak eyes. He goes on to suggest a point of reference well above the surface of the earth in order to

attraper le véritable moment du passage de l'étoile par le méridien ... J'ai donc pensé qu'on pourroit remédier en quelque façon à cet inconvénient, si on pouvoit avoir un point visible et immobile sinon dans le ciel, au moins d'une élévation fort haute au-dessus de la Terre, mais où trouvera-t-on un tel point, puisque les sommets des plus hautes montagnes comme celui du Pic [de Ténériffe], n'ont guère de hauteur perpendiculaire plus grande que d'une lieue, ce qui est trop peu sensible par rapport au demi-diamètre de la Terre: il me semble qu'on pourroit se servir à ce dessein (je hasarde cette idée mais à condition que vous ne vous en moquiez pas) des aurores boréales qui sont fort fréquentes dans les pays septentrionaux où vous allez; il y en a qui doivent être fort hautes, témoin celle de 1726 qui fut vue dans presque toute l'Europe et dont la hauteur réelle suivant le calcul de Mairan surpassa la distance de 230 Lieues.

Bernoulli could not leave the suggestion without its mathematical development, proceeding to accept the hypothesis that the aurora, composed of circular bands parallel to the equator which, having their highest point at the meridian, would allow spectators at different points on a given meridian to make exact calculations of their difference in latitude. One may reasonably doubt if Bernoulli had observed the Northern Lights; he does not seem to have realized the extreme difficulty of finding a point in their shimmering beauty on which one could fix a telescopic sight long enough to establish angular measurements. It is possible that the long passage on the aurora which occurs near the end of the *Relation du voyage fait par ordre du Roy au cercle polaire*, published by Maupertuis after the return from Lapland (Paris 1738), was inserted to answer Bernoulli's well-meant suggestion.

In another paragraph of his letter, Bernoulli discusses the merits of the Gulf of Bothnia for such observations as Maupertuis and his colleagues had in mind. Its northerly position, the extent of the body of water and the long meridian available for measurement, the relatively straight western coast between Gävle and Nora, and the absence of tides would all facilitate observations and make results more useful. Bernoulli adds that for observing the aurora one should choose positions as near water-level as possible, when the sea is calm. A final paragraph on these matters offers a series of questions still of scientific interest:

Voilà, Monsieur, bien au long mes pensées sur cette affaire; vous direz peut-être que j'en parle comme l'aveugle des couleurs; j'en tombe d'accord, mais vous me les avez extorquées. Souvenez vous en voyageant de faire aussi des observations sur l'inclinaison de l'aiguille aimantée, sur la grandeur de la refraction horizontale des astres, sur les hauteurs moyennes du Baromètre à la surface de la mer, sur la pesanteur de ses eaux et sur d'autres curiosités qui doivent se trouver différentes dans les pays du Nord de celles de nos climats tempérés.

Bernoulli expects that this letter will find Maupertuis 'chez Mr Cassini,' to whom he sends his compliments, 'en lui demandant pourquoi à son retour de voyage de Landau (qu'il fit l'année passée pour mesurer les degrés parallèles de Paris) il n'a pas voulu nous honorer de sa présence comme on m'avait fait l'espérance.'

The first months of 1736 were spent by Maupertuis and his colleagues in preparation for their expedition, not only in calculations and programming the work to be done, but in arranging for the various instruments necessary for their innumerable observations. Perhaps the most imposing of these was the nine-foot telescopic sector made with consummate accuracy by George Graham of London (figure 10). Ordered for the expedition by Anders Celsius,[6] this splendid object was sent by ship to Stockholm and thence to Torneå at the north end of the Gulf of Bothnia, which was to be the base of operations. Graham had also made the clock for the timing of observations, as well as some of the pendulums of different types by means of which

6 Anders Celsius (1701-44), professor of astronomy at the University of Uppsala from 1730, traveled on the continent from about 1731, meeting Maupertuis in Paris, where it was agreed that he should accompany the French astronomers. Celsius spent the winter of 1735-6 in London, arranging for the construction and delivery of various instruments, including Graham's nine-foot sector, and joined the travelers at Dunkerque at the end of April 1736.

Richer's experiments made at Cayenne sixty years before were to be repeated under different latitudes.

Letters exchanged in these months reflect Bernoulli's great interest in the expedition as well as that exhibited by Jacques Cassini; the credibility of these two men as scientists depended appreciably on the results Maupertuis would bring home. Bernoulli expected a maximum of accurate observations taken over as long an arc as possible; to this Maupertuis replied that the astronomers could not expect to make triangulations over ten degrees in such high latitudes, adding:

Une telle précision n'est gueres esperable et nous n'en avons pas non plus besoin: jamais on n'aura les dimensions de la Terre avec la derniere exactitude, et je crois qu'il suffira pour ses habitans de sçavoir en general la grandeur et qu'elle est allongée ou applatie et à peu près les bornes de sa figure. Or pour trouver cela il suffira, je crois, de trouver entre le premier degré de latitude et celui que nous allons mesurer, une difference assez considerable pour qu'elle ne puisse pas être toute attribué aux erreurs commissibles dans les operations, et si la Terre a la figure que M. Cassini lui attribue il doit y avoir entre ces 2 degrés une difference d'environ 1500 toises et si ceux de Perou et nous mesuroient un intervalle de 2 ou 3 degrés les differences seroient deux ou trois fois plus grandes. Si la Terre a donc quelque figure qui s'écarte autant de la spherique dans l'un ou l'autre sens que celle là, son allongement ou son applatissement sera sûrement decidé a moins qu'on ne suppose que son Meridien differe sensiblement de l'Ellypse et que sa courbure ait des augmentations et diminutions alternatives dans chaque quart de sa circonference.

Nous partons la semaine de Quasimodo pour nous rendre à Dunkerque ou je pourrai encore recevoir votre réponse si vous ne tardez point à la faire ...

Je ne doute point que vous n'aiez une maniere de consilier vôtre systeme sur l'inclinaison des orbites avec l'applatissement de la Terre s'il a lieu. Je suis si accablé d'affaires que je n'ai point pû avoir l'honeur de vous écrire plus souvent

je suis toujour monsieur mon cher ami avec les sentiments les plus tendres

Vôtre trés humble et trés obeissant serviteur

Maupertuis

De Paris 27. Mars 1736

There is no need here to recount the adventures and strenuous labor of Maupertuis and his associates between their departure from Dunkerque on 2 May 1736 and their return to Paris on 20 August 1737. In his *Relation du voyage fait par ordre du roi au cercle polaire pour déterminer la figure de la terre* (Paris 1738) Maupertuis gives much detail concerning the methods adopted, the difficulties encountered, particularly in the various means of transportation utilized in a still primitive and forested region. Their ship reached Stockholm on 21 May, and Maupertuis arrived at Torneå on 18 June; he would not leave the region until nearly a year later. During these months the members of the expedition set up nine signal beacons for triangulation on the hills along some sixty miles of the valley, made innumerable observations of the angles thus established (figure 9), twice moved the heavy Graham sector and other equipment by boat and sleigh from Torneå to Kittis at the northern end of the grid and back again, all the time suffering either from insect life or the cold and privations of a region far from the comforts of Paris.[7] Maupertuis' account of this year is recommended to anyone who delights in travel literature from another epoch, describing a part of the world where tourists are not numerous.[8]

7 Maupertuis makes few references to temperature in his *Rélation du voyage au cercle polaire*. At one point he indicates the precautions taken to maintain a temperature of 15° around the *toise* brought from Paris which served to establish the length of the base used to calculate the dimensions of the triangles of the grid; elsewhere he mentions that the mercury thermometer recorded an extreme of cold, minus 37°, during the month of January in Torneå. The thermometers carried on the expedition were largely of the type devised in 1730 by René Antoine Ferchault de Réaumur, and still in an experimental state. In 1724 Gabriel Daniel Fahrenheit had perfected his scale after several trial efforts; in the same year, Joseph Nicolas Delisle suggested still another scale based on the boiling point of water and the temperature of the cellars of the Paris Observatory. Since none of the three scales offered the two essential elements, a secure base in natural phenomena and an acceptable unit of measurement, Anders Celsius proposed his centigrade scale in 1742, without much doubt the result of his experience with the as yet imperfect instruments carried to Lapland. In its final form, the Celsius scale, inverted on the suggestion of C. Linnaeus, and calibrated on more perfect glass tubes, has been the basis of scientific thermal comparison ever since.

8 Claude J. Nordmann, in 'L'Expédition de Maupertuis et Celsius en Laponie' (*Cahiers d'histoire mondiale* 10 [1966]: 74-97) offers the fullest account of the background and circumstances of these months, based on numerous archives in Paris and much secondary literature. The abbé Reginald Outhier kept a diary for the period 20 April 1736 to 21 August 1737, *Journal d'un voyage au nord en 1736 et 1737;* as published (Paris 1744, Amsterdam 1746), this record was accompanied by the log of the 'Prudent' for the voyage from Dunkerque to Stockholm, and illustrated by maps and drawings made by Outhier himself. The work of a skilled cartographer and draftsman, these sketches and plans give some idea of the conditions under which the astronomers worked.

Figures 7 and 8, taken from Outhier's *Journal*, show the daily progress of the small vessel in which Maupertuis and his company traveled to Stockholm, and a perspective view of Torneå, based on measurements made by Outhier; the latter shows the church tower which formed the southern apex of the grid of triangles, the town hall, and the narrow bar which usually connected the island of Swentzar with the mainland (see pp. 180, 181).

CARTE
d'une Partie de *L'EUROPE*
Pour servir au Journal du Voïage de
Messrs de Maupertuis, Clairaut, Camus,
le Monnier, de l'Académie Royale des Sc.^{ces}
et de Mr Outhier,
Prêtre Correspondant de la même Académie
Accompagnés de Mr Celsius
Professeur d'Astronomie à Upsal.
Fait par Ordre du ROY,
Au Cercle Polaire l'an 1736.

ECHELLES
Cent Cinquante üries de France de 25 au Degré.
Soixante Mils ou lieües de Suede et de Dannemark.
Quatre vingt lieües communes d'Allemagne.

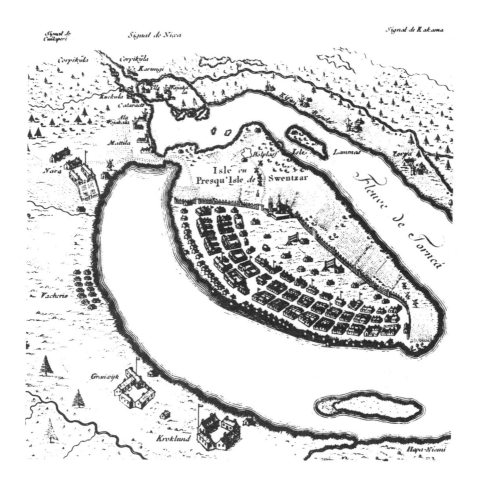

FIGURE 7 (opposite) Map of Maupertuis' voyage to Lapland (photo Metropolitan Toronto Library Board) (see footnote 8, page 179).

FIGURE 8 (above) Detail from Outhier's perspective view of Torneå (photo Metropolitan Toronto Library Board) (see footnote 8, page 179).

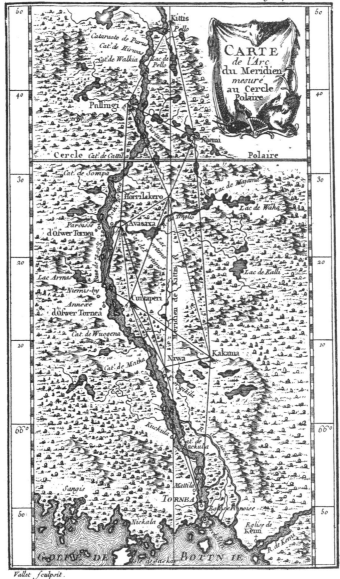

FIGURE 9 Outhier's map of the terrain between Torneå and Kittis (see continuation of footnote 8, page 184).

Fig. 1.re

Dheulland *Sc*

FIGURE 10 Sector made by George Graham for the Lapland expedition (see continuation of footnote 8, page 184).

A letter dated 'sur le Zuidersee 11 Aoust 1737' gives us the best picture of Maupertuis on his return from what eighteenth-century France somewhat generously described as 'le Pôle.' This could not give Bernoulli the detailed conclusions reached by the scientists, which had to be reserved for communication to Maurepas and the Académie des sciences, but there is no doubt that the tone of the letter, and its clear indication of the average result of observations of the pendulums, conveyed a precise idea of the final result. A note of quiet confidence exudes from the passages we quote:

Les tems, les lieux, les plaisirs, les peines ne me feront jamais vous oublier, mon cher Monsieur, et quelque longtems qui se soit passé, sans que j'ai eu le plaisir de vous écrire, je conserve toujours pour vous les mêmes sentimens où j'étois lorsque j'avois le bonheur de vous voir, et de vous entendre, et j'ai cru que vous pardonneriez mon silence à la vie que j'ai menée en Lapponie.

Nous voici de retour, et je n'ai pû attendre à etre à Paris pour vous dire quel a eté le succez de notre voyage, quoique je ne puisse vous faire part du resultat de notre operation, avant que j'en aie rendu Compte au Ministre, et à l'Academie. Je vous dirai donc seulement que nous avons eté assez heureux pour vivre, et même nous bien porter pendant un an dans la zone glacée, ou sur ses confins; que nous y avons mesuré sur la glace du fleuve de Torneå une distance de 7400 Toises, qui mesurée deux fois, ne nous a donné que 4 pouces de difference; que cette distance nous a servi de Toise pour mesurer par des Triangles un Arc du Meridien de 57½ minutes, qui a un tiers dans la zone glacée; et que le petit nombre, et la disposition de nos Triangles, et

Figure 9 is Outhier's map of the terrain between Torneå and Kittis, with the triangles as he drew them; the meridian is superimposed. The importance of the river Tornio to communications in a trackless wilderness is clearly seen, as well as numerous obstacles to their work. Eight 'cataracts' can be counted on the map; the base-line, established across a bend in the river, 7,400 *toises* in length (slightly over 14 km) gives some idea of the distances involved. The triangulated length of the arc was estimated at 55,023½ *toises* (107.24 km, taking the *toise* at 1.949 metres); its amplitude 57′ 28³/4″ (*Œuvres de Maupertuis*, Lyon 1756, 3: 166).

The last figure in this group, 10, shows the massive sector made by George Graham of London. The heavy timber of *bois des Indes* which gave stability to the instrument, essential to the observation of stars at the zenith, was about 2.4 metres in length and 39.4 by 31.2 centimetres in lateral dimensions. This illustration is derived from the small octavo volume, *Degré du Méridien entre Paris et Amiens déterminé par la mesure de M. Picard, et par les observations de Mrs de Maupertuis, Clairaut, Camus, Le Monnier, de l'académie royale des sciences; d'où l'on déduit la figure de la terre* (Paris 1740), in which further diagrams show the various controls, graduated scales, micrometers and other devices which made this an altogether exceptional instrument.

enfin l'excellence de l'Instrument avec lequel nous avons observé la difference des deux Zeniths qui terminent notre Arc, et la précision qui s'est trouvée dans cette operation repetée par 2 Étoiles differentes ne nous laissent rien à souhaiter. J'espere que tout le monde sera content de ce travail, et que la Question sur la figure de la Terre sera pour jamais decidée. Je ne vous parlerai point de la vie qu'il nous a fallu mener pour parvenir à cette fin heureuse, des froids, des peines, des fatigues, des perils, tout est passé, et sur 15 personnes que j'avois à conduire, il n'y a pas eu un de mort, ni de malade. M. Celsius Professeur d'Astronomie a Upsal étoit de notre compagnie, et le Roy vient de recompenser les service qu'il nous a rendus, par une Pension de 1000 [livres]. Je crois qu'on peut demontrer qu'en comptant les Erreurs de la Mesure sur la Terre, et celles qu'on peut avoir commises pour determiner par les Étoiles l'Amplitude de notre Arc, il est impossible que l'Erreur totale passe 50 Toises, et qu'il est morale-ment sûr qu'elle en est bien eloignée. C'e[st] la dans l'Instrument avec lequel nous avons pris la distance de l'Étoile au Zenith, une précision presque incroyable, mais dont on conviendra lors qu'on le Connoîtra, et qu'on verra les verifications que nous en avons faites. C'est un secteur de 9 pieds de rayon, et qui ne porte que 4¹/₂ degrez, fait a Londres par M. Graham et auquel l'excellence de la construction, le Microscope, et toutes les Commoditez donnent un grand avantage sur des instrumens qui seroient beaucoup plus grands.

Nous avons fait aussi dans la Zone glacée plusieurs experiences sur la Pesanteur, et toutes nous ont fait voir qu'elle est dans ces pais considerablement plus grande qu'à Paris; mais il nous y est arrivé des choses assez remarquables. Pour etre plus sûrs d'appercevoir les plus petites differences qu'il est difficile de determiner par la mesure actuelle des Pendules, et pour eviter aussi les objections qu'on fait sur les Pendules appliquez aux Horloges, outre deux Horloges faites exprés pour ces Experiences, nous avons fait faire plusieurs Pendules simples, de differentes figures, et de differentes matieres, dont nous avions eprouvé le tems des oscillations à Paris; quelques uns de ces Pendules etoient des globes attachez à une verge de fer, les autres pour etre plus invariables etoient de grosses Barres de fer d'environs 4¹/₂ pieds, et de 1¹/₂ pouce de Diametre, tous oscillants si librement, qu'ils pouvoient conserver le moindre mouve-ment pendant 8 et 10 h. et quelques uns pendant plus de 20. Tous ces instrumens nous ont donné des augmentations differentes de Pesanteur.

Maupertuis offers further comment on the behavior of pendulums and con-cludes by saying that he is proceeding to Paris at once, where he hopes to have word from Bernoulli.

The next letter in the sequence is not Bernoulli's reply, which has been lost, the draft most probably destroyed, but the announcement by Maupertuis of the formal result of the expedition:

J'ai reçu, mon cher Monsieur, votre lettre du 25.Août, à mon arrivé à Paris, et puis vous dire maintenant que la Terre est applatie; et que cet applatissement même est si considérable qu'il est impossible que les erreurs qu'on auroit pû faire en approchent...Il est bien vrai que cette nouvelle a fait de la peine à M. Cassini, mais elle n'en a pas moins été démontrée dans l'Académie. Quant à ce que vous dites qu'il eût dû venir lui-même assister à cette mesure, il n'a tenu qu'à lui, mais je ne crois pas que quand il y auroit été, les choses en eussent été mieux faites.

This letter, dated 8 September 1737, is mostly devoted to a reply to a number of rather acrid comments which Maupertuis found in Bernoulli's of 25 August, of which the first dealt with the absence of Cassini from the expedition. Other points raised by Bernoulli were that the base line should have been measured a third time, that it should not have been established on the inclined plane of a river, that the Cassinis had made four measurements which did not accord with the Lapland results, that the members of the expedition were all prejudiced in favor of 'l'applatissement,' and finally that Bernoulli himself should have been invited but was omitted as a Lutheran while Celsius, who was Lutheran, was included and rewarded by Louis xv. These captious comments brought replies in detail. The measurement of the base line was performed twice with ample checking at every stage, and the difference of four inches was not important in view of the considerable length involved. The base may have been inclined, but that makes no difference as such a variable may be allowed for; Cassini's measurements in France may have indicated a different result, but they were two and not four and 'le nombre ne fait rien à l'affaire.'

As for the accusation of prejudice, Maupertuis adds:

Quant à ce qu'on pourroit croire que la Préoccupation pour l'un ou l'autre Système pût avoir part au Résultat qu'on trouve sur l'allongement ou l'applatissement, nous qui étions une compagnie entière, composée même de différentes Nations, avons bien moins cela à craindre, que ceux qui seuls ont retrouvé ce que leurs Pères et Grands Pères avoient trouvé. Je ne crois pas même encor malgré cela qu'il fût permis de faire aucun soupçon de cette espèce, qui attaque l'honneur des gens, et si quelqu'un s'en avisoit, on n'y pourroit opposer que le Mépris.

And when it comes to the final point, on Bernoulli's introduction of the issue of religion, Maupertuis does not conceal his annoyance:

Il est vrai que M. Celsius est Luthérien, et Luthérien fort de mes amis; il nous a rendu de fort bons services dans notre ouvrage, et il étoit juste et honorable que le Roy l'en récompensât. Pour vous, mon cher Monsieur, je n'ai garde de croire que vous parlez sérieusement, lors que vous dites que vous seriez venu avec nous si je vous avois invité; c'étoit une Proposition, que je n'aurois jamais osé vous faire. Mais ce qu'il y a de certain, c'est que la Diversité de Religion n'etoit d'aucune Consequence dans notre Expedition, et qu'elle n'etoit ni Sainte, ni Croisade, nous n'allions ni pour Conquerir le Pays, ni pour Convertir les gens.

There does not seem to have been anything in this letter to offend a scientist; the chief points raised by Bernoulli had been answered one by one, and while Maupertuis conceded nothing, it could not be denied that he had seen the work done on the site, and could speak with an authority of a sort to which the sedentary Bernoulli was not accustomed. Maupertuis referred in this letter to a disagreement with Clairaut about pendulums, and finally expressed a willingness to defer to the younger scientist's view, 'et quand je suis seul d'un avis différent du sien, je n'ai pas grande opinion du mien' – a statement which may very well have pricked the notoriously thin skin of the recipient of the letter. Maupertuis' conclusion quickly covered up the irritant: he sent compliments to Madame Bernoulli, conveyed those of his father to Bernoulli – for whom the elder Maupertuis had been acting as business agent – mentioned the mathematician Klingenstierna whom he had met in Upsala, and closed with the compliments usual in that century.

This letter, however, did little to pacify Bernoulli, whose theory of the universe was being destroyed by the verification of the principles of his much disliked Newton. A letter, also lost and of which no draft has been preserved, must have been written in the latter part of September; Maupertuis referred to it in a letter to Johann Bernoulli II (1710-90), who was at this time becoming one of the French scientist's closest friends, and to whom we shall refer as 'Jean,' in which he said, 'Je suis très sensible à la manière dont Monsieur votre Père en use avec moi, et à la lettre remplie de sarcasmes que j'en ai reçue; s'il croit ne m'avoir pas offensé, il se trompe bien.'

Maupertuis did not reply to this missing letter before the end of the year; under the date of 31 December 1737 he writes:

Il y a déjà quelque temps, Monsieur, que j'ai reçu votre écrit d'*Aimables rémontrances*: quoique j'y aie trouvé plusieurs choses qui pourroient me faire de la peine, et qui me jetteroit dans de grandes discussions si j'entreprenois de les détailler ici et qui ne seroient point du tout capables de rétablir entre nous la bonne intelligence que je souhaitte qui y soit; comme j'ai cru appercevoir dans cet écrit quelques marques d'amitié, j'y ai été plus sensible qu'à tout le reste, n'ayant jamais rien souhaité plus ardemment que de trouver un peu d'amitié dans un homme pour qui j'ai autant d'estime que pour vous.

It is apparent from this letter that Maupertuis had not replied fully to the earlier letter from Bernoulli, that of 25 August. The discussion over religious differences was still open, and Maupertuis' refusal to pass one or two problems to Clairaut was still a sore point with Bernoulli. A witty and perhaps too pointed remark at this juncture may have contained an allusion which Bernoulli took to heart: 'Monsieur Clairaut comme bien d'autres, aura peut-être le défaut de sacrifier de petits devoirs d'amitié à l'envie de passer pour grand Géomètre.' But Maupertuis seems here to be making a serious effort to mend his fences with Bernoulli, stopping short of flattery, but paying the kind of respect that younger men of the new century appropriately owed their seniors who had opened the way to the new world of mathematical physics. The Cartesian view died hard, old friendships cooled, and the correspondence between the two mathematicians became less frequent, somewhat more formal, and less satisfactory on either side. In the letter of 31 December Maupertuis admits his failure to respond to an invitation to revisit Basel as well as his neglect to express thanks for assistance in a problem concerning pendulums. He keeps his letter brief, for

une réponse plus complète pourroit peut-être réveiller les altercations, pour lesquelles j'ai un éloignement infini, ne souhaitant que paix et amitié, surtout de vous, que je considère infiniment. C'est dans ces sentimens que je vais commencer la nouvelle année, que je vous souhaite remplie de bonheur, tant pour vous que pour Madame Bernoulli, et pour toute votre famille.

Relations with the elder Bernoulli cooled soon after the Académie reached a decision concerning the earth's shape, and Maupertuis' letters become ironically distant as he takes more pleasure in corresponding with the younger Jean. A final note may be found in lines from a letter of 12 April 1739, in which Johann 1 chides Maupertuis for not instructing Madame du Châtelet more precisely in the theory of *les forces vives*:

Je m'étonne, Monsieur, que depuis si longtemps que vous connoissez cette Dame philosophe, vous ne lui ayez pas donné de meilleures instructions sur cette importante matière. Je m'apperçois bien que Mr de Voltaire croupit dans la même erreur, mais je le lui pardonne, car il a épousé les sentimens de Newton et des Anglois en général, il n'ose donc pas être plus clairvoyant qu'eux.

After which he closes the discussion of their disagreement by saying he has never doubted Maupertuis' friendly feelings towards him, and that

ce qui de ma part Peut avoir excité ces nuages, c'est je vous jure, uniquement mon imprudence et point du tout ma volonté; c'est donc votre extrême délicatesse, votre sensibilité qui y a contribué le plus. Mais sans accuser ni l'un ni l'autre de nous, laissons dissiper ces nuages ...

He ends with protests of a continuation of the esteem of his family and his own 'dévouement parfait.'

There are just six more letters from Maupertuis to Bernoulli in these papers, and no drafts of letters in the other direction. After Maupertuis' invitation to Bernoulli to come to Berlin as a member of the reorganized academy there, and the rejection of this offer, correspondence ceased, and Maupertuis' relations with Basel must be studied in his letters to Jean.

With Maupertuis' announcement of the findings of the Lapland expedition to the Académie des sciences and to the chief exponent of the theory of the elongated earth, we come to the dénouement of this half-century of intellectual drama: fifty years separate the publishing of the *Principia* from the return from Lapland. There was little need to await the return of 'Messieurs vos Amériquains' from their prolonged travels in the Pacific Ocean, the Andes, and Brazil. The results of measuring an arc of a meridian north from Torneå offered sufficient evidence of *la Terre applatie.*

Yet in spite of the unhappy posture of Johann Bernoulli after 1737, his importance to the whole enterprise must be recognized. He had had a significant influence in the development of Maupertuis, encouraging him from the beginning of their friendship in the most flattering terms, criticizing his work, offering suggestions for its improvement, and singling him out from among French mathematicians of the day for friendship. The correspondence which passed between the two from the time of Maupertuis' first visit to Basel deserves publication in its entirety, and study for what it may contribute to the history of science, the personal aspect of the biography of two men, and the influence of temperamental idiosyncrasies on intellectual relations. Bernoulli was representative of the best traditions of seventeenth-century mathematics – rigorous in method and inventive in thought – although working, as he admitted, in his study, with slight reference to observational astronomy or the technical arts.

Bernoulli's wisdom and experience and that of the members of his family were of great value to Maupertuis. One cannot read the *Relation du voy-*

age ... au cercle polaire and the other texts associated with it, in connection with the correspondence that passed between the two men, without sensing the debt owed to the older savant. The Lapland expedition gained because Maupertuis, who was in large part responsible for it, had to face the intellectual positions taken by Bernoulli, perhaps less by his positive suggestions than by the necessity of meeting his theoretical objections and his criticism of its postulates.

Taken as a whole, this episode, springing from an idea in the mind of a mathematician, and conducted to a successful conclusion with the cooperation and sometimes lively criticism of a man of similar interests and yet diametrically opposed views, who knew that his position would meet shrewd argument and precisely observed fact, is perhaps the event that did most to consolidate the position of Newtonian physics as a central element in the movement known as the Enlightenment. The scientists, Maupertuis, Clairaut, La Condamine, Bouguer, and their colleagues, knew that the natural world could not be understood from libraries and laboratories, nor from measurements taken in the central provinces of France. Facts had to be determined by observations made at extreme points on the earth's surface, sometimes under it, sometimes involving considerable expense of effort and time and the facing of great hardships. They knew also that these arduous experiences, accompanied by accumulated precise calculations, would lend authority to the conclusions finally presented to the scientists and academies of Europe. Their determinations would be interpreted and popularized and pass into the literature of generations yet unborn. Voltaire's *Micromégas* was but a hint of what the stimulus of Newtonian space would do for poets, whether for André Chénier in his *Hermès*:

> Je vois l'être et la vie et leur source inconnue,
> Dans les fleuves d'éther tous les mondes roulants;
> Je poursuis la comète aux crins étincelants,
> Les astres et leurs poids, leurs formes, leurs distances;
> Je voyage avec eux dans leurs cercles immenses.
> Comme eux, astre, soudain je m'entoure de feux;
> Dans l'éternel concert je me place avec eux:
> En moi leurs doubles loix agissent et respirent;
> Je sens tendre vers eux mon globe qu'ils attirent;
> Sur moi qui les attire ils pèsent à leur tour.
> Les éléments divers, leur haine, leur amour,
> Les causes, l'infini s'ouvre à mon œil avide ...

or for Shelley, in whose poems the Newtonian universe is the tacitly accepted stage on which the action takes place. This is perhaps most clearly expressed in his *Ode to Night*:

> Palace-roof of cloudless nights!
> Paradise of golden lights!
>   Deep, immeasurable, vast,
> Which art now, and which wert then
>   Of the Present and the Past,
> Of the eternal Where and When,
>   Presence-chamber, temple, home,
>   Ever-canopying dome,
>   Of acts and ages yet to come!
>
> Glorious shapes have life in thee,
> Earth, and all earth's company;
>   Living globes which ever throng
> Thy deep chasms and wildernesses;
>   And green worlds that glide along;
> And swift stars with flashing tresses;
>   And icy moons most cold and bright,
>   And mighty suns beyond the night,
>   Atoms of intensest light.

Under the impact of such imagery, the vortices, dreamed up on the desk of another mathematician, disappear without trace except as a historical curiosity. Science continued its perpetual revolution, ceasing even more to be something learned from books or calculated by deduction from accepted systems, and increasingly recognized as an on-going process in the hands of professionals who undertake difficult and sometimes hazardous quests among realities of immense distance and mass, time and energy, where the authority of traditional philosophy has no power, and the world lies open to new and even radical innovation of method and theory. This is the kind of world where Maupertuis' prophetic *Lettre sur le progrès des sciences* was born, typical of the *mouvement philosophique*, the most significant contribution of the eighteenth century to the ages that follow.

In the summer of 1740, Maupertuis was in Paris, and ready for new ventures. His work on the shape of the earth was finished, many of his colleagues in the

Académie had accepted *la Terre applatie*, and while his mathematical researches could be continued indefinitely, his taste for travel had been stimulated, and he was more than ever ready for an opportunity to visit new places. There is reason to think he was contemplating another journey towards the pole, this time to Iceland, just south of the Arctic Circle, of which the account in Moreri's *Dictionnaire* would stir an imagination much less lively than that of the man who had come back from Lapland.[9]

In any case, about this time he had invitations from two northern monarchs. In a letter of 21 May 1740 to Jean Bernoulli, he tells of an invitation to come to the Academy of Sciences in St Petersburg; this he rejected, perhaps wisely, as the reign of the Czarina Anna was nearly over, and Russia was in turmoil. He may have had some hint of what was pending in Berlin, for on 13 August he announces that Frederick II has invited him to come to Wesel for a conference, adding that he is on his way.

On 2 September he writes from Wesel that Frederick is

Un prince fort aimable, qui a de grands projets pour toutes choses et qui veut rétablir l'Académie de Berlin... Je ne sçay point ce qu'il fera de moy. Il me comble de bontés, me fait souvent l'honneur de me faire souper avec luy, tant avec la cour qu'à son petit couvert. Cependant on ne m'a presté à luy que pour un temps et j'ay donné ma parole de retourner en France. Cela s'est fait d'une manière très agréable et très glorieuse pour moy tant de la part des ministres de France que de ceux de Prusse.

9 In a letter dated 8 June 1738 from St Elier, an estate near St Malo belonging to the Moreau family, Maupertuis had proposed to follow up a suggestion made by Celsius to measure an arc of a meridian over the ice of Lake Vättern, crossed by the 58th parallel of north latitude. Triangulation from hills on either shore would permit the determination of the length of an arc whose terminal points would serve as bases for measuring the angular distance between zeniths, thus contributing to knowledge of the curvature of the surface of the earth. Maupertuis adds: 'Malgré tout ce qu'il m'en a deja couté dans l'autre voyage je feray toute la depense necessaire pour cette entreprise, et aimeray beaucoup mieux que nous fassions ainsy que de la faire pour le compte de personne et de rugir de n'avoir que du chagrin au retour. Je partiray donc seulement avec des mesures, une pendule et l'Instrument de Mr Graham pour la méridienne que je puis faire venir de Paris à St Malo sans que l'on sçache pourquoy. Je ne crois pas qu'on puisse rien voir de plus beau que ce projet s'il peut réussir; il nous mettra en état de déterminer par nous-mesmes la figure de la terre independamment de la mesure de Picart et de Godin.'

Nothing came of this project; Celsius rejected the idea, most probably because of personal circumstances, but also because he knew much more about the treacherous condition of the ice on Lake Vättern than did Maupertuis.

These letters are preserved in the library of the University of Uppsala, in a volume, *Brev till A. Celsius*, A 533.

From Brunswick, on 20 September, he writes that he will be in Berlin in two days, adding that the academy will not begin to make progress very soon.

The autumn was spent in the capital; on 20 October he writes that 'nous attendons Voltaire ici'; and in December, having discussed the possibility of bringing Jean Bernoulli to join the academy, he describes the life that might be expected there:

Je crois que vous pourriez être fort bien à Berlin; c'est une belle ville où vous trouverez de la société, du plaisir, et la Cour la plus aimable et la plus brillante de l'Europe. La vie par conséquent n'y est pas à bon marché, mais les appointements y suppléeront pourvu que les projets de guerre n'apportent de retardement aux grands établissements que le Roy veut faire.

But no progress was made in this direction at this time; on the last day of the year he says there is still talk of the academy.

At Frederick's request, Maupertuis had drawn up plans for the reorganization of the society, and wished to report on it to Frederick, so that he would be able to return to France; the Iceland expedition was still in his mind, and the desire to return to high latitudes. In January he ventured to suggest that the headquarters of an army on active service was not the place to discuss academic matters, and that if Frederick did not require his services he would like to go home, for a time at least, returning when he might be needed. Afraid apparently that Maupertuis would not come back to Berlin so soon, Frederick sent a curt reply, 'Venez ici, l'on vous attend avec impatience.' This was on 17 or 18 March, and Maupertuis was in Frederick's suite at the battle of Mollwitz, on 10 April 1741, when Frederick, thinking for a bad moment that the day was lost, took horse and fled, only to find that the Prussian foot had stood firm and finally won a victory. Maupertuis had the misfortune to lose his way and become separated from the rest of the royal aides, and was found by peasants who stripped him of his fine blue coat and other clothes. Finally he fell into the hands of Austrian soldiers who took him for a Prussian spy and would have killed him, if there had not been an officer who recognized him, and lent him clothes and money so that he could make his way to Vienna and so to France.

The Mollwitz adventure is a well-known episode in Maupertuis' life, but his own comments, in a letter to Jean Bernoulli of 1 August, from Paris, have their ironic bitterness:

Tous les projets scientifiques ont abouti à me faire courir la prétentaine et enfin me faire prendre dans une armée où je ne devois pas être. Je ne crois pas qu'on fasse grand'chose en Prusse pour les sciences que la paix ne soit faite … La cour, la ville, tout s'est intéressé à mon aventure et m'ont fait voir que j'aurois de la peine à trouver ailleurs ce que je trouve ici.

On 27 November 1741, and again on 3 December, Maupertuis had another pressing invitation from Frederick, but his duties in the Académie des sciences prevented his leaving Paris; he was asked to come at once, if possible, and if not, then for the academic year 1742-3. Frederick, he said, apparently 'travaillera sérieusement à l'érection de l'Académie,' counting on Maupertuis for the direction of the task. The next two years were spent largely in Paris; in 1743 he was elected to the Académie française, where he delivered the usual 'harangue' required of all new members. In this he made an attempt to find a relationship between the geometrician and the man of letters, in a discourse not entirely free of the pungent irony already observed in his writings. In any case, he wrote of the episode to Jean Bernoulli, on 15 July:

Vous verrez par la Harangue que je vous envoye qu'on m'a pris aussy ici pour un homme éloquent; quelques amis m'ont entraîné à cet honneur; quelques ennemis ont voulu s'y opposer; et il a fallu en être. Vous ne sçauriez croire les indignités qu'on avoit suscitées contre moy, jusqu'à vouloir faire croire que j'avois fait des livres contre la Relligion. Vous sçavez bien que la plupart des gens appellent des livres contre la relligion, des livres contre eux. Quoyqu'il en soit, ils en ont le démenti, et sans cela je n'aurois pas été fort avide de l'honneur qu'on m'a faict, quoyque l'Académie Française soit asseurément celle de toutes où il est le plus agréable d'être, par les gens qui la composent, par l'égalité et la liberté qui y règne.

If one can detect a certain discontent with the institutions of Paris in this letter and even in the 'harangue,' it will perhaps seem even clearer in a passage from another letter of 2 November 1743, written from his native Saint Malo, this time concerning the awarding of prizes by the Académie des sciences. The procedure was to establish a committee of five who would read the papers submitted and make a selection of one or more candidates to whom the prize was awarded; the decision was to be unanimous. 'Il arriva,' he writes,

(à ce qui m'a conté Clairaut qui étoit commissaire aussy) une assez plaisante histoire. Quatre des commissaires vouloient partager le prix entre les trois pièces de votre père, d'Euler, et de Maclaurin: Mr de Réaumur le 5e commissaire dit qu'il ne signeroit point le jugement si l'on n'y mettoit au moins une pièce cartésienne, et l'on prit comme au hazard celle du Jesuitte. Malgré cela le Cartésianisme est foutu même dans l'Académie.

This is the low period of his life; in Paris, nothing can be changed, nothing constructive can be done, and, even if life is pleasant and there are charming people about, serious work cannot be achieved in the atmosphere described by Voltaire in his *contes* of this period: *Zadig, Le Monde comme il va*, and a little later, in the twenty-second chapter of *Candide* and the tenth section of *La Princesse de Babylone*. Away from Paris, Voltaire could laugh at its frivolity, its stupidity, its luxury, and its politics; condemned by his profession to live with it, Maupertuis, the imaginative, sensitive man, would be content to leave it well behind him.

The evidence is, contrary to Pierre Brunet, that Maupertuis spent most of 1744 in Paris, leaving for a visit to Basel in September; while there he found he was not far from Freiburg im Breisgau where his friend the maréchal de Coigny was conducting a siege; when the city fell, Maupertuis was asked by Coigny to take the news to Frederick in Berlin. There he stayed at least until 19 January 1745; he dined with the queen, and says 'les bontés du Roy m'y retiendront jusqu'à ce qu'il parte pour se mettre en campagne ... Mon adresse est le château à Berlin.'[10]

During the spring of 1745 in Paris, Maupertuis reached a final decision; the prospect of usefulness in the Berlin Academy, under the authority of Frederick, outweighed any probability of happiness in Paris. He was weary of the endless round of reading prize essays, of struggling against the remnants of Cartesian physics in the Académie des sciences, and of the niggling criticisms of his writings. On 25 May he writes to Jean Bernoulli:

Il est vray que je retourne en Prusse. Je n'ay pu resister à toutes les bontés que le Roy et toute la famille Royale m'ont témoignées. J'ay obtenu mon congé icy quoiqu'avec assez de peine, et ay sacrifié 8000 [livres] que j'avois tant des Académies que des autres bienfaits du Roy. Les 12000 [livres] que le Roy de Prusse me donne ne sont pas asseurément ce qui m'a déterminé à prendre ce party, mais j'ay cru ne pouvoir faire assez pour luy marquer la reconnoissance que je dois à toutes ses bontés. Je compte partir dans 5 ou 6 semaines, et ce sera le plutost que je pourray car depuis mon retour je n'ay eu icy que reproches et combats à essuyer.

Tout le monde m'a blâmé de quitter la France où ma situation étoit fort agréable, pour un pays fort différent et où, quelques avantages que je trouve, ils ne me paroissoient pas avoir la même seureté; mais j'ai calculé de mon mieux et il m'a paru que je devois faire ce que j'ay fait.

Normally a member of the Académie des sciences who withdrew from

10 Letter to Jean Bernoulli, 19 January 1745

active association with the body was granted certain privileges and the rank of *vétéran*; these prerogatives were refused to Maupertuis, which added to his grievances, real or imaginary. He returns to his present situation and prospects in a letter dated 16 June 1745:

Je n'ay pris aucune précaution contre les changements, et ne me suis réservé aucun retour dans ce païs cy; cela n'a pas été possible par le mécontentement que le Ministre a eu de ma démarche quoyque faitte de toutes les manières le plus respectueuses. Mais on m'a fait l'honneur de mettre beaucoup d'humeur dans cela, et j'ay veu le moment qu'on me refuseroit ce qu'on n'a jamais refusé à personne. On m'a flatté, on m'a menacé, on est venu à me donner tous les dégoûts possibles ...

Ce qu'il y a de seur c'est que j'ay bien pensé et que j'ay cru voir avec évidence que malgré les hazards malheureux qui sont dans le cornet, je devois m'y abandonner. Je ne sçaurois vous dire combien je seray heureux à Berlin, si seulement la dixième partie des bontés qu'on a toujours eues pour moy subsiste. Si cela ne subsiste pas, nous irons faire l'Epictète dans un grenier; car on m'a ôté tout ce que j'avois icy.

A postscript explains much: 'C'est président de l'Académie que le Roy veut que je sois.'

After a silence of some months, Maupertuis writes from Berlin (9 April 1746) that he is chiefly distressed by the active social life which his position and his recent marriage to Éléonore Catherine Von Borck, a member of an old Pomeranian family, have imposed on him. Academic routine and duties at court leave him small time for writing letters. Frederick has asked him to revise the constitution of the academy; conserving as much of the old as possible, the president has been given increased powers, which have produced deep internal stresses in the body. The curators and the minister no longer have the final power of decision, which now passes to the president; the four sections are no longer autonomous, but are directed by the president, who is responsible solely to the king.

An impediment to progress and change was the pensioned membership, consisting mostly of local aristocracy and burghers, not at all easy to control. Numerous small pensions paid out at this time made it difficult to assemble sums large enough to attract savants who would bring prestige to the academy. However, at the end of 1747 he was able to write that he had between 150 and 200 rixdalers which could be made available to a good man:

Voici maintenant ce que je voudrois, un sujet qui eust de l'esprit, quelques connoissances mathématiques et qui pust soutenir notre classe de métaphysique; peut-être que si j'avois créé la forme de l'Académie, je n'aurois pas eu le courage d'y introduire une telle classe, mais puisque je l'y ay trouvée, je suis bien aise qu'elle y soit; et je voudrois seulement qu'elle jouast dans le monde un bon personnage.

He finds German metaphysics 'une étrange science,' the fault rather of Germans than of metaphysics.

Letters like these offer rapid insights and impressions rather than a considered opinion. He finds there is not enough money for the academy, but on the whole as much each year as there is for the Académie des sciences in Paris. Berlin is 'la plus belle et la plus agréable ville de l'Allemagne, et où l'on peut trouver le plus de spectacles et de plaisirs'; there is 'un aussi grand théâtre que Paris et que Londres.' While some things are reasonable in price, many others are dear; firewood comes to as much as in Paris, because one needs so much of it.

Maupertuis was much interested in the *Mémoires* of the academy; he wanted to improve their quality, in content and appearance. Good articles were hard to come by; Euler alone kept up the standard in physical sciences, while the section for *philosophie spéculative* lacked substance; its various branches, metaphysics, ethics, natural law, and related questions, all needed development. The lack of suitable papers suggests the reason for much of Maupertuis' own work in the next few years, for his *Cosmologie*, his *Essai sur la philosophie morale*, and the diversity of his contributions to the weekly meetings and the annual volume. He would like to see 'un esprit accoutumé à la géométrie et qui a des connaissances mathématiques' apply his skills to metaphysics; such a man could make applications of his knowledge and 'se distinguer beaucoup des Métaphysiciens ordinaires.' This would be more profitable than to stay with geometry in competition with 'le grand Euler.'

He has obtained certain privileges for the academy; they are to have the censorship of everything published in the Prussian states, as well as the copyright of all maps, and to receive the product of an import tax on maps of foreign origin.

As one looks back from the learned societies of the twentieth century, existing as they do for the promotion of the varied interests of an academic profession, including the publication of the results of research in fields already in full development, it is difficult to envisage the kind of work necessary two centuries ago, when disciplines, scientific as well as historical or philological, were still ill-defined, even embryonic, in the hands of mostly unspecialized amateurs. Away from the great centres, Paris, London, and some university towns, the career scientist was not common. Conditions favorable to science and scholarship were not always available; humanists, even if one could describe them as professionals, were not yet categorized in narrow disciplines, but ranged widely over the field of Greek, Latin, Hebrew, and other literatures and thought, according to the text they happened to be interested in. Sometimes one could not be sure how to distinguish the professional scholar from the amateur.

Most of those with whom Maupertuis had to deal in Berlin were amateurs in any sense of the word. The academy was a social activity; it rewarded its members with local prestige, giving them status as an incentive, a status that in most cases extended hardly beyond the boundaries of the city. Frederick's interest in the academy led to a vogue in the limited social circles of Berlin, a vogue that intensified the struggle for recognition of the kind that it now lay in Maupertuis' hands to offer. In comparison with the kind of respect for the sciences that Maupertuis had seen in London and was accustomed to in Paris, the theological and provincial outlook of many of his new associates was a serious handicap to free inquiry. Research for its own sake, solutions for theoretical problems, and finally the application of new methods and devices to the improvement of the human condition – all this seems to have been something rather foreign to the members of the academy as their new president met them. The leading figures were socially and hierarchically acceptable personages in Berlin life, not creative and inventive scientists, imaginative writers, or penetrating thinkers.

As a result, much time had to be spent on prose and verse, even by the ineffable Baculard d'Arnaud, setting forth the grandiose program of an all-inclusive academy. Local dignitaries had to be eulogized lest they be too soon deservedly forgotten. There was besides an almost continuous stream of business sessions in which properties and employees of the academy were discussed, prizes awarded, new competitions set, papers read, and local sensibilities soothed, while a general plan was kept in somewhat distant sight. One hardly wonders at Maupertuis' exasperation, when he was led to exclaim that the academy in Berlin had begun several centuries too soon!

Experienced in the methods and problems of scientific societies, Maupertuis had standards of behavior and achievement, and hoped that with the authority given him by Frederick he could attain results in the relatively undeveloped community of eighteenth-century Berlin that had not been possible in older academies. One of his plans was for a cosmopolitan organization, drawing together men of many nations, not only Prussians and other Germans, from Saxony, Bavaria, and Austria, but also Swiss, Netherlanders, Italians, Frenchmen, Englishmen, and Scots, who could move forward on a broad intellectual front, exploring many fields and solving problems by combining different methods. For this project, Berlin offered many advantages, for from the time of the Great Elector, Frederick William of Brandenburg (1620-88), the city had become an important capital, with many embassies and frequent foreign visitors and residents, including an active colony of Huguenot refugees. There was no university, but the academy founded at the turn of the century under the counsel of Leibniz was still in existence when Maupertuis arrived, and offered a basis on which to build. Religious questions hardly arose; the regime was Protestant, but Catholics and Jews suffered from no disabilities and there was no faculty of theology to resist new ideas in philosophy, no school of medicine to set limits to anatomical research by unlicensed practitioners. The only censor was to be the academy itself; and the mood was very much against obstacles to speculation in theology and ethics.

On paper, conditions were good and prospects favorable. Freedom of action, some money for publications and pensions, an intelligent program for the four sections representing the disciplines commonly pursued in the eighteenth century, public assemblies three times a year for the enlightenment and entertainment of the general public, an experimental farm at Köpenick, and a staff of employees to keep a mass of material possessions in order – all these factors promised well for the future.

In actuality, difficulties soon arose. It was not easy to move idle and uninspired incumbents out of pensioned appointments, or to make philosophers and philologists produce scholarly papers with regularity. Leonhard Euler could make a dozen contributions in mathematics and physics every year, but Maupertuis, responsible for the general program of the academy, had to fill in where the organization was weak, reading eulogies, occasionally of men whom he had had to offend, and speaking on broad topics of common interest, sometimes quite foreign to his personal scientific background. These productions are relevant to the purposes and scope of the academy; they reveal that he was taking the writings of Francis Bacon as a guide, particularly after about 1749. The *New Atlantis* and the *De augmentis scientiarum* seem to have inspired Maupertuis; their author, who, as William Harvey had said, wrote of science like a Lord Chancellor was obviously a suitable mentor for a *président d'académie*.

To come to a specific case, of crucial interest in evaluating the work of Maupertuis in the Berlin period, his *Lettre sur le progrès des sciences* of 1752 is perhaps the most typical example of his powers of programming for a broad spectrum of disciplines.[11] In the eighteen brief paragraphs of this little

---

11 The *Lettre sur le progrès des sciences* appeared as one of a group of letters on different subjects in 1752 and was reprinted separately in the same year. Revised and rearranged in several ways, it took its final form in the *Œuvres de Mr de Maupertuis: Nouvelle edition* (Lyon, chez Jean-Marie Bruyset 1756) 2: 345-99.

book he outlines the directions in which different branches of science can advance, 'quelques recherches utiles pour le genre humain, curieuses pour les savants, et dans lesquelles l'état où sont actuellement les sciences semble nous mettre à portée de réussir.' The *Advancement of Learning* was admittedly in his mind as he began his book, but while Bacon had taken all knowledge for his province, Maupertuis confines himself to the useful and the feasible. This was certainly wise when one was writing for the economy-minded Frederick.

He begins with anthropology and geography, with *Terra Australis incognita* and the rumored giants of Patagonia. The great unknown land occasionally glimpsed by travelers carried by winds further south than Capes Horn and Good Hope, an area made more tantalizingly extensive by maps on Mercator's projection, demands exploration and poses questions hitherto unanswered; promising much for commerce, it surely offers 'de merveilleux spectacles pour la physique.' The primitive races of the Pacific islands, intriguing all eighteenth-century minds, and the ice of the polar regions, with the devices needed for survival, navigation, and communications, suggest that investigation will lead to useful results. Turning to the remains of giants reported to have been found in Patagonia, Maupertuis sees that the question is not merely that of determining the truth or falsehood of these tales, but of treating the question from an anthropological point of view, and examining both relics and rumors for what such evidence may show.

The search for the north-west passage to China, which for two centuries had haunted the imaginations of sailors and readers alike, becomes, in the third paragraph, a scientific operation, with emphasis on positive results. Questions to be answered will add to knowledge, most of which will be useful: Is the north pole on sea or land? Is the aurora borealis caused by luminous matter given off at the pole or is it a precipitation from outer space? And finally, what are the navigational problems of sailing in high latitudes? Polar areas fascinated Maupertuis; their study could be a great school for research, leading to many benefits for mankind.

A natural transition leads to the next topic, the magnet, which Maupertuis expects will possess properties as yet unknown, useful to many besides the navigator. Edmond Halley's voyage of 1698-1700 had raised the question of the variation of the position of the magnetic pole, from point to point and year by year, a question that could be resolved only by the use of better instruments and observations made the world over. Voltaire's comments on these points, as on others, show his incapacity to appreciate the nature of scientific work; he could not see that instruments constructed to altogether new levels of precision would make traditional methods obsolete and a hindrance to knowledge. In this book Maupertuis represents the transition often remarked on as characteristic of the middle of the eighteenth century, from a science accessible to almost all men of the customary schooling to forms of knowledge that demand special skills and a familiarity with increasingly esoteric language; the scientists were turning toward the development of a new literature based on new concepts and new standards of measurement, a literature written for other scientists, with small regard for the general reading public. In this particular case, Maupertuis had to be intelligible to the enlightened amateur, of whom Frederick 11 was one; but his subject-matter was still recondite, rejecting much that current prejudice accepted. A professed progressive like Voltaire, for all his work at Cirey and elsewhere, was simply out of date; the revolutions of science passed him by; his historically oriented outlook was profoundly disturbed.

An interest in ancient structures turned Maupertuis' attention to the relics of ancient African cultures. The technical devices that had been used in building them could suggest methods and materials which modern man could adopt, thus increasing their value as historical monuments. The pyramids told of a distant and mysterious past; they were also a challenge to man's knowledge of techniques and understanding of motives, posing questions that could be answered only by the application of modern tools of investigation, including the judicious use of explosives. This led naturally to the further question of the exploration of the earth's crust and nucleus; the highly effective skills and devices of German miners, properly applied and used for scientific purposes, could solve the enigma of the nature of the earth's core. Gravitational forces could be evaluated, and barometric pressures recorded, as well as the chemical nature of the deepest rocks and the temperatures of the lower levels. By a process of careful selection and exaggeration Voltaire makes both of these projects seem ridiculous, but no one familiar with modern geophysics and the temporarily suspended Mohole project can justifiably sneer at Maupertuis' enlightened program.

From specific suggestions for the use of royal funds on behalf of science, Maupertuis turns to practical proposals of a distinctively Baconian nature for the organization of research on a broad and comprehensive basis. He proposes a *collège des sciences étrangères* which would gather men of learning from everywhere, even from the most backward cultures, so that knowledge could be pooled and the collective wisdom and experience of humanity made available for all. For this, a *ville latine* was a necessary step; young men from all nations would be brought into a community where they would be immersed in Latin, so that a *lingua franca* for philosophic and scientific communication could be developed. Here Maupertuis' experience in Berlin was clearly useful. If Frederick desired to put his academy in the very front of the intellectual stage of Europe, Maupertuis was quite prepared to devise a plan which would go beyond anything yet seen in the learned world, in its scope rather larger and more inclusive than even the Christian churches.

The *Lettre sur le progrès des sciences* is rounded out with a series of discussions of specific scientific problems; astronomy is treated briefly in terms of its present state and needs, with some stress on the desirability of spreading observers widely over the continents with particular tasks and radically improved instruments. Knowledge of anatomy and physiology could be augmented by the use of criminals destined for torture and the kind of execution sometimes used in that still inhumane century; there would be no less and no more total suffering, but useful ends in surgery and other aspects of therapy could be served. Superstition and false knowledge should be combated on all fronts; audacity, not timidity, is needed, for only radical initiative will lead medicine out of the routines which have had so little success in curing the innumerable diseases from which humanity has suffered all over the earth. Chance and tribal usage have given us medicines; but we have not yet reached anything that can be described as medical science. And Maupertuis proceeds to speculate on the uses that might be made of the promotion or prevention of perspiration, on the rotary motion that might be used on patients with difficulties of circulation, on Japanese remedies and acupuncture, and on the strenuous measures that might be enforced by law for the control of epidemics. Finally, he suggests that there might be much value in considerable specialization in the practice of medicine, so that intensive progress could be made by the combination of clinical work and research by a single physician, free from the distractions of a diversified clientèle. The passage is derived from Francis Bacon, brought up to an eighteenth-century date.

There is not much need here for further review of the contents of this much maligned little book. Let it suffice to say that here Maupertuis gives a glimpse of steps that will be taken by science and scientists over the two centuries and more that have passed since it was published. His general trend is towards observation as opposed to systematic thought; it may be recalled that Voltaire often paid lip-service to that outlook. The most famous of the satirist's obscurantist irresponsibilities distorts a passage in which Maupertuis well summarized the considered view of a sympathetic layman as he looked at eighteenth-century medicine:

La médecine est bien éloignée d'être au point où l'on pourroit déduire le traitement des maladies de la connoissance des causes et des effets; jusqu'ici le meilleur médecin est celui qui raisonne le moins et observe le plus.

The nine words which Voltaire picked out for one of his sharpest comments, 'le meilleur médecin est celui qui raisonne le moins,' attribute to Maupertuis a judgment which was by no means his; if one compares the whole passage with a phrase from the succeeding paragraph, his meaning is perfectly clear. Speaking of animals and tests which could be made on them, he asks that we should seek not classification, even in the Linnaean manner, but 'des recherches qui nous fissent connaître, non la figure particulière de tel ou tel animal, mais les procédés généraux de la nature dans sa production et sa conservation.'[12]

This search for general laws of nature rather than an indefinitely extended catalogue of details is typical of the real scientist that Maupertuis was, and marks him as no amateur. His desire to see menageries placed under the control of naturalists rather than practical husbandmen, so that genetic experiments could be made, monstrous births scientifically recorded, and even tissues grafted, as had long been done on shrubs and trees, was an imaginative extrapolation from the common fund of eighteenth-century lore and practice.[13] He wanted better microscopes, which could easily be achieved within the limits of contemporary optical theory and the glass-maker's art; he saw the need for temperatures higher than those attainable by using coal and wood, particularly in the analysis of substances to be used in industry. He was much interested in electricity, although he could not at this time take part in its experimental study; well before Galvani he proposed its possibilities in the phenomena of growth and paralysis.

Finally, and here he passed entirely beyond the limits of Voltaire's comprehension, he suggested the possibility of useful study of the mind in sleep, natural or induced by opiates, or in a state of reverie, in which illusion is created by affecting the fine nervous structure. He foresees a link between such investigations as these and the study of madness, leading to the alleviation of this affliction, which men of the period were beginning to think of as natural and not induced by imperceptible and uncontrollable spirits. He has much to say on the phenomena of the mind, on *les esprits*, which might yield

12 The *Diatribe du Dr Akakia, médecin du Pape*, with its numerous accessory pamphlets, is a prime example of Voltaire's savage skill in mocking satire, as well as an illustration of his capacity for distorting evidence and destroying reputations. Its success as a literary tour de force has contaminated much of the literature devoted to the eighteenth century; only a ruggedly independent mind can forget Voltaire's wit and discover his motives.

13 Maupertuis' suggestion that princely menageries could be turned to scientific uses by experiments in cross-breeding different species and by grafting limbs and organs, much as botanists create monstrous trees by trimming and implanting scions, points in the direction of H.G. Wells' grim fantasy of 1896, titled, perhaps significantly, *The Island of Dr Moreau*.

knowledge to scientific study. The same approach is extended to the consideration of the mental apparatus and behavior of Australian aborigines and the natives of the islands of the southern oceans; and still further, to the formation of language among children, isolated, like the wild boy of the Aveyron a little later, so that the growth of linguistic phenomena apart from cultural milieu could be recorded for its use in analyzing the speech of various national types.

Maupertuis does not tell us to whom this challenging letter was addressed. The one person whom it fits is, of course, Frederick himself, to whom he could very well, in a moment of international peace, suggest a program of support for the sciences and scientists. The eighteenth century was an age of projects of all sorts, for international peace, for political reform, for reform in the churches, for radical improvements in systems of mensuration, weights, and measures of all sorts, and changes in educational systems and methods, as well as in the techniques of the fine arts and the criteria of criticism. Maupertuis' comprehensive and imaginative program was quite literally the culmination of his career, the point at which his varied experiences came into focus; his proposals are the product of his work for the Berlin academy, but they are also in the line of the vision of Rabelais as he imagines the development of the arts in the final chapters of the *Tiers Livre*, and the free associations in Pascal's mind as he reaches the climax of his fragment on the disproportion of man. Thus it is not surprising that there is no reference to the Berlin academy in this letter; he could not have written with such freedom if he had felt that his words would be read by his colleagues in a more or less jealous search for hidden intentions and ulterior motives. The program was national at least, international really, because he must have realized that many of his proposals were completely out of reach for a nearly landlocked power like Prussia, whose political instruments were military rather than naval. In any case there was no money for such enterprises, nor were there men to direct them.

It was a dream; it belongs with the *New Atlantis* rather than with the documents that founded the innumerable academies of eighteenth-century Europe. Now, Maupertuis challenges the literal-minded Voltaire and his like, when he announces, with emphasis:

Il y a assez longtemps que nous écoutons les philosophes, *dont la science n'est qu'une habitude et un certain pli de l'esprit*, sans que nous en soyons devenus plus habiles; des philosophes naturels nous instruiroient peut-être mieux; ils nous donneroient du moins leurs connoissances sans les avoir sophistiquées.

Après tant de siècles écoulés, pendant lesquels nos connoissances métaphysiques n'ont pas fait le moindre progrès, il est à croire que s'il est dans la nature qu'elles en puissent faire quelqu'un, ce ne sauroit être que par des moyens nouveaux et aussi extraordinaires que ceux-ci.

Among the *philosophes* of his age, Maupertuis occupies a place apart. Others had been and would be secretaries of academies – Fontenelle, Grandjean de Fouchy, and later Condorcet; some, like Diderot, fought long and stubbornly for the *Encyclopédie*. Buffon, in the higher ranks of the civil service, combined administration over an extended period with the compilation of a massive *Histoire naturelle*. But often they were, like Voltaire and J.-J. Rousseau, free-lance writers, without civil responsibilities and regular duties, in a position to write and speak pretty much as they pleased, publishing without regard for the expectations of any but the public they cared to seek for their own immediate purposes.

Maupertuis, on the contrary, was given an opportunity to do something practical for the enlightenment of the public, on a relatively grand scale, with considerable resources at his disposition, and with freedom to plan and execute in circumstances which presented a minimum of official inertia and resistance. As a professional scientist, he thought in terms of what could be done for science; coming from the rich intellectual milieu of Paris, he could not be content with a merely Eulerian concentration on mathematical physics. He was a man of the broad movement, and it fell on him to create what Leibniz had not been able or perhaps had not desired, to create – a focus of intellectual activity that lasted long after he had left it in great distress and failing health, an institution which after many vicissitudes would rank high in eminence and influence. The Berlin academy, as envisaged by Frederick and Maupertuis, was more inclusive than the Paris Académie des sciences, more rationally organized than the Royal Society of London; in some respects it foreshadowed the Institut de France as set up in the year III of the French Republic. Unhampered by tradition, Maupertuis found it possible to propose areas for research, to seek out members who could develop new fields of study; he could go to the writings of Francis Bacon and derive from that copious source the ideas and even concrete proposals which more than a century of scientific progress had not yet made stale.

One concludes that in his work, not only in his writings in book form and in discourses for his academy, but in the project for the scientific organization he had led, one finds the Enlightenment in its most fruitful form, a force that moves among men, within the framework of a polity, capable at least of good, even if it sometimes is guilty of the petty. More than a *philosophe* – a vague and limited term at best – Maupertuis was a philosopher, and in some ways he had the power of a king; it would have been better for the whole movement, and for the prestige of French thought, if the climate of Berlin had been more propitious for his health, and utterly impossible for Voltaire.

The opening half of this chapter has been revised from a contribution under a similar title to *Literature and History in the Age of Ideas: Essays on the French Enlightenment Presented to George R. Havens*, Charles G.S. Williams ed., (Columbus, Ohio State University Press, 1975, pp.69-94). These pages appear here by courtesy of Professor Williams and the Ohio State University Press. Several paragraphs in the latter half have been derived from a paper read at the First International Congress on the Enlightenment held in Geneva and Coppet, 'Maupertuis *philosophe*: Enlightenment and the Berlin Academy,' published in *Studies on Voltaire and the Eighteenth Century* 24 (1963) 255-69. Permission to use these pages has been courteously granted by Dr Theodore Besterman. Work for this chapter has been done in part in the library of the University of Basel, as well as in the Bernoullianum in that city. Some documentation has been derived from letters in the British Museum and the Royal Society of London, and factual material from the article by I. Bernard Cohen, 'Isaac Newton, Hans Sloane, and the Académie Royale des Sciences' in the *Mélanges Koyré,* Paris 1964.

CHAPTER NINE

'L'homme ... tel qu'il est'

L'un est dernier esprit de l'ancienne France, l'autre est le premier génie de
la France nouvelle.

(Journal des Goncourt, 11 April 1855[1])

THE TRANSITION from the science of the *ancienne France* of Voltaire to that
of the *France nouvelle* of Denis Diderot is well represented by Maupertuis, as
he turned about mid-century from the mathematics and physics of his Newtonian period to the study of biology, in particular genetic theory. In his
earlier years he had been generally understood by Voltaire, who could learn
to write acceptably about optics and the theory of gravitation. Now Maupertuis' new interests baffled the one-time disciple. The creativity of the *Vénus
physique*, the *Réflexions philosophiques sur l'origine des langues*, the *Essai
de philosophie morale*, and the *Essai de cosmologie* (all published between
1745 and 1751) quite left Voltaire behind, content to ignore new lines of
investigation and speculation, happy with others of his day to mock the
intellectual adventures of the president of the Berlin academy.

If a man of letters like Voltaire could become spiritually uncomfortable in
the presence of the scientist Maupertuis, there is little doubt the sentiment
was reciprocated. While Maupertuis could live within the internal life of
science, serene in the awareness of an intellectual continuum largely independent of the external world of politics and society, the irritable and hypersensi-
tive Voltaire was impelled to give expression to his discomfort. The literary

---

1 Quoted by Jean Thomas, *L'Humanisme de Diderot* (Paris 1938) p. 23

success of the *Diatribe du Docteur Akakia* and its innumerable echoes could not quite exorcise his sense of intellectual inferiority; the recurrent allusions to the *philosophe du nord* and the snatching of phrases from the *Lettre sur le progrès des sciences* in *Candide* and *L'Homme aux quarante écus*, in various miscellaneous writings and the correspondence, are evidence of a scar, in part self-inflicted. There is little doubt that Maupertuis' science irked Voltaire beyond measure; the success of the Lapland expedition, the rise of the Berlin academy, and the development of scientific disciplines available to specialists and professionals rather than to amateurs no matter how gifted illustrate what one humanist has described as the 'dissociation of sensibility,' a phrase which hardly does justice to the divergence of the intellectual aims and the methods involved. What was lacking in Voltaire was what Charles Coulston Gillispie has described as the 'edge of objectivity,' the 'consciousness of a real world outside himself in nature ... to be grasped rather by measurement than by sympathy.'[2] It was not helpful that Maupertuis had shown himself, in his 'Harangue' on being received in the Académie française, like Pascal before him, an enemy of the conventional poet, critical of the jingle and ornamental glitter that interfered with the presentation of an account of the interests of humanity, of man's place and purposes in the world. This was an outlook that Voltaire could not fully grasp, much less share.

In the wake of the Koenig affair and Voltaire's brilliantly acrid *Akakia* satire, Maupertuis was happy to find, in the summer of 1753, an understanding reception for new ideas and a new outlook in the open-minded intelligence of Denis Diderot. He brought to France the separate publication of the *Lettre sur le progrès des sciences* and the pseudonymous *Dissertatio inauguralis metaphysica de universali naturae systemate* published at Erlangen in 1751 under the name of an imaginary Dr Baumann. Traces of these small books and of the conversations with Maupertuis may be found in Diderot's *Pensées sur l'interprétation de la nature*, not only in a footnote with date and specific reference,[3] but also in several passages which parallel various sections of the *Lettres*, in a detailed discussion of the theories of 'Dr Baumann,' and, perhaps most important, in a general redirection of Diderot's scientific interests, especially in an awakening to the importance of the molecular aspects of biology.

2 Charles Coulston Gillispie, *The Edge of Objectivity: An Essay in the History of Scientific Ideas* (Princeton, Princeton University Press 1960) p. 42
3 In *pensée* 12 of *De l'Interprétation de la nature*, Diderot writes, 'Il me semble que la Nature se soit plu à varier le même méchanisme d'une infinité de manières différentes,' and adds a footnote: 'voyez l'*Hist. Nat.* Buffon Tome IV, l'Hist. de l'Âne; et un petit ouvrage Latin intitulé *Dissertatio inauguralis metaphysica de universali naturae systemate, pro gradu Doctoris habita*, imprimé à Erlang en 1751, & apporté en France par Mr de M**** en 1753.'

Diderot's gentle, politely ironic rejection of the Baumann theories, his judicious quotation from the *Dissertatio inauguralis*, and a certain resemblance to the *Lettres* made a favorable impression on Maupertuis, who had not previously enjoyed much serious and intelligent discussion of his ideas. His reaction took the form of a 'Réponse aux objections de M. Diderot,' which he was able to interpolate in the second volume of the edition of his *Œuvres* in preparation at this time under the direction of the Abbé Trublet.[4] Quoting freely from the *Interprétation de la nature*, Maupertuis restates his position, that he is in no way to be regarded as an atheist, nor does his thinking in any way lead to impiety or vice. Having decided that little was to be gained by defending 'des choses qui ne mériteroient peut-être pas d'être défendues,' and that philosophical positions are of so little interest to the public that they are usually maintained only for *amour propre*, he now finds that

il n'est qu'un seul genre d'objections auxquelles on soit obligé de répondre, et sur lesquelles le silence seroit une faute ou contre la société ou contre soi: ce sont celles qui pourroient donner des impressions fâcheuses de notre religion ou de nos mœurs.

In this way he recognizes the need to carry on a controversy with a kindred spirit whom he esteems, 'qui fait tant d'honneur à notre nation,' but whose very eminence offers an advantage, in that 'il fait disparaître à nos yeux et aux yeux du Public éclairé' all the other critics and criticisms that might appear, 'et que lorsque nous lui aurons répondu, nous nous mettrons peu en peine de répondre aux autres.'

There is no need here to enter into the details of this unusually friendly debate. Maupertuis ends his 'Réponse' with the remark,

M. Diderot n'a peut-être pas rendu justice à notre ouvrage, mais il a rendu justice à nos sentiments, lorsqu'il a dit: *Il faut lire son ouvrage pour apprendre à concilier les idées*

---

4 The 'Réponse aux objections de M. Diderot' does not seem to have been published separately. It appears in volume 2 of the *Œuvres de Mr de Maupertuis* (see chapter 8, note 11) directly after the *Système de la nature*, Maupertuis' translation of the Baumann *Dissertatio*, which occupies pp. 139-68 of the volume, including of course the inserted signature κ 2me, pp. 145*-160*.

In order to insert the 'Réponse,' two of the original gatherings had to be removed; signature κ was renumbered κ 1er, and new signatures were inserted, κ 2me, L 1er, L 2me, and a new M; the pagination was interrupted to read 1-160, 145*-60*, 161-76, 161*-76*, 177-406. The 'Réponse' occupies pp. 169-84, thirty-two pages in all, exactly two gatherings of the reconstructed volume. This interpolation and the careful wording of the 'Réponse' are congruent with Maupertuis' concern that this edition of his works should contain nothing harmful to his friends or hostile to his critics.

philosophiques les plus hardies avec le respect le plus profond pour la Religion ... Nous regarderions comme un outrage fait à la Religion, si l'on pensoit que quelque conjecture philosophique ... fut capable de porter préjudice à des vérités d'un autre ordre et d'une toute autre certitude.

It seems clear that Maupertuis sensed that he was on common ground with Diderot in matters of method and objectives. As a Newtonian of the second generation, devoted to the destruction of *a priorist* mechanism and insisting on the importance of observation as opposed to theory and systems, with Diderot he was one of the men who, as Jacques Roger writes, were to 'révolutionner la biologie et les sciences naturelles,' scandalizing the old professionals, Réaumur, Haller, and Spallanzani, 'bousculés dans leurs habitudes par des amateurs, et justement exaspérés, souvent, par l'inexpérience et les prétentions des nouveaux venus.'[5] In the strange company of La Mettrie and Buffon, along with Diderot, Maupertuis accepts the terms imposed by the physical world as made available to him by new instruments extending the senses, by new methods demanding ever more precise sensory discrimination, and by new standards and criteria. Trained in the tradition of the Académie des sciences, he was a professional who saw the world in terms of precise measurement, rigid distinction between quantities and qualities, and critical evaluation of recorded observations, leading to conclusions irrefutable in the light of accumulated fact. This attitude had evolved from the methodical thinking of Francis Bacon and Descartes and their followers, elaborated through a century of experience and experiment, debated and criticized, satirized and mocked by some, and eulogized by others with equal enthusiasm and excess.

As the century wore on, the findings of the scientists became less and less understood by the untrained mind, and were largely lost on the popular author and his public. The sensibility of the artist took what it could from science, sometimes little and often distorted. It is exceptional to discover lines like those spoken by the Moon in *Prometheus Unbound* (act 4, lines 456 ff.):

> Thou art speeding round the sun
> Brightest world of many a one;
> Green and azure sphere which shinest
> With a light which is divinest
> Among all the lamps of Heaven
> To whom life and light is given;

---

5 Jacques Roger, *Les Sciences de la vie dans la pensée française du XVIIIᵉ siècle* (Paris, A. Colin 1963) pp. 458-9

I, thy crystal paramour
Borne beside thee by a power
Like the polar Paradise,

...

Maniac-like around thee move
Gazing, an insatiate bride,
On thy form from every side.

...

Brother, where soe'er thou soarest
I must hurry, whirl and follow
Through the heavens wide and hollow,
Sheltered by the warm embrace
Of thy soul from hungry space.

In these lines, as Mrs Shelley wrote, the poet endowed 'the mechanism of the material universe with a soul and a voice,' instead of clothing 'the ideal with familiar and sensible imagery.' As the findings of science become more and more remote from the general reader, one finds that the biological inaccuracies of 'La Mort du loup' and the mental flabbiness of 'La Bouteille à la mer' are forgiven as the poet De Vigny satisfies a Romantic need for dramatic, even melodramatic, justification for common attitudes and sentiments, with small regard for the realities of the external world.

The course of intellectual history does not follow a rational straight line; as Gillispie says, 'History is made by men, not by causes or forces,'[6] and the historian has to take account of the importance of the irrational in human affairs. While various explanations have been offered in sociological patterns of normal growth and maturing of organizations, in material conditions of civic life, and in the development of instruments and tools, the hardware and software of technology, historians know the imponderables remain – the characters of individual men. Sooner or later, the narration must return to the comedy of situation, of character, of manners, of errors and happy hunches, of animosities and affinities, to find that there is no single, simple explanation of how and why the development of ideas is hindered or advanced, why great leaps forward occur at certain times, in irregular alternation with equally significant failures of nerve.

And finally, one questions whether we should really speak of two cultures, whether there is an inevitable division of the intellectual faculties, a schism in the mind between opposing, even antagonistic and uncomprehending, ways of thought and life. If some are devoted to the contemplation of things, the

6 Gillispie, *The Edge of Objectivity* p. 521

material world and its motions and changes of state, and the systematic explanation and sometimes creation of such phenomena, at the same time that others concern themselves chiefly with words and ideas, with communication, with speech and thought, with the arts from music to architecture, with aesthetics and philosophy – are these the only great classifications of men? Is this distinction inevitable? Is it fundamentally impossible to overcome the differences, and find a level of analysis of historical events in which the gulf is lost?

There is a possibility that the divisions are artificial, a product of a desire to partition and distinguish, to mutilate the essentially unitary activity of the mind in the interests of a Cartesian classification, in which individual occurrences are isolated and examined on the assumption that only thus can the critic obtain accurate descriptions of reality, a basis for valid argument and acceptable conclusions. But while the academic process separates, discriminates, opposes factors and aspects in the even tenor of life, in the flow of consciousness, there is no inevitable and inherent reason or cause to resist the desire to know, to satisfy curiosity about the world and its sequences. Still less can man neglect the inevitable impulse to tell of events, to record observations in forms chosen to express with precision the visual and auditory experience and the imaginative reverberations of the phenomena in question. Authors such as Rabelais, Pascal, Molière, Boileau, and their epigones, Voltaire, Montesquieu, Maupertuis, and Diderot, made no distinction such as that imposed by academic critics and historians; they had no disciplinary empires to defend. They were men of a world whose margin faded forever as they moved; experience for them was an arch opening on an unexplored and untravell'd universe of fact and fancy, awaiting the passing mind that would make of it what sense or poetry it could. For some there would be an accumulation of new data, to be correlated and systematized into new science; for others the outcome would be images, visions with color and emotional tone, aesthetic patterns and intuitive insight, communicable through the skills of art. In the most comprehensive minds the visions coincide: knowledge, assured by general assent and common experience, structured by logic and the intuition of genius, leads to vistas of new thought and strange association. Beyond the data of contemporary life, the firm ground of what men had done and learned, Rabelais and Pascal could see a technology, a science, a way of living and thinking that would lead to still broader bases for thought and action, and, as the scientific revolution rolled on, men like Maupertuis and Diderot and countless others could agree across the boundaries of religious doctrine and metaphysical system to conceive of realms in which the imagination, scientific and poetic, could work fruitfully and with satisfaction without end.

Index

UNIVERSITY OF TORONTO ROMANCE SERIES

This book
was designed by
WILLIAM RUETER
under the direction of
ALLAN FLEMING
University of
Toronto
Press